THE LUCK OF
NINEVEH

THE LUCK OF NINEVEH

120056

ARCHAEOLOGY'S GREAT ADVENTURE

ARNOLD C. BRACKMAN

M c G R A W - H I L L   B O O K   C O M P A N Y

New York   St. Louis   San Francisco   Toronto
                Düsseldorf   Mexico

Book design by Stanley Drate.

1234567890BPBP78321098

Library of Congress Cataloging in Publication Data

Brackman, Arnold C
The luck of Nineveh.
1. Layard, Sir Austin Henry, 1817–1894.
2. Nineveh.   3.   Archaeologists—Great Britain—
Biography.   4.   Archaeologists—Iraq—Biography.
                    I.   Title.
DS70.88.L3B7   935′.03 [B]   78-1893
ISBN 0-07-007030-X

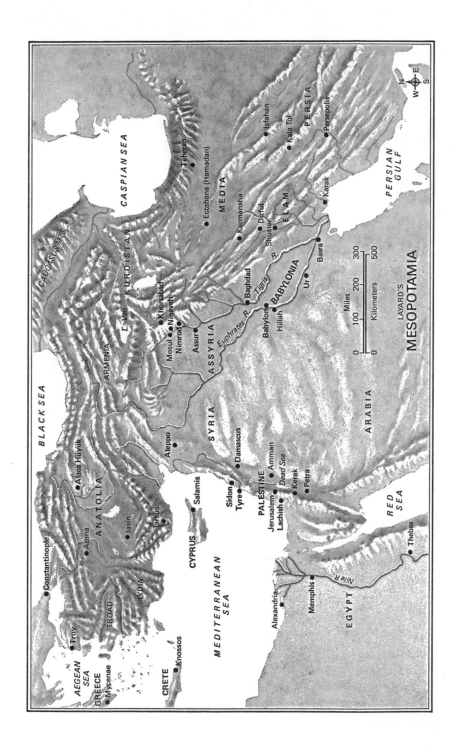

Foreword

In 1817, when Austen Henry Layard was born, there was no tangible proof that Nineveh, the seat of the Assyrian empire, which reputedly had endured longer than any empire before or since, ever existed. For that matter, there was no evidence that there ever was an Assyrian empire.

The Bible, of course, contained numerous references to Nineveh as "that great city," and fragments of its history, preserved by classical Greek and Roman geographers and historians, attested to its former glory, grandeur, and notoriety. Thus, although Nineveh and Assyria had been "familiar to us from childhood," as Layard expressed it thirty-four years later, "it is only when we ask ourselves what we really know concerning the Assyrians that we discover our ignorance of all that relates to their history, and even to their geographic position."

Indeed, Layard considered it one of the most remarkable facts of his day that the records of an empire, so renowned for its power and civilization, were entirely lost.

It was in the course of working on a biography of Heinrich Schliemann, the discoverer of Troy, that I stumbled onto the personal relationship between Schliemann and Layard, the discoverer of Nineveh. The link between them had been lost in history just as had the capitals of the Trojans and Assyrians.

Schliemann's story is the rags-to-riches epic in archaeology; Layard's story, the tale of the greatest adventurer in archaeology.

Schliemann, in his dreams and in the field, spent a lifetime in search of noble Troy—and found it late in life. By contrast Layard, as he openly conceded, "accidentally discovered" Nineveh in his youth. In contemporary argot, he lucked into it. In the process, like Schliemann, Layard brought to light a new world.

Just as Nineveh and Troy are insolubly linked in the legends and history of Western man, so are Layard and Schliemann. I have told Schliemann's story elsewhere.

This is Layard's story.

ARNOLD C. BRACKMAN

London and Paris, 1976
Brookfield Center, Connecticut, 1978

The Assyrian came down like a wolf on the fold.
—BYRON

I More than four thousand
years ago, the dung-colored plains between the Tigris and
Euphrates rivers, a corridor barely 100 miles wide and 400
miles long, spawned the world's first empire. Semitic in origin,
the Assyrian empire stretched at its zenith for a distance of
2,000 miles across the deserts, grasslands, and mountains of
Asia Minor, from Egypt to India, from Russia to Arabia Felix.
"From the borders of the distant mountains," the Assyrians
recounted, ". . . as far as the upper sea of the setting sun."

In double-decked galleys, the Assyrians ventured into that
Western sea, invaded, overran, and occupied Cyprus, and
brought, or at least claimed to bring, the islands on the eastern
rim of Homer's wine-dark Aegean under their sway. "The sons
who dwelt in the midst of the sea came up out of the sea," an
Assyrian monarch inscribed on a memorial stele, "and with
their rich gifts, came and kissed my feet."

During the first eight hundred years of their history, the
Assyrians consolidated their hold on the wedge-shaped area
between the Tigris and the Euphrates. The Greeks called it
Mesopotamia, "the land between the two rivers," a term they
probably derived from either Aramean *beth naharin* (house of
the two rivers), Hebrew *Aram naharain* (Syria of the two
rivers), or Arabic *bain al-nahrain* (the country between the
two rivers).

Then, with the devastating impact of a nuclear explosion,

between 960 and 612 B.C. the Assyrians pushed back the outer frontiers of empire until it embraced the known world.

At the fringes of empire successive Assyrian rulers discovered new lands to conquer, and set about to do it. The annual state-of-the-empire messages of the Assyrian kings set the tone. "I received the gifts of the distant Medes, the name of whose land the kings, my fathers, had not heard," wrote one monarch, "and I made them submit to my yoke."

In the Book of Genesis, Assyria is identified as the first great empire to come into existence after the Flood, and the founder is singled out as Nimrod, a great-grandson of Noah, who is described as "a mighty hunter before the Lord," "a mighty one in the earth." Nimrod established his kingdom in the "land of Shinar," the Mesopotamian delta, but, as a Greek writer later observed, he was seized "with a powerful desire to subdue all of Asia that lies between the Don and the Nile." According to Genesis, whatever his true motivation, "out of that land he went forth into Assyria and builded Nineveh." The origin of the name "Nineveh" is obscure. It may have been derived from Nina, the name of the city's patron, a goddess whose worship gave rise there to the "cult of Nineveh." As modern scholars point out, the cuneiform inscription for Nineveh is a fish enclosed in the sign for a house, possibly indicating a sacred fish pond of the tutelary deity. In any event, situated along the east bank of the Tigris, some 220 miles north of the delta, Nineveh became the seat of empire and the greatest city of its day.

Dotted with majestic palaces, temples, canals, and gardens, its walls rose 200 feet above the West Asian plain. Fortified by 1,500 watchtowers, the walls were so thick, it was said, that three chariots easily drove abreast upon them. Like the kernel of a nut protected by outer husks, Nineveh was defended by five walls and three moats. Each of the city's fifteen gates was guarded by castellated ramparts. And within its perimeter were more than thirty temples, "each shining with silver and gold."

For more than 1,300 years Assyrian monarchs ruled from Nineveh and other royal cities within the immediate vicinity, an irregular trapezium of land which included the Biblical cities of Ashur and Calah, and such hill stations as Dur-Sharrukin, the Fortress of Sargon, "built hard-by the springs at the foot of the mountains . . . above Nineveh," which Sargon the Great dubbed "a palace of incomparable magnificence."

With a remarkable sense of history, the Assyrian kings, a millennium before Homer, permanently inscribed their story of conquest on obelisks, clay tablets, cylinders, prisms, boundary markers, and memorial steles. They decorated the walls of their palaces and temples with sculptured scenes of sieges and battles. They wrote a veritable Iliad in stone.

The names of their kings were legend and struck terror into the hearts of people the length and breadth of the empire, and beyond: Ashurnasirpal, who proclaimed, "I am merciless . . . first in war, king of the world . . . who has trampled down all who were not submissive to him, and who brought under his sway the totality of all peoples"; Shalmaneser, who described himself as "the sun of all peoples, despot of all lands"; Tiglath-Pileser, who boasted, "42 countries and their kings . . . my hand conquered . . . and laid on them the heavy yoke of my rule"; Sargon, patron of the arts, who deported whole populations, overwhelmed Israel, and carried off her inhabitants into captivity; Sennacherib, "a mighty hero clothed in terror"; Esarhaddon, who described himself as a "consuming, unquenchable fire . . . the unsparing weapon which utterly destroys the enemy's land"; and the fabulous Ashurbanipal, "the terrible hurricane . . . who filled the plains . . . with blood," and whom the Greeks remembered as a transvestite tyrant who wore women's robes and painted his lips.

When Nimrod founded his capital, Diodorous wrote, "his design was to make Nineveh the largest and noblest city in the world, and to put it out of the power of those who came after him to build, or hope to build, such another." Even so, Nineveh did not attain the heights of her magnificence until a thousand years later, in 700 B.C., during the reign of Sennacherib, who erected "The Palace Without a Rival," a royal dwelling that outshone all others in splendor. It was so richly embellished with gold that "the whole city shone like the sun."

Nineveh was a wicked city, its rulers coarse, lustful, and

sadistic. Young women, including the wives of Assyrian nobles, danced naked before royal guests; human sacrifice was practiced; the emperor was unimpeachable, his word, law; the palaces were guarded by eunuchs, young men stripped of their virility; temple prostitutes, so designated, practiced their trade openly before idols, half-man, half-beast. Among the gods, Ashur (from which the Greeks derived the word "Assyria") was first, above all.

Justifiably, perhaps, the Assyrian kings bragged that they had built Nineveh "for all time" and "for lordly pleasure." Yet despite the splendor of Nineveh, and the extent of their empire, the Assyrians suffered from a deep inferiority complex. Their civilization was essentially borrowed. Their life style was largely acquired from the Sumerians and Babylonians of the delta, the land of Shinar. Assyria's gods, laws, and language—all were imported. Of course, they made contributions of their own. Their bas-reliefs and other works of art were original in composition and brilliantly executed. They erected arches, dug tunnels, and built aqueducts before the Romans were a glimmer in history's eye. They were masters of industrial processes—smelting, enameling and inlaying. They filled libraries with works on mathematics, astronomy, and astrology. They established the world's first botanical and zoological gardens, and maintained the world's first hunting preserves, a feature which, as Xenophon, the Greek, later observed, "affords the best training for war"—and it was in war that their true genius lay.

They were the first to transform conquered domains into provinces. Until their time, vanquished kings continued to rule their lands as the vassals of the conqueror. The Assyrians, however, replaced defeated nobles with Assyrian magistrates or permitted a vanquished ruler to continue to "rule" with an Assyrian prefect at his side. In effect, the Assyrians developed the world's first colonies, puppet states, and satellites. They introduced other political novelties. Whole populations were deported. Genocide was practiced as an instrument of state policy. Armies were conscripted. Popular opinion was suppressed. Forced labor was instituted. The cult of personality was developed.

According to Ctesias, who lived at the Persian court in Babylon, the Assyrians possessed a military machine of 1.7 million foot soldiers, 200,000 horsemen, and 16,000 war chariots, the most formidable army in the world. Their table of military organization included cavalry as well as chariotry, light and heavy infantry, artillery, and an engineer corps. They maintained a sophisticated intelligence network.

In a word, the Assyrians were the scourge of the known world. The approach of the Assyrian host is characterized in the Bible as "a whirlwind." They came on "roaring like the lion . . . like . . . the sea." And wherever the Assyrian armies trod, the Book of Isaiah lamented, there was "darkness and sorrow."

Assyrian literature is a paean that glorifies war. Cities are "smashed like pots"; "the smoke of burning towns obscures the heavens"; enemy strongpoints are so thoroughly destroyed that they appear as though "devastated by a flood." In the plains, the adversary is "cut down like a reed." In the hills, the mountains are "dyed the color of red wool" with the blood of the enemy.

Not all the passages about war are so lyrical. Much of Assyria's history is recorded on victory steles in a matter-of-fact, expository style.

"The nobles I flayed," the memorial stele of one king reported. "Three thousand captives I burned with fire. I left not one hostage alive. I cut off the hands and feet of some. I cut off the noses, ears and fingers of others. The eyes of numerous soldiers I put out. Maidens I burned as a holocaust."

Surveying the destruction he wreaked against an enemy, another Assyrian monarch, in a description that came back to haunt his empire, boasted: "The noise of people, the tread of cattle and sheep, the glad shouts of rejoicing, I banished from its fields. Wild asses, gazelles and all kinds of beasts of the plain, I caused to lie down among them, as if at home."

In counting their spoils, people and cattle were indiscriminately lumped together in the minds of the Assyrians, as in one campaign when they claimed to have captured 208,000 people, 7,200 horses and mules, 11,703 asses, 5,230 camels, 80,100 cattle, and 800,509 sheep. Even allowing for exaggeration, the checklist demonstrated that the non-Assyrian world was viewed by Assyrians as simply a private hunting preserve.

Assyria's fixation with war is also mirrored in the personal histories of their rulers; for example, the chronicles of Shalmaneser III, the Shalmaneser of the Bible, who ruled for thirty-four years. When he ascended the throne in 858 B.C., he recounted: "At the beginning of my reign, when I solemnly took my seat upon the royal throne, I mobilized my chariots and troops, the passes of Simesi I entered, Aridus, the stronghold of Ninni, I captured." Year followed upon year, and each year the litany of war was restated: "I destroyed, I devastated, I burned with fire." In his thirty-first year on the throne, the last on record, Shalmaneser's year-end review struck the same chord: "In my thirty-first year of reign . . . 250 cities I destroyed. . . . Awe-inspiring terror I poured out over [the enemy] . . . I slew their warriors. I carried off their booty." The booty included silver and gold beakers and bowls, golden goblets and pitchers, copper vessels, objects of ivory, richly dyed cloth, logs of cypress, tame elephants, and wild monkeys and apes. The latter fascinated the Assyrians, who, perhaps, saw in them their own primordial origin.

By their own accounts, the Assyrians reserved their direst cruelty for those who rebelled against their authority. They turned Nineveh into a sinister city that exalted cruelty.

When a group of Egyptians plotted a revolt, Assyria's king dispatched troops and "the curse of Asshur, king of gods, overtook [the conspirators] . . . not a man among them escaped. . . . Their corpses I hung on stakes, I stripped off their skins and covered the city walls with them."

A worse fate awaited the ringleaders of a Babylonian rebellion. The tongues of the ringleaders were torn out ("slit" is the word used on the stele), and their "dismembered bodies were fed to the dogs, swine, wolves, eagles, to the birds of heaven and to the fish of the deep." In a war against neighboring Elam, which lay to the east, the Assyrians not only slew the living but exhumed the dead.

"Of their earlier and later kings, who did not fear Asshur and Ishtar, my gods . . . I exposed [them] to the sun," the Assyrian conqueror averred. "Their bones I carried off to

Assyria ... [where] I deprived them of food offerings and libations of water."

Still worse was in store for the leader of a rebellion in Arabia Felix. "To make known the majesty of Asshur and the great gods, my lords, I laid on him a heavy penalty," an Assyrian king raged. "I put him into a kennel. With jackals and dogs I tied him up and made him guard the gate in Nineveh called *Entrance of the Thronging Nations.*" A similar fate awaited a co-conspirator. "At the command of the great gods, my lords, I put a dog chain upon him and made him guard a kennel," the emperor said with satisfaction.

At the crest of greatness, the Biblical prophet Ezekiel described the Assyrian empire in awesome terms. "Behold," Ezekiel said, "the Assyrian is a cedar of Lebanon ... and under his shadow dwell all great nations." And yet, suddenly, more swiftly than the empire rose, it fell—and disappeared.

Shattered is Nineveh—who shall pity her?
—NAHUM

III Despite Nineveh's dreaded military machine and undisputed political mastery of the known world, Babylon never accepted the "upstart" nation nor the role of a vassal state. In the seventh century B.C., the Babylonians rose in revolt and proclaimed their independence. Similar rebellions flared from Egypt to Persia. The insurgents joined in a grand alliance and marched on Nineveh.

Classical accounts of Nineveh's fall in 612 B.C.—those by Berosus, Ctesias, Diodorous, Eusebius, and Armenian historians such as Moses of Chorene—have titillated Western readers since the Greek Bronze Age. In these accounts, Ashurbanipal—Sardanapalus, the Greeks called him—the last Assyrian king, is held responsible for "the total destruction of an empire which had endured longer than any other known to history."

A voluptuary, Sardanapalus is said to have outdone his predecessors in luxury and sluggishness.

"He lived the life of a woman," Diodorous wrote with disgust. "He assumed feminine garb and so covered his face and indeed his entire body with whitening cosmetics and other unguents used by courtesans, that it rendered it more delicate than that of any luxury-loving woman."

He imitated a woman's voice and at his carousals he not only drank and ate to excess "but also pursued the delights of love with men as well as with women; for he practised sexual indulgence of both kinds without restraint."

As unrest spread through the empire, Sardanapalus figuratively fiddled, as Nero would do literally six hundred years later. Like Macbeth who took comfort in firmly rooted Birnam Wood, the Assyrian overlord took solace in the ancient prophecy that "no enemy will ever take Nineveh by storm unless the river shall first become the city's enemy."

As the rebel forces neared the great city, Sardanapalus committed an act of madness. He summoned help from the wolf against the dogs. He entered into a pact with barbarians from the northern limits of the empire, the Scythians.

By comparison with the Scythians, the Assyrians, for all their lust, repressive rule, and wanton cruelty to prisoners of war, were outriders of civilization. The Scythian warriors still drank the blood of their enemies, made drinking mugs out of their skulls, cloaks from their scalps, skinned them, and used their skin as napkins. In some instances, commented Herodotus, whom Cicero called the father of history, the Scythians "flay the right arms of their dead enemies, and make of the skin, which is stripped off with the nails hanging to it, a covering for their quivers."

In any event, the Scythians descended on Nineveh—and promptly betrayed Sardanapalus. They joined the Babylonians, Medes, and others in the final assault. (An Egyptian army was also en route but arrived too late to participate in the kill.) The rebel strategy included a diversion of the waters of the Tigris, along whose banks stood Nineveh. The ancient Assyrian prophecy came to pass.

In order to avoid capture, according to Ctesias, Sardanapalus built an enormous bonfire in his palace, heaped upon it all his gold and silver as well as every article of the royal wardrobe and, shutting his concubines and eunuchs in the room with the pyre, he consigned them and himself and his palace to the flames. In a Wagnerian flourish, the fiery exit marked the twilight of Assyria.

"I slaughtered the land ... ," Nabopolassar, the leader of the rebel Babylonian forces, later recounted. "I turned the hostile land into heaps and ruins. The Assyrians, who since distant days had ruled over all the peoples and whose heavy yoke had brought injury to the land ... their yoke I threw off."

The world rejoiced, none more than the Israelites. Nahum, the prophet, an eyewitness to the battle, gave a blow-by-blow account in the Old Testament: "The river sluices are opened, the palace walls are crumbling . . . Nineveh is a tomb of water. . . . She is empty and void and waste."

Then he editorialized. "The Lord of Hosts [has] set thee up as a wrong," he exalted, "and all who see thee shall flee and shall cry: Shattered is Nineveh—who shall pity her?"

In his moment of ecstasy, Nahum may have recalled the words of an earlier prophet. "The Lord our God," Zephaniah forecast, "he will make of Nineveh a desolation, dry like the wilderness. Herds shall lie down in the midst of her, all the beasts of the nations. The pelican and the porcupine shall lodge in her capitals, the owl shall hoot in her windows . . . desolation shall be in the thresholds for he has laid bare the cedar work."

As Sardanapalus' funeral pyre sent a column of smoke to heaven, the great palaces and temples, built of burnt and unburnt brick, their ceilings supported by cedar beams, burst into flames. As the "cedar work" burned, the ceilings collapsed. Walls buckled and cracked. The unbaked bricks, exposed to seasonal rains, dissolved. Hot desert winds, the simoon, blew across Mesopotamia and carried with them clouds of fine dust and sand. Gradually, the seared, fire-scarred ruins were filled in. They were covered and transformed into artificial mounds. Wind-blown seeds, watered by spring rains, sprouted from the mounds and covered them with a blanket of grass.

With the passage of time, Nineveh, the capital of an empire which held sway over the earth for longer than any before or since, faded from view. Nineveh, the joyous city that dwelt carelessly, that said in her heart, "I am, and there is none beside me!" dissolved, transformed by nature into grassy mounds fit for sheepfolds.

Nothing remained of either Nineveh or Assyria except vague memories, legends, myths, and traditions handed down in profane and sacred literature. Not a scrap of tangible evidence survived to prove that Nineveh ever existed.

A great stronghold, deserted and lying in ruins.
—XENOPHON

IIII Nineveh sank so rapidly
from sight that when Xenophon led his Ten Thousand Greeks
over the site two hundred years later on their celebrated
reconnaissance of the Persian empire, they did not know that
Nineveh lay underfoot. "[We] marched one stage, six para-
sangs, to a great stronghold, deserted and lying in ruins,"
Xenophon said. The ruins were those of Nineveh, and within
its shadows he skirmished with a Persian patrol. He called the
place Larissa.

By the beginning of the Christian era, mounds were commonplace in Mesopotamia. Strabo, by language and education
a Greek, ethnically an Asian and in his heart a Roman,
observed in his celebrated *Geography* that "mounds are to be
seen throughout the whole area." When he visited the delta
and saw the ruins of Babylon, he applied to it the epithet
pinned to the Megalopolitans of Arcadia. "The great city is a
great desert," Strabo said. As for Nineveh, even though infre-
quent downpours caused slides and cracked open the mounds,
the city was now so lost to view that he did not even refer to
it, although it had been the greater city of the two.

Six hundred years later, in A.D. 627, Heraclius defeated
Chosroes, the king of Persia, in a battle waged at the edge of
the mounds. If the Roman emperor knew he fought within
Nineveh's environs, he, like Strabo, made no mention of it in
his account of the fighting along the Tigris.

(11)

Yet the site was never truly lost in local tradition. Thus, following the Arab conquest of Mesopotamia, Arab geographers such as Ibn Hykal, Edrisi, Abdulfeda, and Ibn Batuta identified the mounds on the east bank of the Tigris, at a point opposite the sleazy trading town of Mosul, as "Ninawi" or "Ninaway." When the Turks succeeded the Arabs and reduced Mesopotamia to an outlying province of the Ottoman empire— an empire which lasted into this century—"Nineveh" was the only legal name that could be employed on deeds and other legal documents relating to the ownership or transfer of land on the bank opposite Mosul.

Despite these rich local traditions, however, Nineveh was, for all practical purposes, lost to the West. Indeed, the first European reference to Nineveh was not made until after the Crusades. In the mid-twelfth century, a Spanish traveler, a native of the kingdom of Navarre, Rabbi Benjamin of Tudela, in the course of a thirteen-year journey from Iberia to the borders of Cathay, visited Mosul and laconically observed that the town "stands on the banks of the Tigris and is combined [linked] by a bridge with Nineveh." Marco Polo, a latter-day Benjamin, mentioned Mosul during his travels in 1295, but he made no reference to Nineveh.

Benjamin's account was circulated privately and eventually published, "in the rabbinic character," at Constantinople in 1543. Thirty-two years later the report appeared for the first time in Latin in a slim volume proclaimed as "the first introduction of this work to the learned Christians, who although they might understand the scriptures in Hebrew were strangers to that style, which is called rabbinic, and in which these travels are written." That same year Leohart Rouchwolff, a German physician, visiting Mosul, confirmed Benjamin's observations. "In the region hereabout years ago," Rouchwolff wrote, "the mighty city of Nineveh was situated."

Nineveh, of course, had never been forgotten in the West. How could it be? In the Old and New Testaments Nineveh is mentioned twenty times, and in the Old Testament there are 132 references to Assyria. In the chronology of Archbishop James Ussher of Armagh, published in 1650 and widely accepted as gospel into the last century, the world was created in 4004 B.C. and the Assyrian empire in 1770 B.C., 114 years after the Flood. An increasing number of skeptics, however, their religious faith diluted by the spectacular scientific breakthroughs accompanying the first stirrings of the Industrial Revolution, sneered at tales about Nineveh and treated it as a legend that belonged to an age of fables. For them, there had never been a Nineveh any more than there had ever been a Troy.

Nonetheless, periodically, Europeans passing through Mesopotamia not only reported the existence of "strange mounds" in the region but returned home with souvenirs, a burnt brick or broken clay tablet inscribed with odd, arrow-headed, pyramidal-shaped characters. In Mosul farmers occasionally plowed them up while planting wheat and barley, and called them, in Arabic, *misimari* (nail-writing). They were either discarded as meaningless and worthless or recycled in making new bricks. Nobody related these finds to the Biblical hint that divine commands were first given to man on stone tablets. (In the Book of Job, the prophet exclaims, "Oh that my words were now written . . . that they were graven with an iron pen and lead in the rock forever!")

In 1700 Thomas Hyde, an Englishman, labeled these curiosities *dactuli pyramidales seu cuneiform*, meaning "pyramidal or wedge-shaped signs." He derived the word "cuneiform" from the Latin *cuneus*, or wedge. The word caught on. Hyde, however, considered the scratches a quaint style of Oriental decoration.

Thirty-two years later, Isaac Preston Cory, in a volume published in London, asked the question that a growing number of scholars had begun to speculate upon. "We are accustomed to regard Hebrew Scriptures and the Greek and Latin writings as the only certain records of antiquity," Cory wrote. "Yet there have been other languages in which have been written the annals and the histories of other nations. Where then are those of Assyria and Babylonia? . . . The literature of those mighty empires? Where are *even* their remains?" (italics added).

Shortly after Cory's publication, a French savant returned to Paris from a trip to the Near East with several specimens of "cuneiform" and agreed with Cory that they might conceal a lost language. Inexplicably, however, he concluded that the tablets "are not meant to be read." This prompted a German scholar to accept the challenge. He attempted to decipher them and deduced that cuneiform was an obscure form of Latin verse. Other academicians fared as badly. Some regarded the marks as talismans, Egyptian hieroglyphics, or Chinese. Indeed, as late as 1878, just a hundred years ago, the distinguished head of a Cambridge college considered the inscriptions "a pagan language which no one could read."

Thus, into the beginning of the Victorian era, and beyond, almost nothing was known about Nineveh. Despite the existence of the mounds and the occasional discovery of "decorations" of unknown origin, it simply never entered anybody's head to dig into the mounds and see what, if anything, lay within them. The city that was founded before the fall of Troy, and that flourished before Exodus, had dissolved into a myth.

May the gods lead him.

—ASHURNASIRPAL

IV

In 1825, the year the British Museum acquired its first collection of mysterious cuneiform tablets—the collection filled a three-foot-square glass case—Austen Henry Layard embarked on his first solo journey. He took a coach from London to Dover, crossed the English Channel by packet, and traveled from Calais to Paris. He put up one night in the French capital and ordered the concierge to bring him a bottle of champagne. By diligence the following morning, he proceeded to Moulins, arriving in the middle of the night. "In the crowd," he recalled later, "I recognized my father, who was waiting for me."

Layard was eight years old.

The journey gave him a large measure of self-confidence, and a taste for travel and adventure. The champagne incident also illuminated his precocious appreciation of life's pleasures. "I well recollect asking for that bottle, which my father, to his amazement," Layard said laughingly sixty years later, "found charged in the bill."

In many ways, the journey was a microcosmic forerunner of his future life style.

As Layard's surname suggests, his family was of French origin; indeed, the family claimed to be of ancient stock, descended "in a somewhat mythical way," his relatives used to say, from Raymond of Toulouse. Whatever the case, when

Louis XIV revoked the Edict of Nantes in 1685, and thereby removed the shield that protected the Protestant minority from religious persecution, the French king set in motion a mass flight of Huguenots, as they were called, from France. Among the refugees was Peter Raymond de Layarde, who slipped across the Dutch border with the assistance of a French Catholic friend, and fled to England.

De Layarde Anglicized his name and entered the British army, rose to the rank of major, married the daughter of a French refugee like himself, and settled at Canterbury, where a French community took root after the Huguenots were granted permission to use a crypt of the cathedral for their service—a service they conduct there to this day.

The Layard family flourished on English soil. By the turn of the eighteenth century, two Layards had risen to the rank of general in the army and a third, Charles, entered the church, became Prebendary of Worcester, Chaplain-in-Ordinary to King George III, and Dean of Bristol. Like many of the orthodox clerical dignitaries of his day, he lived comfortably, frequented good society, enjoyed good food, and, as his grandson Austen Henry Layard was wont to say, "drank freely of old port."

In truth, the dean was a pompous and overbearing figure who was in constant conflict with Christian values. He was not especially fond of children, particularly his own. Indeed, he considered children an inconvenience, if not a nuisance. He solved their interference in his own life by bundling them off at an early age, like a cat's litter, to respectable country families. His second son, Henry Peter John Layard, was dispatched to Ramsgate. Out of sight, out of mind. The dean never corresponded with him and rarely visited him. Incredibly, he never invited his children home for the holidays, not even for Christmas. If his wife had any say in the matter, which is doubtful, there is no record of it.

Young Henry Peter John was fortunate, however. His proxy family was well read and fostered in the boy a taste for English literature and the fine arts. The child also developed a deepening affection for a playmate with merry blue eyes, Marianne Austen, the daughter of a neighbor and local banker.

While he was growing up at Ramsgate, France invaded the

Netherlands and in 1795 reduced Holland to the status of vassal. Automatically, the Dutch overseas empire, which was spread from Surinam on the northern bulge of South America to the Malay archipelago in Southeast Asia, became fair game for the British, who warred incessantly with the French on a global scale. One of the jewels of the Dutch empire was Ceylon, "Pearl of the Orient," rich in spices, tea, rubber, pearls, and other exotic treasures. The British East India Company lost little time in driving its Dutch counterpart from the island.

To the British, Ceylon was a kind of paradise, and their acquisition of the territory set off a wild scramble for postings to the island, particularly for appointments to the newly founded Ceylon Civil Service, which administered the treasure trove. The civil service was considered a shortcut to riches, and the dean shrewdly applied the right pressure in the right places in obtaining appointments for two of his sons, Henry Peter John and Charles Edward, both of them now teenagers.

In short order, the Layard name became a force in the crown colony—and remained so until Ceylon regained her independence in 1948. Through the years, Layards held key posts in the civil service, served as senior officers in the Ceylon Rifles, played prominent roles in the island's judiciary system, from district judges to chief justice, and prospered as tea-and-coffee planters and traders.

But this was not to be the case with Henry Peter John. His brother Charles, and Charles's descendants, reaped the good fortune, while Henry was compelled by poor health—notably an unfortunate mix of asthma and malaria—to leave the tropical paradise. He returned to England with a modest pension, and little else.

In Ceylon, however, the youthful Layard's thoughts had turned on more than making a fortune. No sooner had he disembarked from a square-rigger in the Thames' roadstead than he took the first available stage to Ramsgate and proposed to the blue-eyed Marianne. She promptly accepted the offer. Attractive, diminutive, she possessed an uncomplicated and unassuming nature, and despite a parochial upbringing, she was quite cosmopolitan in outlook. Marianne was a voracious reader—and rarely forgot anything she read. She delighted in history, biography, and travel. Her weakness was a susceptibility to family pressures, real or perceived. The Austens were a large, well-to-do, close-knit clan. Fortunately for Marianne they approved of "the young man from Ceylon," whom they had known and liked as a child and whose father had impeccable Church of England credentials.

Soon after their betrothal, with Napoleon's defeat and the restoration of peace on the Continent, the asthmatic Henry and his bride sailed for France with a view to stretching out his small pension and escaping England's miserable climate. In Paris, on a blustery Wednesday, March 5, 1817, on Rue Neuve des Petits Champs, Marianne gave birth to the couple's first child, a boy, dutifully christened Henry Austen. This was the same year Constable painted *Flatford Mill*, Byron wrote *Manfred*, Jane Austen died, and riots against low wages flared in Derbyshire as social unrest in England kept pace with the burgeoning Industrial Revolution.

Paris, of course, took no notice of Layard's birth. The Parisian press was preoccupied with another Englishman, Tom Belcher, "first of all English boxers," who injured his hand and announced that day his retirement from the ring after six hundred successful bouts in which, according to *Gazette de France*, he broke the jaws of two hundred opponents.

The senior Layard's health, however, fared no better in France than in Ceylon or Britain. In quest of a milder climate, Layard and his family gravitated south, and in 1821, when Henry Austen was four years old, they settled at Florence, where, for the first time since he quit Ceylon, the father was overjoyed to find himself free of chronic asthmatic attacks.

Unlike his own father, the Dean of Bristol, or perhaps because of him, the senior Henry Layard was a doting father, who cultivated in his children—Marianne bore him four other sons, two of whom died in infancy—a lively interest in the fine arts and the world. With young Henry Austen in tow, the father employed Florence's renowned museums and picture galleries as classrooms.

These happy days in Italy, however, were short-lived. Marianne's family was horrified at the thought of her children being raised in a foreign country; worse, among foreigners.

Her brother Benjamin and his wife, Sara, a childless couple, were particularly upset. As young Henry's godparents, they felt a special responsibility toward the boy.

Benjamin Austen was a prominent London solicitor, and he entertained big plans for the lad. When the boy was of age, he proposed to take him on as an articled law clerk. In the back of Austen's mind was the hope that the young man might become a partner in his firm and eventually take over the law business. Like her husband, Sara Austen, a socialite who collected young writers and artists around her dining room table like a lepidopterist collects moths and butterflies, insisted that the boy's proper place was in a proper English school where he would obtain a proper education before taking up the law. "Proper" was one of Sara's favorite words.

The affluent Austens brought pressure to bear on Marianne, who, in character, bowed to her family's desires. Reluctantly, her husband went along with the wishes of his wife and in-laws. After all, he reasoned, there was the boy's future to consider.

Unhappily, the Layards returned to wet and dreary England. But the father suffered so severely from a fresh series of asthma attacks that on medical advice he and his family fled back to the Continent for relief and settled again in Moulins. Before their departure, however, the Layards promised the Austens to give young Henry a "proper" education.

During the family's residence at Moulins, the boy entered a French school. Sheltered through infancy and childhood, Henry Austen Layard came into contact with a new world. Suddenly, he found himself a member of a detestable and detested minority. The Napoleonic wars were over, but the French and English continued to view each other suspiciously, even with contempt and hatred. At school, Layard was denounced as a Protestant and heretic.

He was often beaten up by school bullies, and whenever a scuffle erupted, the headmaster meted out to him a double punishment. The headmaster reasoned, with Gallic logic, that the English lad must have been the instigator of the trouble. After all, the school was peaceful until he enrolled.

Informed that they possessed a "rebellious and unmanageable" son, the surprised Layards eventually got to the bottom of the trouble and withdrew him from school. But the experience gave young Layard a new perspective on life. He developed a persecution complex and, as a defense mechanism, a hot temper and aggressive attitude. Thereafter, in dealing with the world, he was outwardly on the offensive, although inwardly on the defensive.

If the Moulins school episode was disastrous for the son, so was the French climate for the father. The family packed their belongings and, after a brief residence in Switzerland, did what was in their hearts and returned to their beloved Italy and their old haunt, Florence.

This second sojourn in Florence was the happiest period of Henry Austen Layard's youth. He was immersed in a world of painters and soon became as fluent in Italian as in French and English. In a house filled with books, he was drawn irresistibly to volumes about travel and high adventure—the sort of books his mother feasted upon until her death in 1879 at the age of eighty-nine.

One of Layard's favorite authors was Johann Burckhardt, the Swiss explorer who wrote a string of travel books on Asia Minor and had recently discovered the lost city of Petra, built by the Nabataeans, in what is now the Jordanian desert. Petra, he wrote, was a mass of glorious ruins of undetermined vintage and lay in a region so utterly desolate that "it is scarcely possible to imagine how a wilderness so dreary and desolate could ever have been adorned with walled cities, or inhabited for ages by a powerful and opulent people."

Burckhardt's account stirred within young Layard a desire to see Petra for himself and perhaps find a "lost" city of his own. But his favorite book was *The Thousand and One Nights*, that composite of Persian and Indian tales, transmuted into Arabian fables, which to this day, in expurgated form, serves as a Western child's introduction to the Arab world.

For hours, stretched out on the floor under the family's ornate, gilded Florentine dining room table, he read and reread with widening irises tales of genies and ghouls, obese sultans and almond-eyed damsels, of Aladdin, Ali Baba, and Sinbad. That particular book lived in him for more than a thousand

and one nights. Nearly seventy, while working on his memoirs, Layard wrote with a boyish enthusiasm that persisted throughout his life, "I can read [these tales] even now with almost as much delight as I read them when a boy." Significantly, he added, "They have had no little influence upon my life and career."

As a result of his passion for the *Arabian Nights*, he thereafter devoured every available book on Near Eastern travel.

In addition to an adventurous spirit, Layard developed through the thousand nights what he later conceded was a "somewhat romantic disposition." At the age of ten, for example, he fell in love "with a real living damsel," the sister of a playmate over whom he quarreled with another boy. Since both boys were taking fencing lessons, they determined to settle their rivalry with foils—shorn of buttons. "How we were prevented from carrying out our bloody intentions," he reminisced later, "I now forget."

Immediately after having resettled in Florence, the father and son had fallen back into a familiar routine, touring galleries and museums. By the age of nine, young Layard knew the identity, at a glance, of every painter of the Florentine school, and was at home with all the pictures in the great Uffizi and Pitti collections. By the age of twelve, he was an accomplished art connoisseur and critic. Much to his father's delight, and to the astonishment of the experts, the youngster could distinguish the subtle difference between the paintings of such minor artists as Carlo Dolci and his daughter Agnes. Indeed, for a time, the boy considered becoming a painter. But his father, who envisioned his son as an established London solicitor, with wood-paneled office, discouraged the idea. Beauty in art, yes; money, no.

Nonetheless, the father let the son down gently and arranged for the youth to take drawing lessons with a local, indifferent painter who lived in a cell at the Convent of St. Croce. The artist taught the child to copy lithographs of human figures and animals, an accomplishment that proved invaluable to him in later life. Young Layard also visited the studio of Seymour Kirkup, an English painter and student of Dante who is best remembered for his illustrations of the Vernon edition of the *Divine Comedy.* A local celebrity, Kirkup enthralled the boy with the story of how he discovered a lost fresco by Giotto. It was hidden by centuries of whitewash on a wall in the chapel of Borgello. Little did Layard realize that he was destined to repeat Kirkup's actions far afield, and on a stupendous scale, recovering not simply a lost work of art but enough lost art to fill several museums.

In Italy, Layard's father retained his Ceylonese habits and, despite his limited income, crowded his lunch table regularly with local and visiting personalities. They were largely big fish from small ponds, among them, Morgan, a landscape painter; Niccolini, a dramatist; Trelawny, a friend of Byron; and Migliarini, who was in charge of the "department of antiquities" at the Uffizi, the word "archaeology" yet to come into popular usage.

"They all took too much note of me," Layard protested. But he relished the attention. Table talk centered on the fine arts, and travel. These luncheons excited the boy's imagination, instilled within him an intense desire for travel, and turned him, prematurely, into a cosmopolitan lad.

Through their friendship with Migliarini, father and son visited the Etruscan excavations in progress in the region and inspected the ancient walls of Florence, Layard's first contact with "the dig," as modern archaeologists term it.

Archaeology, of course, was in its infancy, stimulated largely by the casual discovery of the ruins of Pompeii at the end of the eighteenth century, an event which stirred the imagination of Europe. But these ruins, covered with volcanic ash, were essentially aboveground. The idea that lost cities and lost civilizations could be brought to light by digging into the core of the earth was novel.

Thus, in the formative phase of Layard's life, fate appears to have pushed him in the direction of archaeology, and its outriders, travel and adventure. The family, for example, frequently picnicked along the banks of Lake Trasimeno, adjacent to the field on which the Romans under Flaminius were routed by Hannibal. According to local tradition, ever since that fateful encounter, the crow of an invisible cock pierced the air at sunrise. The tradition was either accepted or rejected, depending on one's credulity. But the boy exhibited an independent mind: Why debate the issue from armchairs? Why not go into the field and find out?

While others argued over the merits of the tradition, Henry Austen Layard, eleven years old, rose one morning shortly after midnight and posted himself at the scene. In the moonlight, in his mind's eye, he probably saw a replay of the battle, as chariot pressed against chariot, shield against shield, spear against spear. But the cock did not make himself heard that morning. "I had a toilsome walk in the night for nothing," he later remarked, adding, "but I was determined to go, and I went."

As the years slipped by, his godparents back in England were aghast at their godson's freewheeling education. The Austens applied new pressure on Marianne and her husband to reconsider the boy's future. The choice was theirs—either ship him to England for a proper education or raise him among dirty foreigners. True to her character, Marianne retreated and, true to his, her husband retreated with her.

In 1829, at the age of twelve, young Layard's Italian idyll collapsed for the second time. He was packed off to England.

Like a caged bird—shut up.
—SENNACHERIB

V In England, the Austens
placed their heir in a school maintained by the Reverend
James Bewsher, like themselves, a proper Tory and member
of the Church of England. "I found myself," Layard said with
understatement, "among boys who had been brought up
differently from myself."

Not only did he have nothing in common with them, but
the students regarded him darkly. His fluency in French and
Italian made him suspect, the butt of unending harassment,
and Layard was introduced to reverse discrimination. Like the
barnyard, he learned, every society required a pecking order
to compensate for its own insecurities. The experience taught
him when it was diplomatic, and honorable, to retreat. For
example, he was so unmercifully teased and bullied because
of his Italian background that, as he later wrote, "I did my
best to conceal my knowledge of that floral language and to
avoid all allusion to Italy."

Since he was never destined to wear a school tie—the Layards
could not afford to send him to college, and the Austens saw
no need for it—his tutors at Bewsher's school took little
interest in his classical education. "I have regretted it through
my life," he often said. His passion for travel deepened when
he gazed on the square-riggers which tied up in the Thames;
on one occasion he boarded H.M.S. *Coote*, a sloop-of-war based
in Asia Minor, which was being refitted and was open to the
public.

Layard's happiest hours at school were during summer recess. The boys dispersed to their country estates and he remained behind with the caretakers of Bewsher's. His free time was devoted to fishing the Thames, eyeing the girls, and reading the latest accounts of travel and adventure in Asia Minor.

Layard usually spent Christmas and other holidays at the Austen town house or country estate, where Layard discovered he possessed a natural gift for horsemanship. He also regularly visited the British Museum, then located at Montague House, within a few minutes' walk of the Austens' London residence. There he gazed, for the first time, on all that remained of the "great cities" of Nineveh and Babylon, which was scant indeed. The collection had been purchased—the year he was born—by the Museum from the widow of Claudius James Rich. To Layard, the name Rich meant nothing.

The collection filled a solitary display case and consisted of four baked clay cylinders, thirty-two clay tablets, thirteen bricks, one boundary marker, and several smaller bits and pieces. The relics were covered with arrow-headed characters. Whether these objects were truly of Assyrian origin was problematical. After all, nobody could read the strange markings. Although Layard did not know it at the time, that lonely case gave Rich immortality. It marked the first stirrings of Assyrian archaeology.

Layard spent four years at Bewsher's in a desultory fashion. Then in 1834, Layard's parents and brothers returned to England at the insistence of the Austen clan. Young Layard met his parents at Dover, and a warm reunion ensued. The parents were proud. Their oldest son, approaching his seventeenth birthday, had developed into a handsome youth, who wore his golden locks à la Byron and sported a mustache in the dashing style popularized during the early Victorian era.

Benjamin and Sara Austen had virtually adopted young Henry in his parents' absence. At Benjamin's request, he had even reversed the order of his Christian names and signed himself Austen Henry, although family and friends continued to call him "Henry." He was ready to embark upon his apprenticeship in law, and clearly he was being groomed to take over his uncle's firm. At least, that was the family game plan. "My own tastes and inclinations . . . were not considered or consulted," Austen Henry observed with misgiving. "Nor was my character and disposition taken into account."

On January 24, 1834, he was "articled" to his uncle for a period of five years. Under the terms of the compact, a copy of which is now kept in the British Museum together with other Layard papers, Benjamin Austen pledged "to the best of and utmost of [my] skill and knowledge to teach and instruct Austen Henry Layard in the business practise and profession of an attorney and solicitor."

For his part, young Layard swore that he would not "willfully conceal, embezzle, spend, destroy, lend, obliterate or make away with any money, books, papers, deeds, writing or any other goods, chattels or effects of the said Benjamin Austen."

The saids and whereases were sealed at a family dinner at the Austens, where the port flowed freely. Young Layard's parents and godparents were in high spirits. The former had provided their first child with an excellent start in life; the latter had acquired an heir-apparent.

The only individual at the table who was less than enthusiastic was Austen Henry himself. The law did not appeal to him. Secretly, he envied his schoolmates who were going on to Eton and Oxford, "but I knew my father was not sufficiently rich to enable him to give me a similar advantage," he later confessed.

For the next five years Layard diligently and desperately applied himself to the law. The effort was a disaster.

During those years his father bestowed on him an allowance of £2 ($10) a week. From this amount, he was expected to pay for his lodging, food, clothing, carfare, entertainment, books, and incidentals. His uncle had led the Layards to believe that he intended to "do something for the boy" during his apprenticeship. But he contributed nothing to the weekly stipend other than an annual gift at Christmas.

Each morning, promptly at nine, like a young Bob Cratchit, Austen Henry was at his stool in his uncle's chambers, quill in hand, ready to partake in the routine of an attorney's office.

His principal activity was to copy legal documents and to accompany the firm's clerks to public offices to transact business. When not entwined in seemingly endless piles of paper, he was expected to read and master the law.

At quitting time, late in the day, his uncle and staff departed for their homes and the warmth of their winter hearths while Layard went to dinner alone at a dingy eating house just down the street. Dinner was always the same, a single chop and a glass of tepid water, at six pence (12 cents), the cheapest fare he could find. After dinner, he was expected to return to his uncle's offices at Gray's Inn and spend the evening studying Blackstone, before retiring to his cheap boardinghouse on New Ormond Street. Some of the legal tracts, he discovered to his horror, were written in Elizabethan English. He found the law "dry and monotonous . . . difficult of comprehension," he later admitted. His only escape from the morbidity and drudgery of the law was Sunday, when the Austens held open house.

These Sunday dinners were glittering affairs, the more surprising since the puritanical outlook of the Victorian age was beginning to take hold and Parliament had just narrowly defeated the 1837 Sunday Observance Bill which would have barred entertainments, public or private, on the Sabbath.

But like Layard's parents, his aunt and uncle were gracious hosts and crowded their table with a wide circle of writers, painters, and politicians, the latter invariably staunch Tories (the Austens hated the Radicals and had contempt for the Whigs). Unlike his parents' table in Florence, however, his godparents' table was encircled by big fish from big ponds. He dined with such celebrities as Turner, the painter; Robert Plumer Ward, author of De Vere; Charles Fellows, who had found Greek ruins in Turkey; Isaac Disraeli, the literary critic, and his foppish son Benjamin, who wrote Vivian Grey, with the editorial assistance of Aunt Sara, a book that catapulted him into the limelight and, ultimately, into 10 Downing Street. On one occasion, in the course of a spirited debate, young Disraeli brought down the Austens and their guests with the outrageous declaration that when he became prime minister, he would do thus-and-so. As the laughter reverberated around the table, an angered Dizzy, as he was called, shouted, "Laugh as you may, I shall be prime minister!"

Among the Austens' inner circle, the two personalities whom Layard envied the most were Disraeli and Fellows.

Layard, then seventeen years old—Dizzy was thirty—was secretly jealous of the brash, confident young Tory who knew what he wanted and was determined to get it. Like himself, Disraeli had been an articled clerk. One day, however, Dizzy was caught reading Chaucer instead of Blackstone, upbraided for breech of discipline, and told he was unfit for the law. Dizzy required no encouragement to abandon the profession. He fled Gray's Inn and took refuge in the worlds of literature and politics. If only someone would tell Layard that he, too, was unfit for the bar.

As for Fellows, then 35, he was, to employ the euphemism of the period, "a gentleman of fortune"; he had inherited his money—his father was a banker. But Fellows was not an idler. He regaled the Austens and their guests with fascinating accounts of exploration in Turkish Asia and the discovery of such Greek ruins as Xanthus, the ancient capital of Lycia. Fellows brought back tangible proof of his discoveries, sketches and cases of sculpture. Queen Victoria later knighted him "as an acknowledgement of his services in the removal of the Xanthian antiquities to this country," and he was lionized by London society.

Layard was more than fascinated by Fellows—he was enthralled. Secretly, he nurtured the hope of emulating him. If he could only escape the law like Dizzy and spend his free time like Fellows! Oh, how he envied them. But for Layard the die was cast.

After these stimulating Sunday dinners, young Layard returned to his boardinghouse more depressed than ever.

Layard's father, within a year of his reluctant return to England's inhospitable climate, sustained a fresh series of asthmatic attacks. These bouts left him weak, and he contracted tuberculosis, the curse of a rapidly industrializing England.

Young Disraeli, in the hustings during the 1835 election campaign, visited the elder Layard at his Aylesbury home, on the outskirts of London, and was aghast. "Layard in bed," he penned the Austens in his familiar staccato style, "& really dangerously ill."

Austen Henry rushed to his father's side. Shortly thereafter, at the age of fifty-one, this artistically inclined, sensitive family man, who had developed strong bonds of friendship with his sons in an age when fathers and sons were expected to be aloof, was dead. His death stunned the boy. The shock, coupled with a rapidly declining interest in the law, induced a severe depression. Alarmed, the Austens summoned their physician and the doctor prescribed "a change of air."

In the company of a friend of the Austens, William Brockeden, an author and illustrator, Layard spent part of the summer that year on the Continent, chiefly in the Italian Alps. Through "Brock," as his friends called him, he met Camille de Cavour, learned of the Italian struggle for independence, and was quickly enlisted to Cavour's side.

It was during this journey that Layard's serious interest in the world of the distant past surfaced. Brock was gathering material for a new book. In particular, he wished to verify the theory that Hannibal had crossed the Alps during the Second Punic War through a pass now known as the Little St. Bernard. With a frayed copy of the Roman historian Polybius in hand, and with Layard at his side, Brock examined the Alpine topography and announced that he had correctly solved the controversy over the route the Carthaginians took during their invasion of Italy.

During their Alpine sojourn, Brock introduced Layard to Henry Crabb Robinson, a former foreign correspondent of the London *Times* who had turned to law, amassed a fortune, and quit in midstream to "pass the remainder of my life in ease and comfort." Robinson took an immediate liking to the young man and extended him an invitation to breakfast with him in London. Robinson's breakfasts were as justly famous as the Austens' Sunday dinners.

Through Robinson, Layard met literary giants such as Coleridge and Wordsworth, and colorful and unorthodox political figures, including W. J. Fox, the Unitarian minister who was a leader in the successful campaign against the Corn Laws, the most seamy and steamy domestic political issue of the day.

Despite his "retirement," Robinson contributed regularly to

journals and frequently employed Layard as a research assistant. "Soon," Layard recalled, "each moment that I could spare from my work at Gray's Inn was devoted to general reading."

German was hardly a popular language in that era. But as a result of his association with Robinson, who talked endlessly about Goethe and other German writers, Layard sought to acquire a knowledge of it. For the price of a cup of tea and a slice of bread and butter, he recruited a destitute, half-starved Polish refugee to give him evening lessons in German. Through the Pole, Layard learned of Russia's network of Siberian prison camps (the Gulag Archipelago of the Czarist era), and of the Polish struggle for independence.

Thus, he received lessons not only in German but also in foreign affairs. Just as he had become a champion of the Italian struggle for independence, he became an ardent supporter of the Polish cause. "Their unhappy fate taught me to appreciate the blessings of a free constitutional government," Layard wrote, "and of the liberties which my country enjoyed."

Mixing with Robinson and his friends rapidly undermined Layard's Tory convictions and Church of England moorings. He often attended the Sunday service of the Unitarian church and expressed political sentiments about the Corn Laws, for example, that shocked the Austens. He favored their repeal against the interest of the landed gentry.

The change of air that summer had done him wonders, and thereafter he spent his summers on the Continent, missing an occasional chop at dinner or squirreling away a few pence to finance these journeys. In 1836 he spent July and August in France, where he flirted with the pretty *grisettes*, and the year after that he revisited Italy, his true home.

Layard was now a dashing lad of eighteen, and looked as though he had stepped out of a Gainsborough painting. For him, Italy held as much fascination as for the poet whose style of dress he imitated. "O Italia," wrote Byron, "thou who hast the fatal face of beauty!"

And for Layard, in the summer of 1837, Italy's beauty was almost literally fatal. At Lake Maggiore he met the Contessina Galateri, who was several years younger than her husband, a man of violent temper and capricious disposition, who delighted in plucking out the eyes of song birds so that they would sing better, and who was known in the lake district as *il matto,* the madman.

"The Contessina was one of the loveliest woman I ever saw," Layard reminisced. Her hair was brilliant gold; her eyes, deep blue; her complexion, translucent; her features, classic. She was barely five feet in height, graceful and shapely.

Il matto thought the English youth paid too much attention to her, and a quarrel at Locano nearly ended in a duel. Layard protested there was nothing between them, but clearly, he had an eye for pretty women and they had an eye for him. As he confessed in a private letter, "I *am* always getting into hot water." The italics were his.

During this Italian airing, Layard also met Silvio Pellico, whose *Francesca da Rimini* was an Italian literary sensation. "The conversation," Layard recalled, "turned upon Botta, the historian." Carlo Botta had recently died at Paris at the age of sixty. It was the first time Layard had heard the name, but five years later, his meeting with Botta's son, Paolo Emilio, was destined to mark a turning point in his life.

The following summer, in 1838, with the advance of a few extra pounds from his widowed mother, Layard booked a second-class passage on a British steamer for an excursion to Scandinavia and Russia for the purpose of "seeing something of northern Europe."

The visit to Russia was a sobering experience. This was the first Western country he had visited in which the pretense of even a modicum of representative government and civil liberties was wholly lacking. He found the regime "oppressive," and as a result of the trip he acquired "a detestation of Russian despotism and of Russian rule" that he retained throughout his life.

But at Copenhagen he visited the royal library and made the acquaintance of a keeper who obligingly showed him Scandinavian manuscripts that proved Norsemen were the early discoverers of the New World.

"I thus took at Copenhagen," he said later, "my first lessons in antiquities"—archaeology.

Claudius Rich, Esquire, some bricks has got.
—BYRON

VI

Other than short summer excursions, Layard quenched his thirst for travel by haunting London's secondhand bookshops. His focus centered on books about travel and adventure in Asia Minor. In his childhood, it had been Burckhardt and the *Arabian Nights*; now it was Sir Robert Ker Porter.

At a book stall near the British Museum he found worn copies of Porter's two-volume work on Persia and ancient Babylonia. The set had been published in 1821, when Layard was four years old.

Not only Sir Robert's book but his adventurous life style appealed to Layard. Porter had married, to employ Layard's idiom, a "real living damsel," a Russian princess, and he himself was a character as fanciful as any in Scheherazade's tales. An incurable romantic and adventurer, Sir Robert also described himself as "an ardent lover and sedulous practitioner of the arts and the study of antiquity."

During his Near Eastern travels, Porter traced the route of Xenophon and the Ten Thousand Greeks, a land march that took him to nondescript Mosul. There, to Porter's astonishment, he discovered, like Rabbi Benjamin of Tudela three centuries earlier, that according to local legend the large mound on the opposite bank was the site of lost Nineveh. Out of curiosity, Sir Robert crossed the Tigris and found scattered on the mound a number of odd bricks inscribed with chiseled characters "known by the several names of cuneiform, nail-headed, arrow-headed." With astonishing perspicacity, he surmised that the characters might be of Assyrian origin and speculated: "We might not be extravagant in believing these characters to have been used before the Flood."

He also reported the discovery of "curious relics," the fragments of cylinders covered in cuneiform characters and depicting such fantastic figures in combat as a bull, half-man, half-beast. This was indeed a remarkable discovery, for Berosus, in his strange stories of ancient Assyria, claimed that "there was a time in which there existed nothing but darkness, an abyss of waters, wherein resided the most hideous beings ... among them bulls with the heads of men ... and other animals with the heads and bodies of horses and the tails of fishes."

Porter's book captivated Layard. He was also moved by the last paragraph of this 1,589-page tome, in which, in the form of an afterthought, Sir Robert grieved over the death of Claudius James Rich, the East India Company representative who had often been Porter's host at Baghdad and who had succumbed to cholera at the age of thirty-four. Rich had left behind some "literary papers," and Sir Robert ended the postscript with an appeal that the papers be published.

Rich? The name plucked at Layard's memory. Suddenly, he remembered: Rich's name adorned the odd collection of cuneiform tablets in the lonely vitrine in the British Museum.

Layard scurried about in search of Rich's literary papers and learned that they had just been published by his wife, fifteen years after Rich's death. When Layard got his hands on Rich's memoirs, the title alone whetted his appetite: *Narrative of a Residence in Koordistan, and on the site of Ancient Nineveh; with a Journal of a Voyage Down the Tigris to Baghdad and an account of a visit to Shirauz and Persepolis.*

Layard sat up through the night reading Rich and the following day fell asleep on his stool at Gray's Inn.

Like himself, Rich had been born in France—near Dijon, in Burgundy. An extraordinary linguist, Rich was fluent in Arabic by the age of nine—without a teacher and assisted only by a grammar and dictionary. By fifteen he had mastered the Babel of Asia Minor—Persian, Hebrew, Turkish, etc. Two years later he joined the East India Company, rose quickly through its ranks, married the comely Mary MacIntosh, daughter of a company official, and at twenty-five was appointed the Company's resident at Baghdad.

In his journal, Rich referred to the collection of relics he had donated to the British Museum as "the curiosities of Nineveh." But, he confided, "Whether they belonged to Nineveh or some other city is the question."

Rich recounted how he and Mary had visited Mosul on several occasions and had explored together the Tigris's left bank. They found a ruined wall and impulsively scratched their names on it. "Some traveller in after times, when our remembrance has long been swept away," Rich wrote, ". . . . may wonder, on reading of the name of Mary Rich, who the adventurous female was who had visited the ruins of Nineveh."

Layard's adrenalin flowed as he read these passages. The journals, edited by Mary as an imperishable monument to her husband, stirred not only Layard but England. (Although Byron, Layard's hero, may have been less impressed with Rich's sudden claim to fame; in *Don Juan* he quipped, "Claudius Rich, Esquire, some bricks has got.")

Layard was now permanently hooked on Asia Minor. "I greedily read," he said, "every volume of Eastern travel that fell my way." Among these books were Sir John Malcolm's Persian histories and James Morier's adventurous tales of Haji Baba.

And the more he read, the more acute the contrast between his dreams and reality, the more he railed against his fate as an articled law clerk.

In 1838, after four years of legal training, he reached the breaking point. "I could not conceal my feelings on the subject from my uncle and my friends," he said. As a personal friend of Layard's later politely put it, "A lawyer's office failed to satisfy his spirit of adventure."

But driven by a sense of guilt combined with honor and duty, Layard continued to turn up promptly on his stool each morning. Even Uncle Benjamin, however, realized that the boy no longer even attempted to apply himself seriously to the law. Forthrightly, the uncle told his godson, as a young Disraeli had been told a decade earlier, that he was unsuited to be a solicitor and, for that matter, probably unsuited for any other kind of work.

For Layard, the present was bleak, and the future bleaker. "I was almost in a state of despair," Layard said. "My position in England seemed to me hopeless and caused me so much misery that I thought only of getting away."

Layard's depression contrasted sharply with the spirit of the times. That same year a nineteen-year-old girl was radiantly invested as queen of the most powerful empire in the world. Victoria's ascension to the throne heralded Britain's golden age, an age of positive thinking and of positive accomplishment, an age of enthusiasm, of giants—explorers, adventurers, scientists, statesmen, empire builders, writers: Livingstone, Chinese Gordon, Darwin, Lord Curzon, Rhodes, Tennyson. "Of all the decades in our history," an enthusiastic G. M. Young wrote, "a wise man would choose the eighteen-fifties to be young in."

Scholars dubbed the interregnum the Victorian age, a period of faith, purpose, and buoyancy. But Layard, in his state of mind, possessed neither faith nor purpose, and certainly no buoyancy. He was twenty-one and his life lay ahead of him. Gnawed by doubts, he felt his life was behind him.

As his personal crisis deepened, a paternal uncle, Charles Layard, who had journeyed to Ceylon with his father forty-two years earlier and amassed a fortune, reappeared in London on holiday. The Austens confided in him their concern about their mutual nephew, and Uncle Charles took young Layard to lunch to sound him out. Downing a tankard of bitters, Uncle Charles advised his nephew to consider Ceylon, as his father before him. "The island is flourishing," the uncle reported. Moreover, there was no need for young Layard to pass the bar examination to practice law in Ceylon. He needed only a certificate, and surely, after five years of drudgery, he could obtain that modest recognition of his apprenticeship. Once in

Ceylon, if he did not pursue the law, "there were other occupations," the uncle advised him, ". . . such as coffee planting, with every prospect of . . . making a fortune."

Surprisingly, despite his passion for travel and adventure (possibly because he had associated the island with his family and, therefore, not with independence), Layard had never considered Ceylon the solution to his problems. Now the solution was manifest, or so it seemed.

Faith, purpose, and buoyancy revived quickly, as they are apt to do in the springtime of life, and he resolved to go to Ceylon.

But as the fates were to have it, he never got there. He set sail, but instead of a journey to Ceylon, Austen Henry Layard embarked on a journey into history.

A district on the other side of the sea,
a distant place.

—ASHURBANIPAL

VII

In the great age of sail, before the opening of the Suez Canal in 1869, the quickest way to reach Ceylon from England was also the most inconvenient. The traveler embarked in England and sailed to Alexandria, since pharaonic times Egypt's principal port of entry. Then he proceeded overland across the Isthmus of Suez, and caught a ship bound for India via the Red Sea.

The route was heavily traveled by government officials until the opening of the Canal. The road from Cairo to the sun-bleached port of Suez was through desert. It consisted of several parallel tracks, each 12 or 18 inches in width, formed by the tread of the camel. For promoting the journey, the East India Company had erected guest houses or caravansaries at intervals of 8 to 10 miles along the route, and provided them with servants and refreshments. Passengers covered this route by carriage or by camel.

Although arduous, the route was attractive. It avoided the tedious and sometimes perilous voyage around the Cape of Good Hope, the long route. The amount of time saved by the shortcut was considerably more than half the time it normally took to reach India by sea. The prospect of such a journey must have been particularly attractive to Layard, for it would give him the opportunity of visiting ancient Egypt, perhaps exploring the ruins along the banks of the Nile, which were now coming to light with the birth of Egyptology.

(37)

But chance, the fickle goddess, intervened, and Layard found himself contemplating an altogether different route.

As a formidable Ceylonese figure, Uncle Charles was in great demand in London for counseling about opportunities on the island. Among those who introduced themselves was an adventurous Englishman of twenty-eight, six years Layard's senior, staunchly Tory and Church of England, who had spent five years on the Barbary coast of North Africa, largely in Morocco, and was currently unemployed. His brother, a member of the 18th Royal Irish, who had done a tour of duty in India, suggested that he look into the possibility of a job in Ceylon, either in the civil service or in coffee planting. The young Englishman—he had the imposing name of Edward Ledwich Obaldeston Mitford—sought out Charles Layard for advice. Uncle Charles was impressed with his experience and thought he would make an ideal traveling companion for his nephew. He got them together.

They hardly seemed compatible. Mitford was a veteran traveler, reserved and prudent; Layard was inexperienced, incautious, and rash. But they quickly discovered strong bonds. They were, in Layard's words, "equally careless of comfort and unmindful of danger, curious, enthusiastic, and anxious to leave England as soon as possible." Mitford was slightly less romantic in his assessment of the arrangement. "In case of danger or sickness," Mitford noted in his businesslike fashion, ". . . it was a satisfaction to feel that neither would be alone, [and] we were soon agreed."

But Mitford dreaded the sea. He proposed reaching Ceylon by a land march through Europe, Asia Minor, Central Asia, down the Indian subcontinent, and then across Adam's Bridge, the chain of treacherous sandbanks separating India from Ceylon.

The plan appealed to Layard. It was vast, romantic, and extravagant. It contained elements of high adventure—danger—since some of the areas they would traverse were unmapped and Europeans in those regions were regarded as no less strange than visitors from a distant planet. At last, he would realize the dreams of the *Arabian Nights* that had haunted him from his childhood.

The Austens were less enthusiastic about the plan. They thought it preposterous. Even Henry Crabb Robinson, who had encouraged the boy's flights of fancy and his readings on Asia Minor, characterized the proposal as "wild."

But Layard and Mitford, their spirits soaring, plunged energetically into preparations for the journey, heedless of the dangers. They would be without even elementary forms of communications. No telegraph lines had yet been strung across the region. There were not even any post offices along the route—and there were no road maps available.

But, they obtained introductions to a number of Old Asia hands and picked their brains. Among them were the aging James Baillie Fraser, whose works Layard had devoured as a child, and Sir Charles Fellows, whom Layard had met at his godparents' Sunday dinners. "Fellows gave me many valuable hints," Layard acknowledged. Did they discuss the lost cities of the Assyrians, since Layard would cross Mesopotamia? There is no mention of this in any of Layard's surviving papers, although, significantly, Layard did note that Sir Charles "inspired me with the strongest desire to follow his example in explorations."

Probably at Fellows's suggestion, Layard contacted the Royal Geographic Society and outlined the route of their proposed journey. Layard's interest in exploration excited the Society's secretary, who informed him that "the ruins of ancient cities and of remarkable monuments" were certain to exist along the route, especially in western Persia, where "all attempts to reach them have hitherto failed."

The secretary supplemented his meager knowledge of the area with the field reports of Major Henry Rawlinson, a former military adviser to the Shah's court in Persia, a soldier-scholar who would emerge as one of the great Orientalists of the Victorian period. In the course of his activities in western Persia, Rawlinson had discovered many ancient ruins. But he was unable to visit the highlands that were inhabited by the Baktiyari, a tribe that was in an almost perpetual state of rebellion against the Shah. Nonetheless, Rawlinson had received secret descriptions from Baktiyari chiefs of ruins and rock-cut inscriptions in the area around Shushan. These reports excited the Royal Geographic Society, and the clergy, too, for it was at Shushan that Daniel saw the vision of the ram and the goat. The Society urged Layard to try to penetrate the region, and he promised to do so if possible.

Layard did his homework. He read and reread everything available on Asia Minor. He also took lessons in Arabic and Persian; however rudimentary, the lessons gave him an ear for those exotic languages. Curiously, he took no lessons in Singhalese or Tamil, the languages of Ceylon, nor did he read much about the Indian subcontinent. Obviously his heart and mind were in Asia Minor. Ceylon and the Far East held no enchantment.

There were other things to consider before setting out. For one thing, there was the question of money, the bane of many would-be explorers. Layard, who had no funds of his own, was determined to make the journey pay for itself, a familiar theme. Accordingly, he took lessons in taxidermy with the hope of shipping stuffed birds and small mammals to the British Museum. He also accepted a mapmaking commission from the Royal Geographic Society. A sea captain gave him lessons in the use of the sextant, and Layard invested in an artificial horizon, a compass, an aneroid barometer, a Fahrenheit thermometer, a telescope, and a pocket sextant. Since a sextant is useless without a chronometer, he put his last savings into a reliable watch—it was encased in silver, and at the suggestion of Sir Charles Fellows, Layard painted it black "so that the sight of bright metal might not excite the wild tribes through which we were to pass."

Again with an eye to financing the venture, Layard and his companion solicited an advance of £200 ($1,000), a goodly sum in that day, from the publishing house of Smith-Elder. Under the terms of the contract, the pair agreed to "forward to the said Messieurs Smith-Elder Company, within six months after their arrival in the island of Ceylon, a manuscript of their journal in an intelligible and prepared condition for the press." If they failed to produce the manuscript, they agreed to repay Smith-Elder the advance, with interest.

Part of the advance was immediately invested in a couple of double-barreled shotguns, both for protection and with a view to procuring fresh meat. Layard contributed two double-barreled pistols of his own to the arsenal, and to supplement their diet with fresh fish, he also packed away a light rod and flies.

Layard visited the Austens' physician and asked for lessons in medicine. The doctor took the young man with him on his rounds of the University of London Hospital, pointed out various illnesses, demonstrated how to mend broken bones, and provided him with a do-it-yourself kit for treating the three curses of Eastern travel: dysentery, eye inflammation, and fever (the discovery of malaria and its transmission by the female mosquito was still a half-century away).

Both Layard and Mitford agreed to travel lightly, carrying only as much as they could cram into saddlebags. Layard's wardrobe consisted of a change of clothes, some linen, a change of stockings and boots, powder and shot, a cloak or poncho for protection against the rain, and a contraption, popularized by the East India Company, called a Levinge bed. This consisted of a pair of sheets sewn together and attached to a mosquito curtain that was hung from a tree or a nail on a wall—in effect, a primitive sleeping bag. "It formed a complete defense against insects of all kind," Layard said, "whether crawling, hopping, or flying, that abound in the dirty houses and still more filthy *caravansaries* that we were warned we should have to occupy when travelling in the manner we intended to do in the East."

As for the manner in which they intended to travel, they confounded their friends and relatives alike.

In the course of their preparations, Layard interviewed Sir John MacNeill, the former British envoy to Persia, and sought his opinion about the practicality of their plan.

Sir John was among the very few who heartedly endorsed the scheme. But he did so for political reasons. He believed the pair would pick up valuable intelligence along the route about political conditions in the outlying districts of the Ottoman and Persian empires which overlapped in the Mesopotamian borderland, and, more important, about Russia's machinations and expansionist designs in the Near East.

Sir John was warming up to his favorite subject, politics,

when Layard politely asked for advice on how to travel in potentially hostile regions.

"You must either travel as important personages with a retinue of servants and an adequate escort," MacNeill said, "or alone, as poor men, with nothing to excite the cupidity of the people among whom you will have to mix. If you cannot afford to adopt the first course," he added, sizing up Layard, "you *must* take the latter."

"And the latter," Layard said dryly, "we are determined to take."

On learning of their strategy, the Austens no longer considered the whole plan preposterous. They told their nephew that he was "insane."

On June 1, 1839, all was at the ready except for one odious detail. Layard had still to obtain his accreditation as an attorney. For five days he crammed, took the examination, and, as much to his surprise as relief, passed with flying colors. Nine days later Layard was formally "sworn, admitted and enrolled as attorney of Her Majesty's Court of Queen's Bench at Westminster." That was the last the law ever saw of him. He never practiced for a day.

If Layard entertained any misgivings about the journey, it was the separation from his mother. Marianne Layard recognized her son's spirited nature and made no attempt to dissuade him from the adventure. Most probably, she recalled how a young Henry Peter John Layard, his father, had dashed off to Ceylon in search of riches some forty years earlier.

On July 9 she arrived in London to bid her son farewell. She gave him her blessings and, much to his surprise, a going-away gift of £300 ($1,500). This, coupled with his share of the Smith-Elder advance, and a credit of £300 which Uncle Charles had drawn on Coutts & Co., bankers, was his total capital.

The following day, Layard and Mitford embarked—but in different directions. Mitford, whose aversion to the ocean was total, took the shortest sea route to the Continent and landed at Calais. Layard took a steamer for Ostend. They agreed to rendezvous at Brussels.

"As I passed down the Thames I labored under various emotions," Layard recalled. Inwardly, he doubted that he would ever reach Ceylon. Indeed, the concept of an overland journey through Asia Minor had put Ceylon completely out of his mind. He had no idea of where he was truly headed. But for the first time in his life, at the age of twenty-two, he was independent. Relieved at leaving England, where his parents had been unhappy, where his father had died, where he himself was a failure, he mused, "Had I remained in England, I should in all probability have passed through life in the obscure position of a respectable lawyer."

The admission is revealing. Layard was in quest of more than a job. Like the Assyrian kings of the past, he sought a place in the sun.

From the upper sea to the lower sea,
I marched in safety.
—SENNACHERIB

VIII

Three days later, July 13, Layard landed at the Flemish fishing port of Ostend and joined Mitford at Brussels.

The pair had set out on a 9,000-mile journey in an era so primitive in transportation that the railroad was in its infancy and steamers were paddle-driven. The primary mode of travel in western Europe was still the dusty diligence, the lumbering *eliwagen*, and the tedious *vetturino*. "This was supplemented a little further on by springless carts," Mitford recalled, "but even this mode of conveyance ceased south of Trieste and there was a necessity of taking to the saddle in Dalmatia."

The rigors of early Victorian travel notwithstanding, they moved effortlessly through central Europe and on August 10 reached the southern limits of the Austro-Hungarian empire. It would take them eight months more to reach Mosul, the halfway point to Ceylon. Their adventures crossing Asia Minor would be enough to fill several books and, in a sense, did. In their early seventies, still robust and mentally active, Layard and Mitford told their story in separate memoirs. In his two-volume *Early Adventures in Persia, Susiana and Babylonia*, published in 1887, and in his half-completed autobiography, published in 1903, nine years after his death, Layard devoted 357 crowded pages to his experiences between Brussels and Baghdad. Mitford, in his own two-volume account of their travels, published in 1884 as *A Land March from England to Ceylon Forty Years Ago,* contributed another 245 pages.

For Layard his escape from the West was not realized until he reached Croatia, present-day Yugoslavia, where the dress of the peasants was no longer European but Eastern in character. Men and women alike wore red skullcaps, those of the men richly embroidered in black silk, those of the women with gold and colored thread. Both sexes sported jackets adorned with silver coins, and wore their hair plaited in pigtails, like the Chinese of the period. Layard kept a seasoned eye on the girls, who he observed, wore petticoats of gay colors, an abundance of gold ornaments, and large earrings. "Many of the women we passed were tall and handsome," Layard observed, "with black eyes and hair."

The pair next crossed into Dalmatia, where the peasants carried long guns and wore belts crammed with pistols, knives, and yataghans, a short Islamic saber without a crosspiece.

Beyond Dalmatia lay Montenegro, an admirable political fiction that served as a buffer zone between the hostile Austrians and Turks. Montenegro was neither truly Occidental nor truly Oriental, but an exotic pastiche of both.

The travelers' first order of business in Montenegro was to present themselves to the Vladika or bishop, who, like the ancient ecclesiastical princes of medieval Europe, served as the tiny state's temporal and spiritual ruler. En route to his palace, Layard received his first cultural shock. In front of the Vladika's whitewashed, unpretentious palace was a round tower. "On top of it, arranged in array on short poles, were a number of gory heads with their long tufts of hair waving in the wind, the trophies of a recent raid upon the neighboring Turks," Layard said. "It was a hideous and disgusting sight which first greeted the traveller on his arrival at the residence of the priest-prince."

Ushered into the Vladika's presence, Layard and Mitford were astonished to find "a perfect giant," more than seven feet in height. "He seemed to me the tallest man I had ever seen," Layard said. The Vladika wore the long black silk robes and high round black hat of a Greek Orthodox priest. A large gold cross dangled from his neck. He welcomed his guests in

French and invited them to dine with him. After dinner, to their further astonishment, the Vladika led them to a billiard room. His proudest possession was a pool table imported from the West.

In the midst of the game, a party of Montenegro warriors burst into the palace and cheerfully deposited at the bishop's feet a cloth bag filled with the heads of their latest victims. "Amongst these were those apparently of mere children," noted a horrified Layard. "Covered with gore, they were a hideous and ghastly spectacle."

Layard brashly expressed to his host his disgust at what he had witnessed, especially in the house of a Christian clergyman. Coolly, the Vladika acknowledged that decapitation was un-Christian and shocking. But, he explained, his guests must remember that Montenegro was encircled by implacable enemies—Turks, Albanians, and Austrians—and isolated by almost impassable mountains. "I must tolerate the custom to maintain the warlike spirit of my people," he said; otherwise Montenegro would be exterminated. "There is nothing more I dread," the Vladika continued, "than a long peace." The Vladika's assessment had a ring of historical validity. An independent Montenegro no longer exists.

As Layard discovered in the course of talks with his host, the Vladika was in the midst of a massive reform movement. He had introduced a new code of laws; for example, murderers were now punished by death—not, as in the past, by a fine paid to the family of the victim. He had also ordered elementary school books translated into Montenegrin and planned to establish the country's first educational system.

Layard, the Huguenot, found himself empathizing with the plight of the Montenegrin minority, just as he empathized with Italian and Polish patriots. "I was much struck with the superior intelligence and liberal views of the Vladika," he admitted. "He greatly extolled the independent character and love of liberty of his people." These were qualities that Layard understood and cherished himself.

When he and Mitford moved on, the Vladika furnished them mules and an armed escort as far as his border with the Ottoman empire.

They now crossed into the world of Islam, the Fertile Crescent, stretching from the northern rim of Africa to the Malay archipelago. In a spirit of great expectations, Layard wrote, "The change since passing the borders of Christian Europe is now complete, and I feel myself, as it were, in a new world—in a world of which I had dreamt from my earliest childhood."

The bazaars through which they passed were crowded with Turks, Albanians, Greeks, and others. The women wore veils across their faces, merchants sat cross-legged in front of their wares, smoking the narghile or water pipe, Albanians carried yataghans tucked into their belts, and savory, enticing aromas exuded from food stalls.

At the *serai*, the official residence of the pasha, the chief administrative officer in the area, the Franks—as Europeans were still called, harking back to the Crusades—were served heavy black Turkish coffee and amber-mouthed water pipes. The pasha questioned them briefly about the nature of their journey and the wonders of England, and issued a *bouyou-rouldi*, or official pass, for post horses. One of the strengths of the Ottoman empire was its superb communications system. A pony express served the empire. At intervals of eighteen miles were caravansaries, rest and relay stations for the quick change of horses or for spending the night. But travelers could use the system only with official approval.

On August 30, the pair set off for Constantinople, the seat of the Sublime Porte. A fortnight later, in the later afternoon, they rode within sight of the minarets and domes of St. Sophia and entered the Ottoman capital through the Gate of Seven Towers, threading their way through a large encampment of Turkish cavalry. Layard was transfixed. He found himself in the urban kaleidoscope built by Constantine the Great, the city which had served as the eastern capital of the Roman empire and which, for more than eleven centuries, had served as the capital of the Ottoman dynasty. Like a picture postcard, the city was spread out before him—the Seraglio, which contained the Sultan's palaces and harems, St. Sophia, the Hippodrome, the Column of Constantine, the mosque of Suleiman the Great and, finally, the Golden Horn, Constantinople's harbor, filled that day with Turkish caïques, foreign warships, paddle steamers, and four-masted barques. The city's narrow streets were crowded with Turks, Greeks, Armenians, Bulgarians, and Eastern Jews. All the great and lesser powers maintained embassies near the Seraglio.

Layard and Mitford found lodging at Roboli's, a small hotel run by an Italian. There Layard came down with his first bout of what would develop into chronic fever. He suspected that he had contracted the malady at a caravansary adjacent to a marshy plain. The ague—malaria, really—was accompanied by dysentery.

Layard was attended by an Armenian physician who proudly displayed a diploma from Edinburgh University. The method of treating most illnesses at that time was bleeding. Like a mystic, the doctor made a large circle with pen and ink on Layard's stomach and ordered the circle filled with leeches. Layard was bled twice. His loss of strength was so great that he was unable to continue the journey.

For several days he was delirious and was once considered in grave danger. During his convalescence, he was attended by two compatriots, J. A. Longworth, the Near East correspondent of the London *Morning Post* and author of *Travels in Circassia*, with whom Layard formed a lasting friendship, and the fourth lord of Carnarvon, who was en route to Egypt. Incredibly, there is an archaeological link in the Layard-Carnarvon relationship that covers a century. In 1922, after barren years of digging, Carnarvon's son, the fifth earl, found the intact tomb of the Pharaoh Tutankhamen, an archaeological trove that, in its time, rivaled the discovery of Nineveh.

By early October Layard had regained his strength. He and Mitford agreed to abandon the pony express and purchase their own horses, making themselves independent of the caravansaries and enabling them to follow any route that suited their fancy. For £20 they purchased three sturdy animals. They also hired a garrulous Greek, Giorgio, as combination dragoman, servant, and cook. Mitford departed with Giorgio and the horses overland while Layard gained extra rest by following the Turkish coast in a caïque. They were reunited at the dingy port of Mudiania. "We were now about to penetrate into regions untraversed by Europeans," Layard wrote, "and where we should have to rely entirely upon our own resources."

The pair were ignorant of the language and customs of the people, the maps of the interior of Turkey and Asia Minor were almost blank, and they could not have selected a worse time to travel through Turkish Asia. The empire's Egyptian provinces had rebelled, and the insurrection had spread across the Middle East. The region beyond Turkey proper was on the edge of anarchy.

Traveling by horse at the speed of Nelson's ships at Trafalgar, a modest three knots, Layard and Mitford set off across Asia Minor. Their only concession to the warnings of the British embassy was to adopt the prominent red fez of the Turk, with its tassel of blue thread, not only because it was more comfortable than their European riding caps but primarily in the hope that they would be less conspicuous as they passed through the countryside.

As the party pressed ahead, Layard maintained a journal of the route for the Royal Geographic Society, mapping streams and rivers, taking bearings on mountains and other conspicuous objects. He jotted the information down in a notebook which was ruled into equal spaces, each representing half an hour's progress, or about one and a half miles.

Layard had recovered fully from his bout with dysentery, and the experience did not inhibit his culinary curiosity. From village to village he feasted on local food—baked mutton with vegetables; a kind of pastry with minced meat, which vaguely reminded Layard of a Cornish pie; mutton omelets; pilafs; flat cakes of unleavened bread; and a strange dessert of honey and cream made from buffalo's milk, which promptly became Layard's favorite, *kymak*. Watermelons, olives, and Turkish coffee were always plentiful. In Armenian villages, the standard fare was a delightful dish composed of cheese, onions, and flour. On one occasion they crossed a stream out of Hans Christian Andersen's imagination, where "the water is as blue as the petals of the loveliest cornflowers, and as clear as the purest glass." While a crowd of intrigued villagers gathered, Layard dismounted, set up his fishing rod, and selected a fly.

He landed three chub, weighing about three pounds each. The Turkish peasants were flabbergasted. "Neither the people nor the fish had ever before seen an artificial fly," Layard said with amusement, "and both were equally surprised." The fish were delicious, roasted on an open fire.

During these epicurean adventures, Layard and Mitford shared one discomfort. No wine, no bitters. Islam, of course, proscribes the use of alcohol, and they had to make do with black coffee. Occasionally, in a Christian village, they were offered raki, a strong and sour alcohol distilled from grapes or grain.

Not surprisingly, on several occasions the party lost their way. Like peasants everywhere, who constantly look over their shoulder for the approach of the tax collector, the villagers were reticent about giving them directions or passing along the most innocuous information. The evasiveness was deliberate and often amusing.

"How many goats have you got?" Layard inquired upon meeting a shepherd driving his flock.

"As many as you passed," the shepherd replied.

"But," Layard persisted, "I did not count them. How many are there?"

"The same number I took with me to the mountains."

"But how many did you take to the mountains?"

"As many as I had."

On the outskirts of Adana, they came upon classical ruins, a Greek temple of the Ionic order. "I was greatly excited," Layard recalled, "This was the first Greek ruin that I had seen."

In Layard's accounts of the journey there are animated passages about the various ruins they stumbled upon along their route. In Mitford's writing, the most exciting pages deal with the flora and fauna. Mitford was a naturalist, and an ornithologist of some authority. Thus, while Layard wrote glowingly of Adana's ruins, Mitford observed that one of the eighteen Ionic columns, standing 24 feet high, "is crowned with a stork's nest."

And while Layard studied the ruins at Adana and made notes, sketches, and measurements, Mitford was busy freeing a golden eagle, measuring 7 feet across the wings, from a trap. "He lay quite still, not attempting to strike, while I opened the trap, seeming to understand my good intentions," Mitford noted, "and as soon as he felt himself free, he soared slowly into the sky."

As they moved across Turkey, Layard was shocked and angered by the injury caused to many classical ruins in Asia Minor by treasure seekers and others. There was hardly a temple in the region that had not been smashed in the search for hidden treasure. In Adana itself, to Layard's consternation, he discovered that almost every cottage was built of fragments of marble from local temple ruins, some of the slabs exquisitely carved, others bearing Greek inscriptions.

The terrain through which they traveled had been incessantly fought over in antiquity by Assyrians, Hittites, Trojans, Greeks, and Romans. Ruins were their calling cards. At times Layard felt as though he was walking through a vast open-air museum. At Iasin, he and Mitford made a discovery of their own, a city of rock tombs, hypogea cut into the mountainside, not unlike the rock tombs of the pharaohs in Upper Egypt.

Iasin's tombs bore rude crosses and wall paintings of figures in the early Byzantine style. The paintings of saints were mutilated, their eyes scratched out. "As far as I was aware," Layard wrote with the pride of the explorer, "the tombs had never before been visited by European travellers, nor have I seen it described in any modern book on Asia Minor." Actually, it was not until 1886, almost half a century later, that a systematic exploration of these Byzantine tombs was undertaken.

Layard's quickening interest in antiquities, an infectious enthusiasm that spread to Mitford as they penetrated deeper into Asia Minor, evoked little surprise among the Turks. Indeed, one official recalled to them an incident when a marble statue with a Roman inscription was unearthed in the presence of a local pasha. The pasha presented it to an English friend with the comment, "You English set a value on these things."

In southwestern Turkey they encountered their most extensive ruins, and Layard spent a whole day copying inscriptions near a colossal headless statue of Hercules.

Thus, gradually, subtly, the purpose of Layard's trip altered. In letters home, and in private notes, there was not a single mention of Ceylon, ostensibly his objective. Inwardly, he appeared to have abandoned that goal. But he had not found a substitute. Each day he rode anew to the horizon, hoping to reach it and peer over the side. For every step he took toward the horizon, it retreated a step from him. But he had found himself.

In his own words, "[I was] unencumbered by needless luxuries and uninfluenced by the opinions and prejudices of others." On still another occasion, he described this period of his life in these terms: "I had passed many happy days and delightful days, notwithstanding the toil and privations to which we had been exposed and, above all, I felt and enjoyed my independence."

As the pair approached Tarsus, they entered a region contested by the rebellious Egyptians, an area which today encompasses Syria, Lebanon, Israel, Jordan, and, of course, Egypt itself. At Tarsus the character of the people dramatically changed from predominantly Turkish to Arabic. Layard now inspected a great mass of rubble which some local villagers believed to be the remains of an Assyrian monument. But there were no cuneiform inscriptions to prove their suspicions, and even if there had been, nobody would have been able to read them. According to the credulous inhabitants of Tarsus, this was the funeral pyre upon which the Assyrian king Sardanapalus, the founder of Tarsus, had consumed himself, his wives, and his wealth.

This was Layard's first brush with Assyria in the rough, and he wrote, "I viewed the ruins with particular interest." Yet he realized that despite all his reading, he was inadequately prepared for exploring a region so rich in Biblical and classical traditions. "I had turned my attention but little to archaeology," he reflected, "and I had but a mere smattering of scientific knowledge of any kind. I never regretted more the incompleteness and neglect of my early education."

But this burgeoning interest in lost worlds was taking a toll. When he and Mitford reached Aleppo, Layard came down with a second—more violent—attack of ague. Once again he was bled. This time fifteen leeches were applied to his stomach, twelve to fourteen ounces of blood drawn from his body, a strict diet imposed, and heavy doses of quinine prescribed. "It is wonderful," he wrote to family and friends in England, "that I survived this treatment!"

In a figurative sense, Aleppo was their first crossroad. Before them lay two roads, and two worlds. One road, running due east, led across Mesopotamia to Mosul, Baghdad, and the Indian subcontinent. The other led south to the Holy Land. By mutual agreement, they turned south. This was an opportunity neither felt he could afford to miss. Mitford was moved by a natural Christian desire to make a pilgrimage to Bethlehem, Golgotha, and in between. Layard was motivated only in part by retracing the footsteps of Christ. Chiefly, he was seized by a passion to visit the ruins along the Jordan that he had read about as a child. "The description that I had read of Petra and of the other remains of ancient cities to the east of the Jordan in the works of Burckhardt," he confessed, "had given me an intense longing to see them."

For Layard, the detour was unavoidable.

Father of the gods . . .
decide my decisions . . .
determine my destiny.
                    —ESARHADDON

IX   As at the outset of
their journey, Layard and Mitford again parted company.
While Mitford saddled his pony and headed directly south for
Beirut, Layard executed a detour within their detour. "I was
determined to visit the cedars," he said. Whenever Layard
employed the verb "determine," Mitford had learned, he
meant it. There was no dissuading him. They agreed to meet
at Beirut Christmas Day.

Layard's journey through present-day Lebanon was nos-
talgic. Many Lebanese had already acquired a French veneer
from French missionaries. As he crossed a snow-clad gorge,
Layard grazed down on neat white houses nestling along the
mountain slopes, and he heard the peal of a church bell rise
from the valley, "a sound I had not heard for many months."

To his dismay, when he reached the towering forest of
gnarled and majestic cedars, he discovered that many of them
had been freshly hewn by the Egyptians for the purpose of
constructing barracks for their troops quartered nearby. Three
millenniums earlier the Assyrians had done the same thing
for their own army of occupation.

On Christmas Eve Layard arrived in Beirut and joined
Mitford. They had letters of introduction to the English consul,
and they eagerly awaited an invitation to join him at Christmas
dinner. But the consul was a snob; Layard and Mitford were

impecunious travelers. "We were disappointed," Layard wrote, "and had to make the best of a wretched dinner in the small and dirty inn which then afforded the only accommodation to travellers."

The pair left Beirut quickly and crossed into the Holy Land in a spirit of high enthusiasm, taking the same trail as Roman legions and Crusaders before them. But their visit to the Holy Land was disillusioning.

Layard found the place distasteful, the countryside an impoverished wasteland, and the towns dilapidated and in serious disrepair. Jerusalem itself was filled with religious fanatics and imposters. Quarrels and scandalous broils among various denominations for control of shrines offended Layard's Christian sensibilities. Only the previous Easter, he learned to his disgust, the Egyptians had been forced to dispatch armed troops to the Church of the Holy Sepulchre to keep peace among warring religious factions. The principal struggle was waged between the Roman and Greek Catholic churches. Behind them lurked France and Russia, preparing the groundwork for what later became the Crimean War.

Mitford was shocked by the carnival atmosphere of the place. "On the Via Dolorosa," he wrote his mother, ". . . they actually show a dent in the wall against which [Jesus] is said to have leaned his cross!!" But, he observed, the wall was 600 years old, built 1,200 years *after* the event. "I should not be doing my duty," he added, "were I not to raise my feeble voice against these gross frauds."

They were both eager to move on, but they narrowly missed ever leaving. One morning their innkeeper summoned them to breakfast and, Mitford recounted, "We could not lift our heads from the pillow, from giddiness and racking headache, accompanied by retching, faintness and spasmodic pains in the chest." On account of extreme cold that night and in the absence of fireplaces, they had adopted the local habit of burning a large pan of charcoal in their room. They were almost asphyxiated.

While they recovered, they argued over their next objective. Mitford favored resuming the overland march directly to Ceylon, and by the most expeditious route. Layard, however, was "determined"—that word again—to visit Petra, the lost city which Burckhardt had rediscovered less than a generation earlier in the area of the Dead Sea and which he had read about as a child in Florence.

On all sides Layard received dire warnings against his plan. The British consul denounced it as "foolhardy," as did the Egyptian governor of Jerusalem. The Dead Sea was a no man's land, the pasha warned, controlled by neither Constantinople nor Cairo. It was the hunting ground of fanatical Bedouin marauders who were hostile to the "unbelieving" Franks. The Bedouins, who claimed to be descendants of Ishmael, wandered across the deserts with their flocks and herds, dwelt in tents, and subsisted largely on plunder.

In the face of this counsel, Mitford considered it rash and stupid to visit the region. And for what? To look at ruins?

"But I was resolved not to be deterred," Layard said. "I was determined to undertake the journey alone, trusting to my own resources, and fully believing all the romantic stories that I had read of Arab hospitality and their respect for a guest."

On January 15, 1840, while Mitford took the road back to Aleppo before turning due east, Layard left for Petra. En route, his first stopover was Hebron, and he arrived in the town just as several Arabs, in chains, were being lined up in the courtyard of the local pasha. For the first time Layard witnessed the common form of punishment still being meted out throughout the Ottoman empire for even the most minor offenses.

As the crowd gathered, a prisoner was thrown to the ground on his belly and his feet passed through two nooses of line attached to a stout pole. The pole was then hoisted on the shoulders of two strong men, and several stalwart soldiers, in relays, applied whips of hippopotamus hide to the victim's soles as though they were beating a rug. The soles of the prisoner were beaten without mercy, water being constantly poured over the blood-streaked wounds to increase the pain. The victim screamed in agony. After the whipping, the wretched sufferer, unable to walk, was dragged off bodily by guards.

"I felt too much disgusted and horrified with these barbarous proceedings to continue to witness them," Layard said.

At Hebron he hired two camels for the journey to Petra and to the Dead Sea. This was Layard's first camel ride, and he learned one of the reasons these animals are referred to as "ships of the desert." He experienced *mal de mer*.

Along the route he reached a wadi or depression in the desert, and found it dotted with the black tents of nomadic Arabs. In storybook fashion, the sheik invited the stranger to his tent and served him bowls of rice and boiled mutton. The night was bitter cold, and Layard sat huddled by the campfire until he returned to his own tent some yards away.

"I remained for some time at the entrance to my tent, gazing on the strange and novel scene before me," he recorded in his notes. "It was my first acquaintance with an Arab encampment and Arab life. A full moon in all its brilliancy lighted up the *wady*, so that every feature in the landscape could be plainly distinguished. The fires in the Arab tents studded the valley with bright stars. The silence of the night was broken by the lowing of the cattle and hoarse moanings of the camels, and by the long mournful wail of the jackals, which seemed to be almost in the midst of us."

Layard felt he had crossed the threshold of reality and had entered the fabled world of a thousand and one nights.

The sheik, as it turned out, was also concerned about the young Englishman's ambitious plan; as Layard discovered, many, if not most, of the Arab tribes in the region were as wary of roaming Bedouin war parties as Turks and Franks. He took a liking to the youngster and provided Layard with two armed guards to guide him to the next friendly Arab encampment.

As the small party approached the Dead Sea area, Layard found himself engaged in one cliff-hanger after another. As observed earlier, his adventures filled a book. But one incident here will suffice as an example of Layard's daring, foolhardiness, and courage.

He was attacked by a war party of marauding Bedouins who stole many of his belongings. He saved his life—and those of his two companions—by seizing the leader of the Bedouin band in the melee and pointing his rifle at the chieftain's head. Layard threatened to blow the man's head off unless his followers withdrew—which they promptly did. While being constantly tracked from just over the horizon, Layard marched his hostage at gunpoint across the searing desert to the safety of the next friendly Arab encampment.

By this time, the hostile Bedouin was famished. Applying the textbook psychology he read about as a child in Burckhardt and other writers on Araby, Layard invited his prisoner the following morning to join him at breakfast. Out of hunger, the Bedouin leader accepted.

The youthful Layard had outfoxed the older, wiser warrior; for it is the sacred duty of the Arab, including the Bedouin, to protect at all costs a person with whom he has broken bread.

Layard now demanded that his hostage arrange for the return of all his personal belongings. At first the Bedouin resisted, but the Arabs in the camp shouted, "You have eaten bread with this man—he walks with God while you walk with the devil!" Sheepishly, the Bedouin leader arranged for the restoration of Layard's stolen articles.

As a result of this, and similar, incidents, Layard acquired a deep insight into Arab character. The same man, Layard found, "who at one moment would be grasping, deceitful, treacherous and cruel, would show himself at another generous, faithful, trustworthy and humane."

Ultimately, by keeping his wits about him, Layard reached his objective—Petra. The silence and solitude of Petra, with its fallen cornices and broken columns, excited his imagination. In a statement he was destined to amend later, but which mirrored his unlimited enthusiasm for art and antiquities, he wrote in his journal, "The ruins of Petra are unlike those of any other ancient city in the world."

From Petra, Layard turned due north and rode to Ammon, the Biblical city of Rabbath-Ammon, which the Assyrians had laid waste under Tiglath-Pileser. On this very spot the Romans had erected one of the major fortified outposts of their extensive empire; today the site is Amman, the capital of King Hussein's Jordan.

As Layard viewed the massive ruins of Ammon, he was deeply moved by the exploits of the Romans. "That a city so far removed from their capital, and built almost in the desert, should have been adorned with so many splendid monuments—temples, theatres and edifices," he said in awe, "affords one of the most striking proofs of the marvellous energy and splendid enterprise of the Romans."

He had no sooner expressed this lofty sentiment than he was ambushed by another Bedouin band as he approached ancient Tiberias. They robbed him of his camel and most of his belongings but, in a compassionate mood, released him unharmed.

Layard continued on to Tiberias by foot. His appearance was disheveled. So was the city's. Two years earlier, Tiberias had been wrecked by an earthquake and it had still not recovered.

As he stood hungry, tired, and penniless, wondering where he would bed down for the night, a old man in threadbare European clothes and black hat addressed him in Italian. "I begged him to tell me where I could find a night's lodging," Layard said. The man, the hair on either side of his face curled in the manner of the Eastern Jew, took pity on the Frank and invited him to his home. That night Layard slept in a clean European bed for the first time in a month. His host, it developed, was a Polish physician and Jew.

Layard explained his predicament and that he was en route to Damascus to catch up with a traveling companion. The Jew told him not to worry about money matters and loaned him £10 ($50), an incredibly large sum and probably his entire fortune. He told Layard he could repay it to a friend of his when he arrived in Damascus.

"Aren't you showing an unusual confidence in a stranger?" the incredulous Layard asked.

"You are an Englishman and in distress," the Jew replied. "That is enough for me."

The noble generosity of the poor Jew made a great impression on Layard, and he promptly added Jews to his roster of underdogs worthy of fidelity and support. Clearly, he collected minorities the way some people collect cats.

Layard hoped that the journey to Damascus would be uneventful, but no sooner had he left Tiberias on a rented mule than he was accosted by a band of armed conscripts who had deserted from the Egyptian army. They robbed him of all his money and most of his personal belongings, but let him keep his mule, notebooks, and the clothes on his back (torn trousers; soiled shirt, and tattered Arab cloak).

It is a measure of Layard's abnormal interest in art and antiquities that despite his sorry state, he halted briefly at Kaferhowar on the road to Damascus to explore the remains of ancient buildings, marble slabs, the shafts of columns, and the basement of a temple constructed of white marble "which the inhabitants said was built by Nimroud." Nimrod. For the first time in the field he heard the name of the legendary founder of the mighty Nineveh. But Layard had no time to search for inscriptions.

In Damascus, Layard presented himself to the British consul, who opened the door and saw before him an exhausted figure clad in rags, almost shoeless, barely able to stand, bronzed and begrimed by long exposure to the sun and the dirt of desert life. "He was not a little surprised at being addressed by an Englishman," Layard said later. Unlike the snob at Beirut, the British representative welcomed him warmly.

The consul reported that Mitford, after waiting several days, had pressed on to Aleppo, where Layard was to meet him. Then the official offered him tea, a hot bath (his first in more than a month), and a new wardrobe. Since European clothes were nonexistent in Damascus, he wound up in the uniform worn by Egyptian troops in Syria during the cold winters— baggy trousers with tight leggings, a short jacket, a waistcoat fastened up front with numerous buttons, and a colored sash, not unlike a French legionnaire.

Layard felt he owed himself a holiday, and took some time out to visit the bazaars, where shops were filled with "thousands of curious objects," the coffeehouses where customers squatted before ornate narghiles, and the justly famous brothels of Damascus.

He also made plans to leave for Aleppo. But when he learned that by a "short detour" he could visit Baalbek—the Heliopolis of the ancient Greeks, with its temples of Jupiter and Bacchus— he could not resist.

Once again he was warned against traveling alone, but as it turned out, he reached his goal safely and was immediately "lost in admiration and astonishment" among the stately columns and blocks of richly sculptured marble of the temples at Baalbek.

He was now becoming conscious of the pressing of time, the necessity to resume his journey to Aleppo, but he could not resist a compulsion to dally among ruins at the mouth of Nahr-el-Kelb, a roaring, rock-lined river, where he examined a series of remarkable sculptures and inscriptions carved in the rocks. The sculpture was thought to be Phoenician in origin. Layard did not know it, but the inscriptions were Assyrian and told the story of Sennacherib's conquests. This was the third time he had stumbled across the trail of the mythical Assyrians in Asia Minor.

At Aleppo Layard finally found Mitford. Fearing that his companion had been slain along the way, Mitford was completing preparations for crossing the Euphrates and marching on to the banks of the Tigris.

This time there was no argument between the two about the next stage of their journey. They would plunge into Mesopotamia and head straight for the trading post of Mosul on the west bank of the Tigris.

They purchased fresh horses and a change of clothes, including four blue shirts apiece. They also carried a double-barreled gun and a pair of pistols. Together with maps, sketch pads, and a few other articles, their worldly estate weighed 15 pounds. Their bedding, a quilt apiece, was strapped across their saddles, making a comfortable seat. They permitted themselves one luxury—a small box of tea. Apparently they could withstand any privation—sandstorms, rainstorms, marauding Bedouins, fever, dysentery, vermin-infested caravansaries, most anything, but in the Victorian spirit, they could not survive without a cup of tea.

As they saddled up, Layard recalled that he was overcome by a strange sensation. "I now felt an irresistible desire to penetrate the regions beyond the Euphrates, to which history and tradition point as the birthplace of the wisdom of the West," he wrote in his journal.

He sensed that a deep mystery hung over Assyria, Babylonia, and Chaldea, the legendary lands of the Old Testament. "After a journey in Syria, thoughts naturally turn eastward," he wrote, "and without treading on the remains of Nineveh and Babylon our pilgrimage is incomplete."

In an eloquent passage in his journal, he recorded: "With these names are linked great nations and great cities dimly shadowed forth in history; mighty ruins, in the midst of deserts, defying, by their very desolation and lack of definite form, the description of the traveller; the remnants of mighty races still roving over the land; the fulfilling and fulfillment of prophecies; the plains to which Jew and Gentile alike look as the cradle of their race."

In Layard's days, the sphere of rebel Egyptian influence within the decaying Ottoman empire stretched as far as the area which currently delineates the Syrian-Iraqi border. The desert tribes of the region, particularly the Bedouins, exploited the confusion, plundered villages freely, and attacked caravans going and coming across Mesopotamia. But fate rode with Layard and his companion, and they succeeded in reaching Nisbin, halfway to Mosul, unmolested.

On the next leg of the journey they encountered a body of irregular Kurdish horsemen in the service of the Sublime Porte. Their chieftain invited the Englishmen to a sumptuous banquet. A freshly killed kid was the centerpiece of an enormous pilaf of rice. The Kurd leader plied his guests with *kymak*, the concoction of sour milk, dried figs, and honey. In his journal, Layard captured the setting.

"His [the chief's] tent of black goat-hair, supported by enormous poles, was divided into several compartments by screens formed of canes and reeds fasted together by woolen cords of different bright colors, worked into elegant patterns," Layard wrote. "It was carpeted with those carpets of beautiful texture and rich design which are made by Kurdish women, and are greatly valued throughout the East. ... Comfortable mattresses were brought to us to sleep upon. It was the first time that I had passed a night under a Kurdish tent, and I was much impressed by the simple luxury which the chieftain of a roving tribe could display."

Continuing on, they reached another Kurdish settlement at Zezireh, the site of hand-to-hand battles between Romans and Persians in antiquity. Many Kurds, like the Egyptians, were in rebellion against the Turks, and the Kurdish leader of

Zezireh had fortified himself in a castle built on a riverbank and looking down on the town. The rebel chieftain was a superb host and served the strangers platters of pilaf, lambs roasted whole, balls of mincemeat, bowls of cream and sour milk, and other Kurdish delicacies. The chief's retainers sat on their haunches, as did Layard and Mitford, helping themselves to the food with their fingers.

Continuing their eastward journey, they fell in with a band of Yezidis, who had a reputation for ferocity, if not bloodthirstiness. It was said that they worshiped the devil, a belief that sprang from their dread of the power of evil and their endeavor to propitiate, appease, conciliate, and avoid offending Satan. After the lurid tales Layard and Mitford had heard about them, they were surprised to find the Yezidis friendly, and largely misunderstood. "My early impressions, from reading travels, had led me to imagine," Mitford wrote, "that every Turk was a brute, the Albanian a cut-throat and the Kurd next-to-kin to a cannibal. I was agreeably deceived," he continued, "to find the Turks gentlemen; the Albanians, though far from heroes of romance, plain soldiers and harmless if uninjured; and the Kurds hospitable and good natured." Then he added an afterthought: "These remarks will not apply to these races in time of war or when excited by fanaticism; then they are merciless."

In effect, like Layard, Mitford found most people everywhere are like most people everywhere else.

In the course of their trek to Mosul, they stopped to explore the ruins at Nisbin. The town was once the eastern strongpoint of the Roman empire, the residence of the Emperor Trajan during the Parthian War. All that remained were a few splintered shafts of columns, friezes, and fragments of architectural ornaments.

Finally, on April 10, twenty-three days out of Aleppo, the pair came in sight of Mosul. It was built against a backdrop of vast mounds. Layard had read about them in the works of Rabbi Benjamin of Tudela and Claudius Rich, but this was the first time he had seen them. "I was deeply moved and impressed," he said, "by their desolate and solitary grandeur."

He would have been astounded to learn that in this desolate and solitary setting, he would find his place in the sun.

The mound was visible for a distance of many
stadia, and this mound,
they say, stands even to this day.
—STRABO

X From a great distance, as
Layard and Mitford approached Mosul, its walls, minarets,
and gardens glittered alluringly along the right bank of the
river. "It was only when we entered it," Layard said, "that we
realized the condition of ruin and decay to which it had been
reduced by long misgovernment and neglect." Mosul was a
backwater.

A British naval officer, contemporary and friend of Layard's,
Lieutenant F. Walpole, provided in his journal a vignette of
the town. "Two round towers of mud ... women beating dirt
out of clothes ... bathers in their timid nakedness ... bad
smells ... decayed walls ... masses of houses, none good
... more bathers ... more washers ... a picturesque fort."

The interior of the town was no more appetizing than the
riverfront. Most of the people dwelt in hovels. There was not
a hotel in town worthy of the title. The caravansaries crawled
with vermin. Mosul did not even possess a mosque of distinction, although one, curiously, was shaped like an octagonal
pyramid. The two banks of the Tigris were linked by a
makeshift pontoon bridge of boats, moored head and stern
abreast. In a seemingly endless procession, people, donkeys,
horses, and camels crisscrossed back and forth.

"Few Eastern towns of its size ever struck me as so wretched
as Mosul," Walpole wrote, and Layard found the place equally
appalling. "It had a mean and poverty-stricken appearance,"
he said.

The only charitable view of Mosul written in this period was by the Reverend George Percy Badger, one of the East India Company's chaplains in the diocese of Bombay. He conceded that "many of the houses are in a very dilapidated state," but attributed this state of affairs "in great measure to the calamities which have befallen the city during the last century."

Fourteen years earlier, in 1825, Mosul was visited by a famine which lasted for three successive years. This was succeeded by a plague which raged for nine months and claimed 18,000 lives. Then in 1831–32, the Tigris rose to such a height that Mosul and much of the surrounding country were flooded for months. "And," Badger added, "if we add to these misfortunes the ruin of the native manufactures by the importation of cheaper and better articles from Europe, chiefly the produce of our machinery, together with the misrule to which the town has been so long subjected, we cannot wonder that this once flourishing city has been impoverished, and its prosperity well nigh destroyed."

During the classical Greek period, Mosul was apparently a thriving township, and some early scholars thought the city's name a corruption of the Mes-Pylae of Xenophon. Most historians, however, attributed its present name to the Saracen conquerors of Mesopotamia, since Mosul was situated between the fortress-city of Diarbekir and Baghdad, the capital of the Caliphs. In Arabic, Mosul means "place of arrival" or "junction." Some geographers claimed, and some still do, that the place was the site of New Artaxerxes, a name it acquired from the Medes or from the latter-day Persians. Strabo, for example, spoke of a Persian city called Artagira, and Ptolemy referred to the same city as Artasisgarta.

Whatever its early history, Mosul was strategically situated, like a roundhouse in a railroad marshalling yard. The town linked Van and Armenia in the north with Baghdad and the Persian or Arabian Gulf in the south. It served as a terminal warehouse for caravans from the east (Kurdistan, Persia, Afghanistan, India) and from the west (Constantinople, Damascus, Aleppo).

And although Mosul was impoverished, it had a cosmo-

politan air. Among its fifty thousand citizens were Moslems,
Jews, and members of various Christian sects. The Christians
were largely Jacobites, Papal Syrians, and Chaldeans, as Nestorian converts to Roman Catholicism were then called.

Races and religions were conspicuous by their distinctive
attire. Turks, Kurds, and Christians wore short, straight-cut
felt jackets and enormous turbans which seemed as perilously
affixed atop their heads as cotton candy on a stick. The Turks
were conspicuous by their bright red headwear. Yezidis, or
devil worshipers, wore distinctive dark turbans. Sedentary or
"town" Arabs, those who pitched their tents around the city
and along the Tigris, and nomadic Bedouins who filtered
through the marketplace, wore gay, flowing desert gowns, the
gabiliyah.

Despite its shortcomings, for a weary Frank traveler Mosul
had its compensations. Almost on the eve of Layard's arrival,
the British had opened a consulate, the city's first foreign
diplomatic mission. High over the city, as if capable of
swathing it in its folds, floated the British flag.

The new consul, Christian Rassam, was an extraordinary
figure, one of eight children and the son of Anton Rassam,
archdeacon of the Chaldean Christian community. In his
journal, Mitford wrongly described the Rassam family as
Armenian. But the Rassams considered themselves, like other
Chaldeans, to be the Biblical descendants of the Chaldeans of
Ur.

Christian Rassam was well selected by the British to represent their interests. He spoke a half-dozen languages fluently,
and had served as interpreter and guide to the Royal Navy's
first charting expedition on the Tigris. He had married Matilda
Badger, the sister of the Reverend Badger whose eloquent
defense of Mosul was cited above.

Rassam insisted that Layard and Mitford put up at the
consulate. There was one other European visitor in town, also
a guest of the Rassams, Roger Ainsworth, who had arrived
only recently with a commission from the Royal Geographic
Society to explore the ruins of Hatra, a Parthian desert fortress
which had resisted the Romans until A.D. 195.

Rassam's consulate, clean and spacious, boasted several

splendid terraces and a huge courtyard. In a slum like Mosul, it was a veritable palace and impressed upon the local inhabitants the power, authority, and majesty of Victoria.

That first evening in Mosul, over cups of thick black Turkish coffee, Rassam entertained his guests with the checkered history of the town. Gibbon, for example, assumed Mosul to have been a suburb of Ninus, the city that presumably gave rise to Nineveh, and Rassam recalled that he once read an old Syriac manuscript that claimed that Mosul rose on the very ruins of Nineveh. In more recent times, Mosul had been plundered first by Genghis Khan and then by Tamerlane, and at about the time of the American Revolution, it was shelled by the Ottoman Turks and absorbed into their empire.

As he listened to these tales, Layard's mind raced back to the mysterious cuneiform tablets in the British Museum and to Rich's speculation about Nineveh's former existence on the bank opposite Mosul. His first impulse the following morning was to rush across the pontoon bridge and inspect the strange mounds on the other side of the river. Two huge mounds dominated the left bank, Nebbi Yunnus (Prophet Jonah) and Kouyunjik (a bastardized Turkish word for sheepfold).

Nebbi Yunnus covered an area of about 40 acres and was the loftiest of the two mounds. According to local tradition, this was the burial place of Jonah, who preached Nineveh's destruction if it did not mend its ungodly ways. The eastern half of the mound was a Moslem cemetery, and the prophet's tomb occupied the northwest corner, surrounded by several dilapidated houses. Their inhabitants were Kurds and Turcomans, and they owned the sheep pastures on both mounds. According to an estimate made by Major Rawlinson, whose report Layard carried in his saddlebags, Nebbi Yunnus was covered by half a million tons of earth. Almost anything might be buried beneath that artificial mountain, including the venerable bones of the Prophet Jonah himself.

Kouyunjik lay just to the northwest of its sister mound and was oval-shaped, its surface nearly flat, furrowed with numerous ravines created by the torrential rainstorms that periodically buffeted the parched region. This particular mound overlooked the Khoshor, a tributary of the Tigris, and it rose

95 feet above sea level. The artificial hill embraced about 100 acres. Rawlinson estimated that it was formed by 1.2 million tons of earth.

What lay within it? That was anybody's guess. And it was doubtful that anybody would ever find out. For example, Rawlinson, a compulsive figure filbert, estimated that it would take 10,000 men twelve years or 20,000 men six years to clear the earth and rubble which formed the mound. Obviously, nobody had the funds or forces—or the interest—to do the job.

When Layard visited Kouyunjik that first day, it was still early spring and the mound was covered with young grass. A few impoverished Arabs had pitched their black tents on the spot and tended flocks of sheep.

The two mounds fascinated Layard beyond description. He had never before seen anything comparable, and he spent a week "searching," he confessed, for fragments of marble and bricks with those curious arrow-headed characters he had seen at the British Museum eons ago whenever he escaped from Uncle Benjamin's dungeon. But he found nothing, not even a clue to indicate that the mounds were anything more than monstrous heaps of rubbish.

If Kouyunjik was truly the ancient site of Nineveh, Layard concluded, "the city had perished with her people and left no wreckage behind."

But as he wandered back and forth across the vast mounds, intuitively he changed his mind and became increasingly convinced that they must cover some vestiges of the past, that they had some story to tell the present. "I felt an intense longing to dig into them," he wrote in his journal. But the idea was out of the question.

In his physical condition, it is remarkable that he spent so much time among the mounds. No sooner had he and Mitford arrived at Rassam's house than Layard came down with another bout of ague. Each night he was racked by fever and chills, and all the blankets of Rassams' household failed to melt the ice in his bones.

That week Ainsworth and Rassam completed their plans to ride into the desert and explore Hatra. Mitford agreed to go along with them, and despite his fever, Layard insisted on joining the party also. On the day they left for Hatra, Layard suffered another sharp attack of malaria and was delirious for several hours. "I was consequently very weak," he admitted, "but in the fine air of the desert I soon regained my strength."

Hatra's remains had been originally discovered a few years earlier by Dr. John Ross, the resident physician attached to the East India Company's Baghdad station. He published an account of his discovery in *The Journal of the Royal Geographic Society*. But he was unable to linger at the site, because it was infested by marauding Bedouin tribes. Since then, as a result of an outbreak of plague at Hatra, the ruins were reportedly deserted, affording the Society the opportunity of a comprehensive study of the place.

Ross had reached the site from the south, traveling north from Baghdad. No European had ever approached the ruins from the north, and this was Ainsworth's mission. Despite the reports that the area was cleared of Bedouins, Mosul's Arabs refused to guide the party to the site. The local Turkish governor also warned Ainsworth against the project and feared Victoria's wrath on his head if the British expedition ended in disaster. But when Ainsworth insisted on going ahead with the plan, the governor provided him with a *cawass* or janissary as an armed escort. The pasha apparently felt that the *cawass's* presence, in a bright, distinctive army uniform, would frighten off any remaining Bedouins in the area.

On their first night out of Mosul, the party slept at a hot sulfur spring—the region was dotted with them*—and from that campsite, on the horizon, Layard saw his third mound. Tradition, Rassam told him, attributed the mound to Nimrod. Nimrod! Once again Layard heard the magic name.

"As the sun went down, I saw for the first time the great conical mound of Nimroud rising against the clear evening sky," he said. "The impression it made upon me was one never to be forgotten."

The following day, the party struck deeper into the desert. Their *cawass* panicked and deserted them, fleeing back toward

* This area today embraces Mosul, Iraq, one of the world's principal oil-producing fields.

Mosul. He never got there. The fate that he had anticipated for Layard and his friends befell him. He was captured and murdered by Bedouins.

Layard must have suffered horribly during the desert trek, as anyone who has ever suffered from malaria must know. The early morning air was bitterly cold, and as he was still suffering from fever, Layard matter-of-factly noted, "I was not the better for sleeping on the bare ground with only a light cloak to cover me."

As the expedition wandered deeper into the Mesopotamian wasteland, they came upon still another mound. It had an extraordinary shape. One corner rose like an inverted ice cream cone. Ross had mentioned the discovery of this mound in his paper and said the popular name for it was Khalah Sharghat. Layard and his party would have been astonished to know—as would Ross—that they were gazing on the ruins of Ashur, the Ashur of Genesis, the first city of the Assyrians and the very name from which the Assyrians derived their name.

At the mound, the party took measurements. They also climbed atop it and discovered traces of cuneiform inscriptions. "In the ravines formed by the winter rains," Layard reported, ". . . we found walls of sun-dried brick and the foundations of buildings."

Layard was struck by the novelty of Mesopotamian ruins. Everywhere, it seemed, these tantalizing mounds popped out of the earth. What lay under them? In the west—Italy, Greece, Egypt, Turkey, and the Holy Land—the terrain was also dotted with the ruins of vanished civilizations, but they lay above the earth: graceful Ionic or Corinthian columns; the gradines of amphitheaters, the richly sculpted cornices or broken capitals of temples, and giant pyramids. These were visible ruins. "Were the traveler to cross the Euphrates to seek for such ruins in Mesopotamia and Chaldea as he had left behind him in Asia Minor or Syria," Layard observed, "his search would be in vain."

Yet, Layard confessed, "these huge mounds of Assyria made a deeper impression upon me, gave rise to more serious thought, and more earnest reflection, than the temples of Baalbek, and the theatres of Ionia."

In search of Hatra, the party abandoned Khalah Sharghat and pressed ahead.

At daybreak one morning, the small party of Franks, guided by Rassam, awoke to find themselves enveloped in a thick white mist. Like vessels at sea, they were immersed in fog. Suddenly, as also occurs at sea, a light wind sprang up and lifted the mist before them like the lifting of a windowshade. "Not far from us rose a vast and magnificent pile of buildings, and a long line of walls," Layard recorded, ". . . the walls had equidistant towers." They had found the Hatra of the Parthians.

Along the outer edge of the ruins were flocks of sheep, herds of camels, and a series of Bedouin tents with spears, tufted with ostrich feathers, implanted in the ground before them. "It was so fairy-like and unexpected that I could scarcely believe my senses," Layard said, "and [I] fancied myself in a dream."

If Layard and his group were surprised by the presence of Bedouins, so were the Bedouins surprised by the presence of Franks. "Their principal astonishment," Mitford wrote later, "was that we had come so far without being killed or plundered."

However distasteful to the Bedouins, they were forced by their code of honor to extend the hospitality of the desert to the strangers at their tent flaps. The sheik invited the Franks to his tent and served coffee and huge bowls of sour curds and camel milk. The women of the harem scurried off to prepare a hot breakfast. Soon the tent was crowded with the sheik's warriors, whose savage countenances, Layard wrote, "were rendered still more ferocious by their bright, restless eyes and their white teeth, which gleamed through their lips."

What brought the Franks to Hatra?

Rassam, who acted as diplomat and interpreter, explained that the travelers had come to study the ruins and to gratify their curiosity. Nonsense, the sheik said. Obviously, the Europeans were in search of buried treasure. At this point, several of his warriors grumbled loudly that the infidels should be forced to point out where the gold of Hatra lay hidden. This was the land of the Bedouin and, they reasoned, the treasure of Hatra belonged to them.

The sheik, who had visited Mosul and was—in Layard's words—"somewhat more enlightened," pacified his followers. But as the Franks toured the ruins, the Bedouins tagged along and waited impatiently for the Europeans to reveal the location of the gold. When Layard and Ainsworth began to make sketches of the ruins, and take measurements with a tape, the credulous Bedouins suspected that they were employing black magic. By midday, the sheik and his followers had convinced themselves that the strangers were probably the reconnaisance party of a Frank army or how could their audacity be explained? The Bedouins hurriedly folded their tents and stealthily slipped away—men, women, children, sheep, and camels. Ainsworth and his party were relieved to see them withdraw.

After several days at the site, the party returned to Mosul, where they found that the town's European community had doubled with the arrival of three Frenchmen at Rassam's house—M. Texier, who had been traveling in Asia Minor for seven years for the Académie Française, and his companions, Comte de Guichemand and Comte de la Bourdonnais. The French were en route to Europe after inspecting the ruins at Persepolis, the fabulous capital of Darius which had been overrun and destroyed by Alexander.

Layard's fluency in French, his Huguenot background, and his childhood residence at Moulins won the confidence of the French, and Texier showed Layard his drawings of Persepolis. Layard and Texier got along especially well and spent several days together clambering over the mysterious mounds opposite Mosul. They speculated whether or not this marked the true site of Nineveh. Texier expressed serious doubts. Layard felt differently.

"I was convinced," Layard said, "that [relics] were yet to be found beneath these vast and shapeless masses of earth."

Adown the Tigris I was borne.
—TENNYSON

XI While Layard was content to tarry among the mounds, Mitford was impatient to push on toward Ceylon via Baghdad, which lay 250 miles south of Mosul. The desert route was too dangerous, too costly, and too time-consuming. Accordingly, despite Mitford's aversion to boats, they decided to make the journey down the Tigris in quaint but traditional fashion, on a raft.

Two millenniums earlier, Herodotus, more at home as a journalist than as an historian, wrote ecstatically about this style of travel. Passing through Mesopotamia in 450 B.C., he said that after Babylon, "what surprised me most in the land" was the popular means of transport from north to south.

"The boats which come down the river to Babylon are circular, and made of skins," Herodotus reported. "The frames, which are of willow, are cut in the country of the Armenians above Assyria, and on these, which serve for hulls, a covering of skins is stretched outside, and thus the boats are made, without either stem or stern, quite round like a shield. They are then entirely filled with straw, and their cargo is put on board, after which they are suffered to float down the stream. . . . They are managed by two men who stand upright in them, each plying an oar, one pulling and the other pushing. . . . When they reach Babylon, the cargo is landed and offered for

(73)

sale; after which the men break up their boats and sell the straw and the frames. The current is too strong to allow a boat to return up stream, for which reason they make their boats of skins rather than wood."

In Layard's day the circular raft was as popular as ever— and, indeed, it is as popular today, more than a century later.

Rafts varied in size and price and were custom-built at Mosul. Some rafts were built with six hundred or more goat and sheep skins. For 400 piasters, about $20, Layard and Mitford ordered a small raft of sixty skins. It was 12 feet long, had an 8-foot beam, and required only one boatman. In the center of the raft, in the midst of their meager belongings, were two newly acquired luxuries, two bedsteads. Neither Layard nor Mitford, in either their notes or their journals, explained how they acquired these odd objects. For the next four days, as they floated downstream, this was to be their home.

When Mitford saw the contraption, he blanched. The raft lacked freeboard and was practically awash. "We found our baggage on the raft and the water bubbling up between the skins, which our additional weight brought very low down in the water," he wrote in his journal.

Insouciantly, the pilot pushed off and they shot down the river as though they were riding a canoe through the Grand Canyon rapids. The water boiled furiously as they were swept over an ancient barrage and the ruined foundations of a bridge built by the Assyrians.

Then, within a short distance of Mosul, a great conical mound appeared abeam of the raft. Layard immediately recognized it. "The ruins of Nimroud," he said.

The mound was green and the fields stretching around it were covered with flowers of every hue. From the raft, Layard could clearly make out the outline of ramparts. Once again he felt a longing to dig into the mound and find what, if anything, was hidden within its core. He was overcome, as he said, by "a kind of presentiment that I should one day seek to clear up the mystery." Now he knew the where of his fate. He still did not know the when and how. And, like everyone else, he would never truly understand the why.

After they passed through the broken water, the Tigris suddenly turned flat calm and the raft glided swiftly and silently along with the placidity of a gondola in a Venetian canal. During the first day's journey, they passed, to Layard's surprise, other mounds. He obtained a fix on them, using his compass and chronometer, and made pencil sketches of them in his journal. The Arab boatman at the tiller recognized Layard's unusual interest in the mounds and, as they swept along, pointed out traditional sites. "He was telling me of the histories and fates of the kings of a primitive race," Layard said, "still the favorite theme of the inhabitants of the plains of Shinar."

The banks of the Tigris were covered for long stretches with tamarisk jungle, and occasionally the party tied up to shoot game and cook dinner. On the first night out they reached an Arab riverine village and Layard saw his first palm grove. Beneath the shady fronds were clusters of orange, lemon, and pomegranate trees. They were filled with spring blossoms.

The Arab villagers, Layard wrote, were "kind and obliging." The girls wore no veils and were usually not afraid to show themselves to strangers. Layard found them "singularly grace-ful and well-made," and he noted that their faces as well as their bodies were tattooed with designs. He learned about their tattooed bodies because occasionally an Arab girl raised her solitary blue shirt and brought it over her head to hide her face from the inquisitive Frank. She wore nothing underneath. (He also may have learned about their tattoos in a more intimate fashion. "All my *Arabian Nights* dreams were almost more than realized that first night ashore," he said.)

On the fourth day of their journey, the fabled Baghdad of Haroun Al Rashid rose majestically from the banks of the Tigris, her domes and minarets sparkling and glittering in the sun. Layard almost felt like rushing into the Al Karkh bazaar shouting, "Old lamps for new! Old lamps for new!"

In the river's roadstead, as they drifted along on the current, was a gunboat flying a British Jack at her bow staff. She bore the name *Nimroud*—again that tantalizing name—and she was one of two British iron-clad paddle-wheelers controlling the sea route between Baghdad and the Indian Ocean.

These vessels, in an age of gunboat diplomacy, plied the Tigris, the Persian Gulf, and the Arabian Sea. They were armed with six swivels and two large guns, one fore and one aft. As Mitford observed, "This flottila is here more with a political object than for any service it may render in forwarding the mail or merchandise." But the presence of gunboats had had strikingly beneficial side effects. River piracy almost ceased, and with it, the slave trade. Many Arab tribes along the banks gave up their tradition of robbery and plunder and engaged in peaceful trade. Western imperialism had brought a measure of law and order to an area which had inclined toward anarchy for centuries.

Layard and his companion landed on the left bank of the river, beneath an enormous white building that flew a British flag, the residence of the East India Company's political resident in Turkish Asia, Colonel Geoffrey Taylor.

Before disembarking from their raft and presenting themselves to the British resident, Layard and Mitford donned their only clean clothing, spruced up, and combed out their unkempt, curly beards. As Layard stepped from the raft onto the dock, he slipped and fell into the muddy harbor. On being introduced to Colonel Taylor, Layard expressed the hope that the resident would accept him for what he was—"an adventurous traveller with small means." And, he added, with a not very good sense of balance.

They laughed over the incident.

Taylor was a small, slight, and wizened man, considerably past middle age, with a bright and intellectual appearance. This was not an age when diplomatic hacks or political appointees were sent out on important missions. Taylor possessed a good command of Arabic and Persian, had amassed a valuable collection of Arabic and Persian manuscripts, and maintained an enormous library. His wife was an Armenian who was born in Persia; one of their two daughters was married to Captain (later Admiral) Lynch, who was then in command of an expedition charting the Euphrates. Like the *Nimroud* anchored in the roadstead, Lynch and his officers and men were not members of the Royal Navy but of the Royal Indian Navy. They were equally at ease in Hindustani as well as Arabic and Persian and possessed considerable detailed knowledge about Eastern customs.

Taylor warmly welcomed Layard and Mitford and gave them free run of his impressive residence.

The pair lingered at Baghdad for almost two months. Layard spent much of the time fighting recurring malarial attacks, studying in Taylor's library, and, whenever he felt fit, inspecting mounds in the vicinity and engaging in what he himself described as "riotous living." The officers and crews of the English gunboats knew all the proper dens of iniquity operated by Hindustani, Arabian, and Persian madams.

A French mission was the only other European diplomatic representation in the city, and through its members Layard learned that the French planned to open a consulate upriver, probably at Mosul.

Taylor arranged for Layard and Mitford to call on the local pasha, or governor. On the day of the audience, the temperature in Baghdad's streets was 104 degrees Fahrenheit and the pasha greeted them from a divan, his hairy chest naked from the waist up. Layard found him repulsive. "Masses of fat hung about him," he wrote, and, aside from food, he "thought of little but the delights of the harem." For the first time, Layard understood the rot that was eating at the Ottoman empire.

"When one saw the kind of men to whom the government and welfare of the Sublime Porte's subjects were confided," Layard wrote, "the condition of his empire, the sights of poverty, misery and decay which surrounded one on all sides, could scarcely be a matter of surprise."

The empire had been established in 1453 when the Turks conquered Constantinople. By the sixteenth century its writ extended from Budapest to Aden, from the Caspian Sea to the Atlantic. But in Layard's day Turkey was rapidly acquiring the sobriquet "sick man of Europe." The Ottoman empire was in serious decline, but it would take another three-quarters of a century before it was dismembered after World War I and disappeared in 1922.

The situation in Baghdad was a classic example of the rot. Although Baghdad was one of the richest pashaliks of the empire, it was being reduced to ruin by corruption and maladministration. Roads were insecure, the people restless, the regime repressive, commerce almost at a standstill. Only the presence of British gunboats maintained a veneer of order. To the politically astute Layard, Baghdad, like Singapore and Gibraltar, could serve as a linchpin of the expanding British empire. It linked the Mediterranean and the Indian Ocean. Layard was convinced that in time the city would revive as a commercial center. "I trust that it may be the destiny of England to bring about the change," he wrote.

During their sojourn at Baghdad, Layard was intrigued by Taylor's reports of the existence of mounds in the vicinity, especially at Hillah, the site of ancient Babylon, and Ctesiphon, where the Sassanian rulers of Persia built their palaces.

Layard succeeded in talking Mitford into joining him on an excursion to Hillah. It was May 16, 1840. Layard was stunned by what he saw—a long, low series of mounds. The desolation, the solitude, the shapeless heaps—this was all that remained of one of the greatest and most renowned cities of antiquity. He could hardly compose himself when he gazed on the horizon and viewed for the first time the place the Arabs called Birs Nimrod—the Tower of Nimrod. In the Bible, the tower had a different name. It was called Babel.

Regularly, he learned, the few inhabitants of Hillah dug into the mounds for bricks, either for their houses or to sell at construction sites in Baghdad. Many of the bricks bore "nail-headed designs," he was told.

"The characters had not been deciphered, and the meaning of the legend was unknown," Layard observed. "I picked up many of these bricks." They were the first examples of cuneiform that he had ever collected, and he would have been astounded to know that most of them bore the name of Nebuchadnezzar, the Babylonian king who leveled Solomon's temple.

Itinerant Arabs also occasionally discovered cylinders covered with strange figures, and other odd objects baked in clay or fashioned from bronze. Many of these relics turned up in Baghdad's bazaars and were eagerly bought up by Europeans as souvenirs and conversation pieces. Colonel Taylor, for example, possessed a large collection of them; so did the mission's surgeon, Dr. Ross, the same Ross who was the first Westerner to discover and explore Hatra.

As Layard and Mitford rode back to Baghdad, Layard was again struck by the long lines of mounds which traversed the plains around Hillah in almost every direction. Suddenly, he realized that these were the remains of great canals and his thoughts turned to the Hanging Gardens of Babylon.

Upon returning to Baghdad, Layard immediately arranged to visit the ruins of Ctesiphon. But Mitford's interest in ruins appeared to be waning, especially when it was so unspeakably hot, sometimes 120 degrees Fahrenheit in the shade. Layard could not be deterred and decided to make the short journey alone.

Since Ctesiphon was situated along the Tigris and the *Nimroud* was scheduled to pass the spot en route to Baghdad late in the day, Colonel Taylor arranged with Captain Felix Jones to pick him up on his return, so that Layard would be spared the fatiguing ride back to Baghdad by donkey. Accordingly, at dawn that day Layard set out for Ctesiphon with an Arab guide. At the site of the ruins he dismissed the guide, who returned to Baghdad with Layard's mule.

Despite the intense heat, Layard spent the greater part of the day scrambling over the ruins of the ancient Sassanian palaces, some of which rose 106 feet above sea level. The palace foundations were a solid mass of compacted brickwork, almost indestructible. The Caliph of Baghdad had sought to level the palaces of the infidels, it was said, and failed. Out of frustration, he appealed to his grand vizier for advice. "Desist," the vizier counseled, "or the world will say the Caliph of Islam failed to destroy what the king of the infidels was able to build."

In late afternoon, atop the ruins, Layard detected a wisp of smoke on the horizon—the *Nimroud* was churning upriver on her way to Baghdad. Layard quickly descended from the top of the ruins and, to his surprise and dismay, discovered that a broad and deep marsh, formed by the incoming tide, separated him from the main bank of the Tigris.

"I was far away from Baghdad, and suffering from an attack of the ague," he said. "I had sent away my mule, and to return on foot was out of the question." He had no choice other than to wade across the marsh. He stripped off his clothing and plunged into the morass with its leeches and occasional water snakes. Racked by fever and chill, he struggled, waist high and sometimes up to his armpits, through the water, his footing in the deep mud insecure and the sun beating overhead. A lesser individual would have perished from fatigue. He was genuinely frightened, and almost panicked. The paddle-steamer was rushing along, and Layard was afraid the vessel's lookout would take him in the distance for an Arab buffalo keeper and pass him by. In desperation, he waved a handkerchief to attract attention. The vessel stopped, and Captain Jones dispatched a boat to rescue the drowning figure. Jones never quite got over the incident and for the rest of his life told the story of how, "seeing something white waving in the marsh, I looked through my telescope and perceived the head of a European just above the level of the water. I had landed and had fished an English-traveler out of the morass, drenched to the skin and shivering with ague."

According to the law of the Medes and Persians.

—ESTHER

XII

Layard and Mitford now entered upon what was, in Layard's words, "the most difficult and dangerous part of our journey"—the trip through Persia, the last barrier before crossing into British India. Once in India, Ceylon was just a step down the pike. The Persians, however, were a law unto themselves. They were hostile to Christians in general and Europeans in particular. To make matters worse, as a result of Russian machinations, Persia and Britain teetered on the edge of war.

Since Layard felt he would attract less attention in local dress, he discarded his Egyptian uniform and donned the garb of the Persians—long flowing robes, shalwar or loose trousers, and a black lambskin cap, Persian-style. He shaved the crown of his head and dyed his blond hair and beard deep black. With a boyish enthusiasm that persisted through his maturity, Layard relished the guises in which he traveled across Asia Minor.

He and Mitford joined an armed caravan of seventy men, women, and children, and fifty-five animals, on June 22, 1840, bound from Baghdad to the Persian frontier town of Kermansha. In the party were two litters slung across mules, each containing a young woman, the wives of an old Turkish merchant. In a letter to his mother, a frustrated Layard complained, "I haven't been able to find out whether any beauties may be concealed by the obstinate veil which is down day and night."

At Kermansha their journey came to an abrupt end. Britain and Persia had suspended diplomatic relations. Layard and Mitford were ordered to proceed no farther into Persia without the approval of the shah-en-shah or Persian king-of-kings. Under armed guard, they were bundled off to the Shah's camp, a three-day march from Kermansha. For more than a month, Layard and Mitford, suspected of being British agents, were detained as the Shah's "guests." For a man who felt at home among Italians, Poles, Montenegrins, Turks, Arabs, Jews, Yezidi devil worshipers, and the wild tribes of Asia Minor, Layard formed a surprisingly unfavorable opinion of the Persians. He considered them vain, insolent, and compulsive liars. "I have never met with a more consummate set of rascals," he wrote home. He was horrified by their brutal treatment of political prisoners. On one occasion, the Persians drew the teeth of a prisoner and, using the teeth as buckshot, shot the man to death with them.

During their forced detention in the Shah's camp, oddly enough, they were given permission to journey, under armed escort, to nearby Behistun, where Major Rawlinson had reported trilingual cuneiform inscriptions on a lofty, smooth-surfaced cliff. "The . . . bas-reliefs and cuneiform inscriptions . . . were at so great a height from the ground, and so completely inaccessible, that it was impossible to make copies of them," a disappointed Layard reported. The rock was destined to become a Rosetta Stone of Assyriology. It contained inscriptions in Median, Babylonian, and Persian. Scholars—among them Rawlinson, who was the first to succeed in making a copy of the legend—would later determine that it was signed by Darius the Great.

Other than the excursion to Behistun, Layard and Mitford were confined to the Shah's camp (the Shah himself never gave them an audience). The pair had left England almost a year before and were now hopelessly stalled halfway to Ceylon. In part, they idled away the time figuring out their expenditures and estimated that, thus far, the journey had averaged out to four shillings (80 cents) a day. At this rate of expenditure, Layard had visions of wandering through Asia Minor indefinitely. That is, if he ever got out of the Persian camp alive.

On July 10, the first anniversary of their departure from London, the Shah broke camp and marched to Hamadan. Layard felt in luck. He had longed to visit Hamadan, which, as Ectabana, the capital of the Medes, was as famous in antiquity as Nineveh and Babylon. Arbaces is said to have made it his capital after the fall of Nineveh, as he struggled to hold together what was left of the Assyrian empire. In Ectabana, on his return from the invasion of India, Alexander halted to offer hecatombs to the gods. And, according to the Old Testament, Hamadan was the burial place of Esther and Mordecai. Both Jews and Moslems had built a shrine at the spot and squabbled incessantly over its possession.

After the Shah's entourage reached Hamadan, Layard went off to visit the celebrated tombs and came away disappointed. "I found nothing in the building except a vault filled with rubbish," he recorded in his journal.

But something he had not bargained for attracted his curiosity at Hamadan—mysterious mounds like those shapeless piles of earth that he first had seen at Mosul. At the base of the Hamadan mound he found several shafts of marble columns and a figure of a lion rudely sculptured in stone. What lay under the mound? He found it inexplicable that nobody ever tried to find out.

Fortunately for Layard and Mitford, Baron de Bode, the first secretary of the Russian embassy in Persia, arrived at Hamadan on a special mission to the Shah. He was surprised to find the two Englishmen in camp and interceded with the Persians on their behalf to obtain a firman.

A firman was an imperial decree—in this instance, a travel document. Without it, Mitford mused, "we might have been detained an indefinite period."

The firman had a catch. The pair could travel through Persia to India but only along the well-worn caravan routes of northern Persia which stretched into Afghanistan. They were barred from pursuing their original plan of cutting directly through the heart of Persia via Yezd and Seistan, a route rarely glimpsed by Europeans. Before their departure from London, the Royal Geographic Society had expressed to Layard a special interest in having him map the Seistan route.

Mitford eagerly accepted the firman's condition. He had had enough adventures and delays and was anxious to get on to Ceylon. But Layard, as brash as ever, was unwilling to renounce the attempt to cross the Seistan. Instead of accepting the firman to cross northern Persia, he boldly asked for—and received— a firman to travel south to Bushire, a Persian Gulf port on the road back to Baghdad. Layard had concocted a wild plan of returning to Baghdad with a detour through the forbidden Seistan. He sought to cajole Mitford into the journey, but Mitford had had enough of Layard's detours, and the companions parted company.

"We had been together for above a year," Layard wrote later, "and I much regretted that we had to part."

Publicly, Mitford also expressed regret, but in fact a strain developed between the two men. While they remained in touch with each other for the rest of their lives, the warmth was gone from the relationship. Each accused the other of "chickening out." Like little boys, they vied for the honor of having chosen the more dangerous course of action. "I had now to face the worst half of my journey alone," Mitford wrote. And Layard said, "I am now alone [and] the most dangerous part of my journey . . . is before me."

The truth is that they had come to rely upon each other, for counsel and companionship, for sharing perils and observations, for nursing each other through bouts of malaria and dysentery. Suddenly, they found themselves proceeding through hostile countryside—alone. Scant wonder that each viewed the road ahead the most perilous part of the journey.

Nine months later, May 2, 1842, Mitford reached Ceylon, his coveted destination. "[I was] kindly welcomed by the Governor, Sir Colin Campbell, who informed me that he had received a notification of my appointment to the Civil Service of the Colony." Mitford's journey had taken one year and ten months. He had covered 10,000 miles overland, 7,000 on horseback.

As for Layard, nine months later he was still tracking across the heartland of the Shah's empire in the guise of a Persian. This is even more the remarkable considering the precarious state of his health.

Ea, king of the deep, who determines destiny.
—ASSYRIAN INVOCATION

XIII

For the next year or so, Austen Henry Layard wandered through the remote mountain districts of western Persia. He crossed terrain that no European had trod since the days of Alexander. He searched for ancient ruins, and found them, and he discovered, to his astonishment, new mounds.

What makes his adventure in this period of his life so unusual is that, like Rabbi Benjamin of Tudela seven centuries before him, he trod alone.

He left Hamadan August 8, with only a horse and a pair of small saddlebags, and soon came down with yet another attack of intermittent fever and dysentery. He pressed ahead toward the Persian Gulf, but, once beyond Hamadan, he made a detour east and headed for Isfahan. "During my journey from Hamadan," he recorded, "I made careful notes of the country, taking bearings with my Kater's compass of the mountain ranges and peaks . . . as well as . . . the sources of streams and rivers, and the position of the towns and villages through which I passed or which I saw in the distance." The notes were for the Royal Geographic Society. It was a dangerous sojourn, for although his travel documents gave him permission to travel south, he might easily have been taken for a British spy and been tortured and shot. He did, in fact, have some close calls.

At Isfahan, for example, he paid a courtesy call on the *matamet* or governor of the province, a eunuch of Georgian birth, born of Christian parents, who had been purchased as a slave and raised as a Moslem. The *matamet* displayed remarkable administrative abilities, enjoyed the Shah's confidence, and had risen rapidly in the Persian hierarchy.

But the governor was feared and hated. Insensible to human suffering, he spent idle hours inventing new forms of torture, as though he sought vengeance against normal members of his sex. His most recent triumph was a tower which he had constructed of three hundred living prisoners. The prisoners— mountain rebels—were laid on stones in layers of ten, mortar being spread between each layer, their heads left free.

The wily *matamet* entertained suspicions about the young Englishman and detained him, although he was allowed to roam freely through the city.

Layard took advantage of the situation, devoting the days to studying Persian and the evenings to a cram course in the lifestyle of the Persian elite. Members of the Persian nobility often invited him to dinner, which was served in the *enderum*, or harem. While dancing girls performed, as they had for Xerxes and Darius millenniums earlier, bottles of arak and platters of sweetmeats were served.

"Many of these girls were strikingly handsome," Layard observed. Their costume consisted of loose silk jackets, entirely open in front so as to show their bare breasts. Their eyebrows were colored black. Their eyes were large and dark and rendered more brilliant and expressive with the use of kohl. "The dancing," Layard recorded, "soon degenerated into outrageous indecency, for these dancing girls did not refuse the wine and arak that were liberally offered to them."

The *matamet* appeared to be playing a cat-and-mouse game with his compulsory visitor. The governor granted him several audiences and at each audience, Layard's dislike of him deepened.

Unable to receive permission to proceed through the Seistan, which lay to the east, Layard tacked. As the Shah's military adviser, Major Rawlinson had heard of the existence of ancient ruins in the wild Baktiyari mountain district of Persia and had sought to explore them but was unable to do so because of the anarchy that prevailed in the mountains. For young Layard to accomplish the feat would be a rather large feather in his cap. It would also get him out of Isfahan. Accordingly, after a month's detention by the *matamet*, Layard asked whether he might have permission to visit the Baktiyari mountains. To his surprise, the governor acceded to his wish. Unknown to Layard, the *matamet* was plotting a punitive war against the Baktiyaris. Certain that the Englishman would meet with death among them, he planned to use Layard's murder as a pretext for a pacification expedition.

The *matamet*'s permission coincided with the departure of a caravan to Kala Tul, the headquarters of the Baktiyari's paramount chief, Mehemet Taki Khan. Layard joined the trek and for the next several months dwelt among the mountain tribes, the first Christian and Frank to do so.

Much to the *matamet*'s discomfort, Layard was not only unmolested but, on the contrary, was treated as an honored guest. He exhibited in the mountains the same uncanny ability he displayed among the Turks, Arabs, and others to make fast friends among non-Westerners: He accepted people for what they were, judged them by their own standards of conduct, and practiced the hoary adage: When in Rome do as the Romans. In his dealings with the Baktiyari and other mountain tribes, he was neither paternalistic nor condescending. His concept of the Baktiyari, as with other peoples, was that they were neither his inferiors nor his superiors, simply different.

The Baktiyari, he found, were "a splendid race," the men chivalrous, tall, finely featured, and the women fair-skinned, graceful, and of singular beauty.

A genuinely intimate friendship developed between Layard and the paramount chief. Indeed, their relationship grew so strong that Mehemet Taki Khan sought to convert Layard to Islam and, as a tantalizing bribe, offered him in marriage the most stunningly beautiful young woman among the Baktiyari, the famed Khanumi. She possessed exquisite features, her eyes large, black, and almond-shaped. She was as intelligent and lively as sexually desirable. She was the epitome of Scheherazade, and again Layard was overcome by the déjà vu feeling that he was living through a passage of a thousand and one nights.

"The inducement was great," he conceded, "but the temptation was resisted."

Layard's interlude in the mountain districts of western Persia were among the happiest days he had spent since his childhood in Italy. Much of the time was spent exploring ruins, sites never before seen by a European. For example, he visited Manjanik, where—according to tradition—Abraham was cast into the fiery furnace by Nimrod. He also visited what was purportedly Daniel's tomb and nearby, in a gorge near Kala Tul, he discovered a carved figure, larger than life, and thirty-six lines of unintelligible arrow-headed characters. At another place, he came across a set of rock sculptures which he attributed to "the most remote antiquity."

As he went from site to site with his pencil, sketching the cuneiform characters and rock-cut sculptures, his name spread rapidly through the mountains. Many of the tribal peoples considered him a magician to whom the jinns had given extraordinary powers: he wrote with a dry stick from which ink flowed freely.

Mehemet Taki Khan, the Baktiyari chief, was also a pragmatic man. He knew there was friction between Britain and Persia, and he regarded Layard as a hedge against a Persian invasion of his mountain retreat. When reports reached Kala Tul that a British sloop-of-war, on a charting expedition, had temporarily dropped the hook at Karak, a Persian gulf port, about 175 miles to the southwest, Mehemet Taki Khan revealed to Layard his plans to throw off the Persian yoke and proclaim the independence of the Baktiyari. He persuaded Layard to visit Karak and offer the British special commercial relations in return for English support of Baktiyari independence.

Layard, who always empathized with the underdog, required little encouragement to rally to the Baktiyari cause.

Accompanied by a small detachment of Baktiyari escorts, in December Layard made the perilous journey to Karak. In the roadstead, indeed, was a British sloop-of-war. For Layard, it was a heartening sight. "My first thought was a bath," he said. And on Christmas Day, 1841, he dined with the expedition's officers aboard H.M.S. *Coote*, the flagship of the East India Company's Persian Gulf flotilla.

Layard was especially thrilled as he stepped aboard her for the second time.This was the same sloop he had visited eight years earlier, as a wide-eyed sixteen-year-old, when she was tied up in the Thames. As he strode across her teak decks, he felt completely free. What a far cry this was from the Reverend Bewsher's school and Uncle Benjamin's offices at Gray's Inn. Layard's mission, however, was a failure. The *Coote*'s commander advised him to tell the Baktiyari that British policy was to avoid a conflict with Persia and that the Baktiyari could not expect British support for their war of independence.

A disappointed Layard returned to Kala Tul only to learn that the *matamet*, at the head of a large Persian army which included horse-drawn artillery, had invaded the Baktiyari lands. Mehemet Taki Khan was taken prisoner and placed in chains. (He was to die in solitary confinement ten years later.) As for his people, many were taken prisoner; others were slaughtered like livestock.

With a view to freeing their chieftain, a band of Baktiyari organized a foray on the *matamet*'s camp. Impetuously, Layard joined in the attack. The raid was a failure.

Arise, go to Nineveh, that great city.

—JONAH

XIV

Like a Daniel in the lion's den, the audacious Layard rode to Shuster, where the victorious *matamet* now made his headquarters. The governor's camp was given over to feasting, drinking bouts, sexual orgies, and the torture of prisoners. Layard coolly informed the *matamet* that since the mountain districts were in disorder, he had abandoned the idea of examining ancient sites and planned to "push on."

The *matamet*, if nothing else, had a superb intelligence system and was aware of Layard's political activities on behalf of the Baktiyari. "You Englishmen," the *matamet* admonished Layard, "are always meddling in matters which do not concern you." In fact, Layard might well have found himself roasting on an open spit, but fortunately the Shah was set on trying to avoid an Anglo-Persian war.

Instead Layard was once again detained by the governor and spent one of the most terrifying months of his life at his camp. The torture of prisoners was an almost daily occurrence, their shrieks of pain heard at all hours of day and night. The bastinado was commonplace; often, after this form of pillory, the prisoner was revived with buckets of water and hot irons were applied to his penis and testicles. For good measure, needles were driven under his fingernails and toenails.

"The cries of these wretched victims of Persian cruelty,"

Layard said, "were ringing in my ears when I escaped from Shuster." After a month's "education"—most probably as a warning to keep his nose out of Persia's internal affairs—the *matamet* provided Layard with travel documents for Basra, the Persian Gulf port situated just below the confluence of the Tigris and Euphrates. Layard retreated across western Persia to the friendly confines of Turkish Asia.

On the road back he was repeatedly ravaged by recurring attacks of fever. On one occasion, he was compelled to dismount from his mare and lie down on the ground with the horse's bridle fastened to his wrist. "I remained delirious for two or three hours," he said laconically, "as was usual with me."

But his spirits soared as he reentered the domains of the Ottoman empire. "To my great joy," he recorded as he reached Basra in the spring of 1841, "a merchant ship flying an English flag was anchored in the middle of the stream." He hired a small boat and rowed to the ship. When the sailor of the watch saw the dirty, ill-clad Arab approach, he shouted him off in colorful Limehouse argot. "He was not a little surprised when I addressed him in English," Layard noted.

Aboard the *Lord Elphinstone* that night, for the first time in months he enjoyed the pleasant sensation of sleeping between clean sheets. Except for his brief visit to Karak, he had been out of touch with the Western world for what seemed a millennium.

This was Layard's first glimpse of Basra, and from the railing of the vessel, as he took in the view, his eyes focused again on the spectacle of artificial mounds. The area was dotted with them.

Since the vessel planned to lay at anchor for weeks, unloading and loading wares, Layard rowed ashore and inspected several of the mounds. He found odd pieces of pottery and broken bricks. Again he wondered what lay within the mounds.

An Arab courier was leaving Basra the next day for Baghdad—normally a two-day ride—and Layard opted to join him rather than wait for the vessel to weigh anchor. Along the way they were waylaid and plundered by Bedouins, who thought Layard was a Turk. They were ready to kill him on the spot, when one of the party mistook him for Dr. Ross, the East India Company's physician. Ross had ministered to the Bedouins in town, and they befriended and respected him. Even so, they robbed Layard and his Arab companion of their mares and all their possessions, including, quite literally, the shirts on their backs.

Layard was compelled to walk the rest of the way to Baghdad in bare feet. The ground was so overheated by the merciless sun that it burned the soles of his feet, which soon began to swell, blister, and bleed.

When Layard and his guide reached Baghdad, it was sundown and the gates were shut for the night. "I sank down on the ground," the exhausted Layard said, "overcome with fatigue and pain."

At sunrise the following day the city's gates were flung open, and the first party to emerge was a group of European ladies and gentlemen out for a morning ride. "It was the same party that on my previous visit to Baghdad, I had almost daily accompanied on their morning rides," Layard said. The party passed close to him but did not recognize the disheveled Arab figure crouched in pitiful rags at the gate. As for himself, with English women in the party, he was too vain—or Victorian— to call out for help. But at a short distance behind the group rode Dr. Ross and a servant. "I called to him, and he turned towards me in the utmost surprise, scarcely believing his senses," Layard said. Ross gave him his groom's horse, helped him to mount the animal, and took him home.

After four days of confinement in bed, Layard, who possessed remarkable recuperative powers, was restored to his usual strength and health. Nonetheless, weeks passed before he could walk without pain and discomfort.

Baghdad's tiny European enclave buzzed with the news of his return. Nobody had heard from him in more than a year, and it was feared that he had either been killed or, worse, was being held captive in a Persian torture chamber. While Layard's feet mended, Ross sent out a servant to retrieve his mare and his belongings. Within a few days everything was returned intact, including his Kater's compass, precious notebooks, and black-coated silver watch.

Layard was now in a quandary. Ceylon was out of the question. His funds were running low. Physically, he was exhausted. He had no job. His life was still a succession of failures. And he had a touch of homesickness.

He wrote his mother and the Austens about the possibility of returning to England. In his journal, which was later published as *Early Adventures In Persia, Susiana and Babylonia*, he put the delicate decision circumlocutionally. "Circumstances," he wrote, "rendered it necessary that before I decided whether to persevere in my attempt to reach India by crossing the Seistan, or indeed, whether I should continue on to India at all, that I should communicate with my friends at home."

But in his private correspondence he was more direct.

"You will be surprised to find me again writing to you from Baghdad," he wrote his mother September 9, 1841. "I have seriously and after much reflection determined to return to England if my uncle and yourself should approve of my doing so." On the same day he posted a letter to "Uncle Ben" in which, perhaps tongue in cheek, he observed, "You must have seen from my last letter that I was proceeding but slowly towards India." Consuming spoonfuls of crow, he requested his godfather's "sanction to my returning." To demonstrate that, if nothing else, he had learned prudence during his travels, he boasted that during two years of daily travel he had spent less than £200 ($1,000).

In those days, it took three months or more for an exchange of letters between Baghdad and London. Often, the mail failed to get through.

No sooner had Layard dispatched these painful letters than he entertained misgivings. In truth, he did not want to return to England. He did not know what he wanted. In the lengthy interval before receiving replies, Layard took stock of himself. He had an intimate knowledge of Asia Minor. He had exhibited an ability to cultivate the fiercest tribes in that part of the world—Bedouins, Kurds, Lurs, and Baktiyaris, among others. He had developed important contacts in Mesopotamia. He possessed insight into the politics and geography of Turkey and Persia. He could parley in several local languages. He was a good observer, good listener, and articulate. And he was only twenty-four years of age.

Obviously, he had assets. He was splendid raw material for the East India Company or perhaps the foreign or colonial office in London. He also had the makings of a journalist. Colonel Taylor, the British resident at Baghdad, seemed to think so, too, and he wrote the East India Company on Layard's behalf, strongly recommending him for a post in the Near East.

When Layard drafted a blueprint for establishing trade relations with western Persia, especially the mountain district, Taylor had been so impressed that he forwarded a copy directly to Lord Aberdeen, the British foreign minister.

Nor was Layard a complete unknown in London. *The Journal of the Royal Geographic Society*, for example, carried a brief summary of his Persian explorations. "Mr. Layard has forwarded to us a paper," the prestigious journal said, "in which he reports his success in reaching and examining with some minuteness the Bachtiari [sic] Mountains."

And while he awaited word from his mother and Uncle Ben, he engaged a munshi to teach him Persian and Arabic, and he worked on a lengthy article which the *Journal* published two years later. He talked incessantly about the artificial mounds that dotted the region and sought to organize a consortium to finance their exploration. One English trader at Baghdad, Alexander Hector, was so impressed with Layard's presentation that he wrote to Sheffield, England, to raise interest and money for the project. "[I] believe that the objects of antiquity to be discovered would easily repay the expense," Layard told Hector with confidence.

In the midst of these activities, the East India Company planned a quick exploration of the Karun, a river at the mouth of the Persian Gulf, whose head of navigation was at Shuster, deep in Persian territory. The expedition was generated by Layard's paper on the possibilities of developing regional trade. The Karun, Layard had argued, was politically the principal artery for such commerce.

Lieutenant W. B. Selby, the commander of *Assyria*, a small armored steamer of the East India Company, invited Layard to join the expedition. Layard did so not only because of his interest in trade but also because of unconfirmed reports of important ruins along the route. He was not disappointed.

Along the way, as Selby and his crew charted the river, Layard visited the tomb of the prophet Ezra, the great fire temples of the ancient Elymais and reexamined the ruins of Susa, which he correctly identified as "Shushan the Palace" in the Book of Daniel. At Susa he also discovered a new mound and at its base found a slab 9 feet long and 6 inches wide with an inscription in arrow-headed characters. The mound was strewn with bricks, fragments of pottery, and glazed tiles. Layard was more convinced than ever that digging into the mound would restore to light the wonders of lost worlds. For the life of him, he still did not understand why no one else had ever thought of doing so, out of simple human curiosity, if nothing else.

Selby's account of the *Assyria's* ascent of the Karun appeared in the Royal Geographic Society's *Journal*. In glowing terms he referred to Layard as that "indefatigable traveller ... whose forebearance, aptitude, and amiability of disposition well entitled him to succeed in an undertaking of ... much danger."

On returning to Baghdad, Layard found letters from home that led him "to determine upon returning to England." In England, he hoped to land a job and raise funds for his various schemes. He was also motivated by his mother's plight. Since his departure, she said, she had lived in "suspense and anxiety" for his safety. There was also family gossip. His mother's funds were low. She had purchased army commissions for two of his younger brothers, Frederick and Arthur. Edgar, meanwhile, had married before he could find a job. The inference was plain. As head of the family, Henry's place was at his mother's side.

As for the Austens, Uncle Benjamin and Aunt Sara had no objection to his return, but they felt more strongly than ever that their godson had wasted valuable years chasing will-o'-the-wisps in outlandish parts of the world. He could not even support himself.

And so, Layard's adventures had come to an end. He was

homeward bound. His flights of fancy were grounded. The thousand and one nights had run their course, and daylight was breaking.

It was now 1842, and Layard made preparations to return to England by the shortest and cheapest route possible, via Beirut. These plans, however, coincided with news from Constantinople of a border clash between the Turks and Persians and rumors that the Sublime Porte and the Shah toyed with declarations of war against each other.

Taylor was anxious that the British ambassador in the Turkish capital, Sir Stratford Canning, be fully apprised of the latest situation in Mesopotamia. The colonel asked Layard whether, instead of proceeding to England via Beirut, he would consider taking the longer route via Constantinople. Taylor said he had a number of secret dispatches that must be placed in the ambassador's hands and that once Layard reached the Ottoman capital he might furnish Sir Stratford "at the same time, personally, with any information that he might require should he think fit."

"I at once consented to do so," Layard said.

The Turkish pasha at Baghdad also planned to dispatch a *tatar*, or pony express rider, to the Sublime Porte with reports on the situation and, at Taylor's request, the governor permitted Layard to accompany the Ottoman courier.

On the eve of his departure, Layard checked with Alexander Hector to see if there was any reply to his proposal to dig up the mounds. There was none.

As the two couriers departed, the heat on the Babylonian and Assyrian plains rose to 115 degrees Fahrenheit. "But I was accustomed to it," Layard said, "as well as to fatigue and to every manner of privation."

With the *tatar* setting a breathless pace, they rode day and night and in fifty hours arrived at their first caravansary, Mosul. Just as the whale had cast back Jonah, fate had thrown Layard back among his "mysterious mounds."

In front of my horse I saw
the poppy flower for the first time.
—T'ANG DYNASTY POEM

XV

Layard was delayed in Mosul several days while the local governor prepared additional dispatches for the *tartar's* saddlebags.

Mosul was as depressing and evil-smelling as ever. But there was a change. No longer was the British consul, Christian Rassam, the only foreign representative on the Tigris's west bank. A French official, Paolo Emilio Botta, had raised the tricolor, and, to Layard's utter astonishment, Botta was excavating the great mound of Kouyunjik on the opposite bank!

It is a measure of Layard's character at twenty-five that he harbored no jealousy toward Botta. If he was upset, and he was, it was not with Botta but with his failure to stir the interest of his countrymen in probing the mounds. Like many Englishmen of the post-Napoleonic period, he secretly admired the immersion of French officialdom in cultural pursuits, whether the government was monarchial or republican. The fact was that Layard had not succeeded in interesting either individuals or the quasi-public East India Company to underwrite excavations. The latter, like the government itself, was preoccupied with empire-building.

Layard immediately called on the new French consul and discovered in Botta "a delightful companion." The two struck it off magnificently and became enduring friends. Botta was flexible in his views, large-minded and willing to impart what he knew.

They soon discovered they were cast from a similar die.

Botta's name struck a chord in Layard's memory. This was Paolo Emilio Botta, the Turin-born son of the Italian historian whom he first came across a dozen years earlier during his youthful escapades in Italy. The son, now thirty-seven years old, twelve years Layard's senior, was an unusual figure. An accomplished botanist, who opted for French citizenship during the Napoleonic wars, he entered the French foreign service and held various consular posts in Egypt, Yemen, Syria, and China before his posting to Mosul. China was his undoing. There he became addicted to the poppy, "a fatal habit," Layard called it, "which ruined his health and rendered him liable to occasional fits of melancholy and despondency of the most painful nature."

"He is quite a Frenchman ..." H. J. Ross, a Baghdad merchant and intimate friend of Layard, also wrote in his memoirs. "We are great friends in spite of his violent denunciations of England which entirely depends on how much opium he has taken."

Layard and Botta spent three days engaged in a running conversation that was alternately conducted in Italian, French, and English. They talked incessantly about the mounds. Botta was the first person Layard ever met who was willing, indeed eager, to engage in open-ended speculation about the mounds, and what might lie within them.

A gracious host, in the Italian manner, Botta poured a steady stream of arak into Layard's glass, while apologizing profusely over the absence of a good wine. Between sips of acrid liquor, Botta offered Layard a "Chinese pipe." "The result, happily," Layard recounted, "was that I suffered from so severe a headache, accompanied by violent sickness, that I have never made a second attempt."

Layard was puzzled about Botta's interest in the mounds. Julius Mohl, Botta explained, was the catalyst.

Mohl, a German-born Orientalist, had settled in France and, like Botta, adopted French citizenship. During a trip to London, Mohl spied the single vitrine at the British Museum containing all that was known about Nineveh and the Assyrian empire.

It was, of course, the collection of the late Claudius Rich. The bricks, covered with cuneiform characters, hypnotized Mohl. "He was filled with an overmastering belief that these little bricks," wrote William Rogers, the nineteenth-century American scholar, "were the promise of an immense literature which lay buried, awaiting the excavator's hand." Mohl also read and reread every line of Rich's memoirs and concluded that Rich had discovered lost Nineveh and that archaeological treasure lay buried beneath the mounds, even though many people considered Nineveh another Troy, a fable. Indeed, some of the scholars Mohl encountered sarcastically suggested that he also search for Aladdin's lamp in Baghdad.

Mohl, however, persisted in his belief and in 1840, coincidentally the same year Layard viewed his first mound, was named secretary of the French Asiatic Society. Two years later, for reasons of politics and trade, the French decided to establish a consular office at Mosul. Botta, in disfavor with the Quai d'Orsay because of his drug problem, was assigned to that backwater of the Ottoman empire as a form of punishment.

Julius Mohl saw his opportunity and seized on the appointment to impress upon Botta that a great opportunity lay before him and *la belle France*. Botta must not merely explore, observe, describe, and measure the size of the mounds opposite Mosul, like others before for centuries. He must *dig* into them.

Botta, who was amenable to almost any suggestion, promised to do so. As Botta unfolded his story and drew on his Chinese pipe, Layard poured another glass of arak.

Botta told him how he had searched the mounds of Kouyunjik and Nebbi Yunnus and found nothing but potsherds and kiln-dried bricks and a few fragments of alabaster inscribed with cuneiform characters. These items could hardly be taken seriously. For Mohl's benefit, however, he meticulously numbered the cuneiform fragments. The potsherds he threw unceremoniously aside as valueless.*

---

* It was not until the late nineteenth century that Heinrich Schliemann at Troy and other embryo archaeologists recognized potsherds as the time-prints of past civilizations.

Layard was disappointed by Botta's failure.

The following day he and Botta crossed the Tigris to inspect the Frenchman's trenches. Botta was right; there was nothing to see.

Mohl, Botta said, had led him to believe that the mounds were "fruitful mines" of antiquity and that Kouyunjik regularly supplied bricks and stones in the erection of houses at Mosul. "Such, however," Botta dryly observed, "can scarcely have been the case at Nineveh or at any period, and very certainly it is not so in the present period."

"The reason is plain," Botta continued. "All that exists of the ruins of the ancient city, boundary walls, and mounds is formed of bricks which were baked in the sun: these bricks have been reduced by age into an earthy state, and consequently cannot be used again." If Botta was correct in his judgment nothing of Nineveh's past would be recovered.

Botta weakened his case slightly, however, when he added, "There can be no doubt that in the construction of these ancient buildings more solid materials, such as stones and kiln-burnt bricks, were sometimes employed, and this accounts for their being accidentally discovered; but they were merely employed as accessories."

Layard was somewhat dismayed. Yet, intuitively, like Mohl in far-off Paris, Layard clung to the certainty that *something* must be hidden in those artificial mounds.

He sought to buoy Botta's spirits, and his own. "I am convinced," he told Botta, "that remains of great interest and importance are concealed within these shapeless accumulations of earth and rubbish."

But despite Layard's encouragement, Botta, especially in fits of drug-induced despondency, was overwhelmed by quiet desperation. He told Layard he felt he was looking for the proverbial needle in a haystack. The mounds were so large that they discouraged aimless digging. But without clues he had to dig aimlessly. The more he trudged around Kouyunjik, putting his spade here and there, the greater his frustration at not finding anything. And the more despondent he became, the more he turned to his Chinese pipe for solace—and escape.

The Layard-Botta dialogue was interrupted by the *tatar*'s announcement that he was ready to resume the dash to Constantinople. Before galloping off, Layard implored his newfound friend to dig, dig, and dig again. He also extracted a promise from Botta to write him at Constantinople if anything turned up.

His enthusiasm rekindled by Layard's infectious optimism, Botta resumed his single-handed exploration of Kouyunjik.

Thou third great Canning, . .
who wert the voice of England in the Eas..
—TENNYSON

XVI

Layard arrived back at Constantinople on July 10, 1842, bronzed and unkempt after the long trek across the deserts and plains of Asia Minor. He had jettisoned part of his Baktiyari dress along the way and wore "only such European garments as I had been able to secure." Nothing fitted; nothing matched. He bore, he conceded, few marks of a European, either in dress or in complexion.

No sooner had he dismounted than he presented himself at the British embassy with Taylor's dispatches.

An embassy clerk peered down his nose. "Wait a moment," he sneered. Layard waited, and waited. At length a fashionably dressed young prig appeared, cavalierly accepted the dispatches, and remarked coolly that the ambassador, Sir Stratford Canning, was "too much occupied to see anyone." The attaché turned abruptly on his heels and left the reception room. There was not a "thank you. '

Layard was stupefied. He left the embassy for Roboli's hotel, where he and Mitford had stayed during their first visit to the Ottoman capital. Upset by this rude and discourteous treatment after so long and arduous a journey, Layard wrote the ambassador a bristling letter.

"After suffering considerable hardships for three years my face may be somewhat bronzed and my dress after a long absence from Europe might not be within the rules of fashionable elegance," Layard sputtered, "but I cannot admit that my outward appearance could warrant the insolent contempt with which I had the honor to be treated."

Three years of dealing on his own, from the top to the bottom, from camel drivers to pashas, taught Layard to treat the apex and base of the social pyramid with equal trenchancy when the situation demanded it.

Sir Stratford, then fifty-nine, was the third great Canning.* The first was George, who served as a prime minister during George III's disastrous reign, and the second, his son Charles, was the crown's first viceroy to India. Sir Stratford, Charles's cousin, entertained only one ambition as a youth: "To serve England in England." He served England all right, but always abroad.

The third Canning was the terror of the Ottoman empire. In Turkey, each ambassador is designated *buyuk elchi*, great envoy. During three tours of duty at Constantinople, the phrase Great Elchi referred to only one ambassador, Sir Stratford Canning.

Canning's influence was felt throughout the Turkish dominions. In an age of slow communications, he often acted as his own foreign office. Not unlike Layard, Canning was impatient and quick-tempered. He was also a cultivated scholar,** a workaholic, and angered by trifles. Small talk annoyed him, and he chafed at red tape. Committee meetings bored him completely. Surprisingly for a skilled diplomatist, he was often brusque to the point of rudeness.

As necessary, however, he displayed the charm, courtesy, and tone of a *preux chevalier*. Canning, unlike his petty aides, suffered no inferiority complex. On receipt of Layard's letter, he dispatched an embassy *cawass* to Roboli's with a note inviting Layard to tea.

"Sir Stratford received me immediately," Layard wrote some fifty years later. "I was greatly struck by his appearance, and thought him one of the handsomest men I had ever seen." Sir Stratford's hair was silver, his frame tall and spare, his eyes

---

* Oddly, the latest edition of the *Encyclopaedia Britannica* contains brief sketches of the first two Cannings and does not mention the existence of a third.

* *He was a classicist; Virgil his favorite author; and he wrote poetry (Byron praised his poem on Bonaparte which was published in 1813).

gray and penetrating, his brows massive and overhanging, and his air calculatingly reserved and intended to impress callers with awesome respect for his queen, Victoria.

Just as Layard and Botta had got along famously over dirty glasses of arak and Chinese pipes, Layard was equally at ease, sitting on a settee sipping tea from a porcelain china cup in the august inner sanctum of Her Majesty's envoy to the Sublime Porte.

Sir Stratford apologized for the embassy's bad manners (the attaché had been "reprimanded," he said ominously), and he immediately began to pick Layard's brains about the Turco-Persian frontier. Canning was impressed with the young man's intimate grasp of "the great game," as Kipling later called geopolitics.

When Layard was about to leave, the ambassador suggested he remain in Constantinople for a few days, since Britain planned to mediate the dispute between the Shah and the Sultan and Layard could, perhaps, play a useful role in the negotiations.

Layard tarried at Roboli's for a week, his funds running low. A steamer was making ready for England, and Layard sent Canning a polite note informing him that unless the ambassador desired to see him again he was sailing within a couple of days. Receiving no reply, Layard packed his meager belongings, paid his hotel bill, and headed down the steep street leading to Tophane wharf.

As Layard placed his foot on the gangplank, an embassy *cawass*, slightly out of breath, caught up with him and handed him a note from the Great Elchi. "Come and dine here tomorrow," the invitation read.

"After a moment's reflection," Layard said, "I determined to return to the hotel and to accept Sir Stratford's invitation."

At lunch, Sir Stratford disclosed that Britain and Russia agreed to mediate jointly the Turco-Persian row; but, he observed, some time would elapse before the negotiations gathered headway. Canning made a startling proposal. While marking time, would Layard be interested in carrying out a confidential, unofficial mission for him, visiting the Balkans and gathering political intelligence on the growing restiveness to Turkish rule? Sir Stratford stressed that the mission would be unofficial. If something went awry, Layard could not appeal to the embassy for assistance.

"My taste for travel and adventure had not been satiated," Layard said, and he readily accepted the proposal. The idea of embarking on a "secret mission" appealed to him and excited him. "I left Constantinople in high spirits," he wrote.

He still had no job, no regular income, but suddenly he saw his future as a member of the foreign service. "The prospect of entering the diplomatic service," he wrote, "[became] the great object of my ambition."

In his two-volume *Early Adventures*, which ran over a thousand pages, Layard referred to this first mission for Canning somewhat wryly, observing, "Space does not allow me to transcribe from my journal a detailed account of my travels."

His travels took him through Albania, Bulgaria, Bosnia, and Serbia (the latter two incorporated in present-day Yugoslavia). The area was in turmoil as Turk and Russian contested for power.

Layard reconnoitered the political situation at Belgrade and found the local British consul unimaginative and insensitive. The Belgrade situation was critical and demanded Canning's immediate attention. In the grand tradition of Verne's Michael Strogoff, Layard rode *tatar*-style day and night to Constantinople bearing the news to Canning. He covered the 600 miles between the two cities in five and a half days. When he presented himself at Sir Stratford's study, the Great Elchi scarcely believed he had negotiated so great a distance so swiftly. But Layard's saddlebags contained dated letters from Belgrade. Canning's astonishment turned to admiration.

The gist of Layard's reports was that England should stand up to Russian encroachment in the region and support the Serbian independence movement, a conclusion Sir Stratford arrived at independently. But Lord Aberdeen, the foreign secretary, was bent on a policy of appeasing Russia's expansionist appetite, and he rejected the policy.*

Nonetheless, Canning was so impressed with Layard's raw

* Ironically, when his appeasement policy ran out in 1852, Aberdeen was prime minister and he ended up in a domestically divisive battle with Russia, the Crimean War.

ability that he proposed to the foreign secretary the young man's appointment to the embassy as an attaché.

Layard was now introduced to the dirty politics of the large bureaucracy. The consul he had criticized complained directly to Aberdeen that Layard carried on at Belgrade as an official of the British embassy and that he actively worked to undermine British policy. Layard had no difficulty in disproving the charges. "But," as Layard put it, they had "produced an unfavorable impression" on Aberdeen.

The Scot probably would have overlooked the incident had it not coincided with another episode which almost wrecked Layard's diplomatic career before it started.

When Layard left England in 1839, he had deposited with Coutts & Co., bankers, half the £300 his mother advanced him. The bank extended a letter of credit, and when Layard was in need of funds during his Persian adventures, he drew against the letter. But the documents were improperly endorsed and Coutts refused to honor them. Layard was ignorant of the affair when Sir Stratford received a letter from Coutts denouncing Layard as a swindler.

"I was overwhelmed with grief," Layard said.

Layard begged Sir Stratford to withhold his judgment until he could exchange letters with Coutts & Co. For months, he was, in his own words, "under a cloud." Finally, the matter was cleared up. The London bankers expressed regret at what happened and tendered him a formal apology. They acknowledged that he had ample funds to cover outstanding bills and that the withdrawals should have been honored, but "considering the places from which [his] bills were drawn, and the impossibility of communicating with him, they were unable to clear up the matter earlier."

The damage was done. In Aberdeen's view, and that of the foreign office, Layard was a "controversial" figure, clearly unfit to serve in Her Majesty's service.

Everything appeared to be working against him. But Sir Stratford's confidence in Layard was unshaken, and he advised him to remain at Constantinople as his official attaché "with every prospect," Canning assured him, that Aberdeen would eventually come around to his appointment to the embassy.

A disheartened Layard agreed to mark time in the unpaid, unofficial post. This was, at least, an opportunity to remain in the East. It mattered little to him what he did as long as he remained in Asia Minor, where he felt free and independent.

On their first visit to Constantinople, Layard and Mitford, it will be recalled, had fallen in with J. A. Longworth, the *Morning Post* correspondent. Layard looked him up. Longworth was in the midst of writing a book which was later published under the title *A Year Among the Circassians.* Warmly he welcomed Layard and suggested he share his digs. Longworth lodged with an Armenian widow who had a vacant room and three daughters; the youngest, a girl of sixteen, quickly caught Layard's mobile eye. "She was," he said, "of exceptional beauty."

The other member of Longworth's mess was Charles White, the correspondent of the *Morning Chronicle*, who was a student at Eton with Sir Stratford Canning. He was completing a history of Constantinople.

Like Layard, Longworth and White were free spirits, and theirs was an uproarious relationship. As for the widow housekeeper, she was a superb Turco-Armenian cook and her table regularly sagged under platters of pilaf and kebabs.

Layard, of course, had abandoned plans to return to England. "I find," he wrote Uncle Benjamin, "that my mind is too active to admit of my returning cheerfully to any sedentary employment unaccompanied with an extraordinary degree of excitement, and I fear that I should be unable to settle down to the law."

Uncle Ben, who shared the same fears and considered his godson flighty, was hardly surprised by the change in plans. Nonetheless, he encouraged Layard to follow up his relationship with Canning. But the godfather warned him that diplomacy required a "cool judgment," implying serious doubt that his nephew would ever develop this quality. In their correspondence, the uncle advised him that public figures often wring out their subordinates like shipboard limes and then toss them overboard. Layard admitted the possibility in Canning's case, but he revealed a shrewd plan of his own "for the subordinate to make the employer dependent on him."

For Layard, the next three years, 1842–45, were crowded like the masts of a full-rigged ship with sail. Unofficially, he worked as Canning's private secretary; Canning met his food and lodging bills and paid him a retainer of £200 annually. He also worked on a book about his adventures in Persia; but he was so fearful that its publication would further weaken the position of his close friend Mehemet Taki Khan, who still languished in a Persian prison, that he put off its publication for forty-five years and incorporated the manuscript in his *Early Adventures*.

Nor did he forget the mounds. He continued to search for a financial backer, and he infected Canning with his enthusiasm for the project. With an eye to future exploration in Mesopotamia, he took lessons in Turkish, Hebrew, and Syriac, convinced that the latter two Semitic tongues were linked to the arrow-shaped characters of the Assyrians.

In the midst of these activities, Layard also worked as a part-time journalist. When White was recalled to London, he inherited the position of *Morning Chronicle* correspondent (White received £300 annually; Layard was offered, and accepted, £150). When Longworth was reassigned, his job also fell to Layard. Thereafter, Layard's reputation as a free-lance journalist spread rapidly, and he was appointed Constantinople correspondent of the *Malta Times*, the most influential and widely read English-language newspaper in the Near East.

But Layard was never a genuine newspaperman; his journalistic practices were unethical, his conflicts of interest appalling. He reported on foreign affairs while working for the British ambassador as combination private secretary, secret agent, and public relations man. "It was of much importance to Sir Stratford that he should have the support of the English and European press," Layard said openly. Under his orchestration, the most influential journals in England and the Continent raised a chorus of praise for Canning's policies. In plain language, Layard was managing the news as a skilled propagandist. The gullibility of editors turned him off journalism.

"I had no great reason to think highly of the correspondents of the English press from what I had seen of them abroad [including himself?]," Layard said. "The race may improve in the course of time . . . I have known some highly cultivated, upright and independent men amongst them; but I could never bring myself to take them into my confidence."

Newspapering, however, paid political profits. Through his contacts as a foreign correspondent, Layard made many friends among leaders of the Turkish, Armenian, and Greek communities in the Ottoman capital, including Ahmed Vefyk, eight years Layard's junior, who worked at the Turkish foreign ministry. In a manner reminiscent of young Disraeli's outburst at Uncle Benjamin's, Vefyk proclaimed, "One day I will become grand vizier!"—a role in a sultanate equivalent to that of the prime minister in a parliamentary government.

Vefyk's family belonged to the Turkish reform movement. Unlike most families of their rank and station, for example, the Vefyk household included neither eunuchs nor slaves. Through his young friend, Layard came into sub-rosa contact with the leaders of the Turkish reform movement. In short order, Layard became a secret conduit between the reformists and the British ambassador. "The task [Canning] imposed upon me was a very delicate and difficult one and, even in those days, not unaccompanied with danger," Layard said. "But it suited my adventurous and somewhat romantic disposition."

Through Layard, Canning sought to throw England's support behind the reformists. Canning was convinced that unless the indolent, corrupt bureaucracy was streamlined—indeed, unless the Ottoman empire was modernized—"its fall would not be far distant." Layard was of the same opinion. (In fact, the six-hundred-year-old Turkish empire collapsed, in the aftermath of World War I, exactly a generation after Layard's death.)

If Layard's days were crowded with work, his romantic encounters kept him fully occupied at night. During those three years, he confessed, his life was "merry . . . somewhat reckless and riotous." He and his friends were frequent visitors at Constantinople's bawdy houses and on Friday afternoons, he and Charles Allison, the only other member of the embassy staff who was completely in Canning's confidence, spent their time at the "Sweet Waters of Asia," a walk along the seawall where Turkish girls gathered weekly to smoke their narghiles, consume sherbets, and exchange gossip.

One Friday, a richly dressed young woman, accompanied by a retinue of handmaidens, was in the process of boarding an imperial, eight-oared caïque when she cautiously lowered her veil and showed her face to Layard and Allison. Her face, Layard said, was "unsurpassingly lovely." She motioned them to follow. The two Franks lost no time in hailing a water taxi and following. The pursued caïque turned into the sacred precincts of the Seraglio and, as if a warning of things to come, "a dead body rose to the surface of the water close to us." The boatmen refused to row farther. They warned Layard and his companion that the woman was probably of high rank and that they risked their lives chasing her.

The following day, to Layard's astonishment, a closely veiled female servant appeared at Layard's lodging with an invitation from her mistress to visit the Seraglio. The servant refused to reveal the lady's name. That evening a side gate of the palace was left open. Layard and Allison were ushered into a large, richly ornamental hall. At the farthest end, reclining on a divan, was the woman who had boldly lowered her veil.

"She was young and singularly beautiful," Layard said, "with the large almond shaped eyes, the delicate and regular features, and the clear, brilliant complexion ... peculiar to Turkish women of mixed Circassian descent." She was splendidly clad, and around her hovered a number of young female attendants.

The attendants took their places at her side on the divan while Layard and Allison were served thick black Turkish coffee. For the next couple of hours the woman, her attendants, and the two Englishmen engaged in lively conversation; Allison, the embassy's interpreter, was expert in Turkish and regaled the party with jokes and anecdotes.

When the pair left, they still did not know the name of their hostess. Determined to get to the bottom of the mystery, they contacted the reigning Italian madam in the Turkish capital, "with whom we were well acquainted and who kept a small hotel." La Giuseppina, as she was called, had the reputation of either knowing the name of everyone in the capital, or of having ways of finding out. They commissioned her to identify the mysterious beauty. A few hours later, La Giuseppina knocked on Layard's door, Layard recalled, "her face pale with terror." The lady was the Sultan's sister! If Layard and Allison were found in her apartments, they would be put to death summarily and their bodies flung into the waters of the Golden Horn.

Cool judgment, to employ Uncle Benjamin's phrase, prevailed. Layard and Allison abandoned their pursuit. Some years later the Princess caused a stir in Constantinople by appearing outside the Seraglio without a veil. The orthodox Moslem religious community was in an uproar, and the Sublime Porte ordered his sister never again to appear in public. "She disappeared from the scene . . . ," Layard said, "and I do not know what became of her." Neither does history.

Layard sometimes thought of English girls, with whom he had not associated since leaving home six years earlier. He entered into a lively correspondence with Cecilia Berkeley, a friend of the Austens, but nothing came of it. At first the letters were addressed to "my dear Miss Berkeley," but after a while he was writing "my dear Cecilia." The letters were facetious and suggestive.

"Of course, you know I have turned Musselman [Moslem]," Layard wrote. "I say my prayers regularly—an improvement, you will say, on my former habits—I have left off wine, gin and all other ardent spirits." In another letter, he wrote her, "I am married to four—but I will tell you all about this in my next letter."

The next letter was a bit risqué for the Victorian era. "This Mohammedan life is after all very agreeable and the privilege of taking four wives," he said jocularly, "if not abused, that is, if the ladies do not take into their heads to abuse their lord, is a very enviable one."

In this fashion, 1842 dissolved into 1843 and the latter faded into 1844. Layard still had no regular job, no regular income, no future.

But he had grounds for hope. Aside from Canning's efforts on his behalf, Layard, now twenty-seven, had gained a mite of recognition. Lieutenant Selby's account of their ascent of the Karun and Dizful rivers in the steamer *Assyria* was published in 1844 in *The Journal of the Royal Geographic Society*. It contained several laudatory references to Layard and touched on his able diplomacy in gaining for Britain the friendship of Persia's mountain tribes. Major Rawlinson, the renowned soldier-scholar, had replaced Colonel Taylor at Baghdad as British resident in Mesopotamia, and he took the initiative to contact Layard. Rawlinson had been impressed with the copies of cuneiform inscriptions Layard had collected on his travels and deposited in Taylor's library. "I have wished to commence a correspondence with you," wrote Rawlinson, the man who would help solve the mystery of cuneiform, and promptly went on in technical detail about the nail-shaped characters. Layard was flattered.

But Canning, try as he did to obtain Layard an attachéship, was still unable to overcome Lord Aberdeen's prejudices. When a Turco-Persian border commission was established to delimit the frontier between the two quarrelsome neighbors, Canning proposed Layard as a member of the commission because of his firsthand knowledge of the troubled theater. But the foreign secretary passed over him.

Layard was crushed. His position at the embassy had become increasingly embarrassing, and he was overcome by so acute a desperation that he again thought about returning to England and Uncle Benjamin's law offices. Canning counseled patience and suggested he take a holiday.

Layard joined Lord Somers, then a member of Parliament traveling in the Near East, in the autumn of 1843 for a journey around the Turkish "elbow" and across the Aegean. In his autobiography, Layard described Somers as "my dearest and truest friend. I was never more intimate with any man, nor loved any more."

They visited the Troad, or Plain of Troy, and, like travelers before him, Layard was disappointed that he could find no trace of Homer's citadel. But, then, only a romantic would look for evidence of noble Troy's existence. In Layard's day, it was the almost universal belief that Troy and the Trojan War were flights of Homer's soaring poetic imagination.

The brief holiday, however, gave Layard only a temporary

lift. The winter of 1844–45 was his winter of discontent. "I [passed] the winter in a state of uncertainty and expectancy which weighed considerably upon my spirits, and was only alleviated by the extreme kindness of the ambassador and Lady Canning." Her ladyship, the daughter of a member of Parliament, was twenty years Canning's junior (she was wed at nineteen) and eleven years Layard's senior. Both she and her husband were fond of Layard, and by 1844 they had taken him into their residence as a member of the family and gave him a private room.

This drift in his life reached the crisis stage in the summer of 1845. Lady Canning and her three school-age daughters had left for England, and Sir Stratford was making plans to follow suit on home leave. Canning, who never lacked confidence in his diplomatic skill, was convinced that once he talked to Aberdeen, he would remove the difficulties which had stood in the way of Layard's appointment as an attaché. But, Canning conceded, this might take two or three months.

Sir Henry Wellesley was already en route from London to take charge of the Turkish mission during Sir Stratford's absence. "I was not desirous of remaining at Constantinople after Sir Stratford Canning's departure," Layard said, "and I was anxious to find some means of spending my time profitably until he had been able, after his return to England, to obtain for me from Lord Aberdeen the permanent appointment in the Constantinople embassy, of which I had the promise."

But how was he to mark time "profitably"? Suddenly, it struck him. It was there before him during this whole unsettled period. The limbs had obscured the trees. Layard proposed to Canning that during his absence he proceed to Mosul and dig up the mysterious mounds.

Let some future prince repair its ruins,
my name inscriptions let him restore to its place.
—ASHURNASIRPAL

XVII

Layard's proposal to excavate the mounds was hardly surprising. Rarely, during his three years of aimless drifting in Constantinople, was Nineveh far from his thoughts.

Botta had kept his word and had maintained regular contact. The tone of the Botta-Layard letters was almost invariably the same. Botta complained that his excavations turned up nothing. Layard entreated him to continue to dig. Layard even suggested, in despair, perhaps, that Botta shift his operations from Kouyunjik to the strangely shaped mound at Nimrod, the artificial heap that fascinated him above all others and that he considered—however irrationally—*his* mound. But Botta, his energy drained by opium as much as by Mesopotamia's climate, argued against it because, he said, it was "too far away." The distance between Mosul and Nimrod was 14 miles.

Then, in the spring of 1843, Layard received the dismaying news that Botta had abandoned Kouyunjik. Layard railed against his decision. So did Mohl. If Botta thought of Layard and Mohl wining and dining in Constantinople and Paris, while he dwelt in sweltering, foul-smelling Mosul, he kept his opinion to himself.

For months, Botta's activities at Mosul had kept the town's coffeeshops filled with gossip. What did the crazy European want with nail-headed inscriptions? The previous December, in the midst of his explorations of Kouyunjik, an inhabitant of Khorsabad had turned up at Botta's house with two kiln-baked bricks inscribed with cuneiform characters. He claimed that he had found them near his village and offered to procure for Botta, at a modest price, as many as the crazy foreigner desired. Khorsabad was filled with them, he alleged. Botta was accustomed to the soaring imagination of Arabs and stifled a yawn.

But when he abandoned Kouyunjik, he recalled the incident, and he sent several of his workers to Khorsabad, a place about as far from Mosul as the Nimrod mound.

Three days later, his workers returned in a state of frenzy. They had dug up a statue inlaid with nail-headed inscriptions. Botta dispatched his foreman, Naaman ibn Naouch, to make an investigation.

Botta had complete faith in Naaman. "He has two qualities which are very rare in this country," Botta said, "namely, intelligence and probity."

Naaman returned from Khorsabad highly agitated. Botta hesitated no longer. He journeyed to the mound. There he saw what his workmen had uncovered: an incredibly magnif-icent alabaster bas-relief. As he gazed on the sculpture with disbelief, he realized that he was looking at a lost world.

Every writer since that historic day, with one exception, has hailed Botta as the first modern man to view Assyrian ruins in situ. The exception is Botta himself. Modest and unassuming as ever, he insisted, "It was Naaman who I charged to go and explore Khorsabad, and it was he who discovered its hidden treasure."

Botta was as confused as he was astounded by the discovery. The origin of the sculpture baffled him. The bas-relief depicted scenes of a monarch, accompanied by soldiers attired in strange garb, leading a column of prisoners into captivity. Botta realized that it was a mere fragment of what must be a large building buried in the mound. He tested his theory by sinking shafts at random. "I caused a trench to be dug," he said, "[and] ... my workmen immediately found a wall displaying two very remarkable colossal figures, eight-and-a-half metres [27.5 feet] high."

On April 5 Botta announced his discovery in a letter to Mohl. No regular mail service existed at that time—England's Penny Black, the world's first postage stamp, had been issued only three years earlier and the French would not print their own for another six years. Botta sent his letter by *tatar* to M. de Cadalvene, the director of French overland posts at Constantinople, who arranged to forward it by ship to Paris.

"My workmen have found the remains of a monument, very remarkable for the number and character of the sculptures adorning it," Botta wrote. "I continue to excavate, and with so much the greater interest, that I believe myself the first who discovered sculptures that may, with some probability, be traced back to the epoch when Nineveh flourished."

He enclosed several rough sketches of the scenes depicted on the bas-reliefs, figures clothed in armor, soldiers in combat, a woman captive leading a naked child by the arm. Each of these figures was 3 feet high and was inscribed with cuneiform legends, many of them in bad condition. But Botta found that his letters and sketches barely touched the surface. "To describe each detail would require a written volume," he said. "The art, as far as I know, is unique." And upon discovering an altar of triangular shape, he wrote, "The *tout ensemble* has so Grecian an air that I should have doubted its origin, had not the circumference of the platform presented me with a cuneiform inscription."

The altar may have born a striking resemblance to Greek art, but the figures upon it were carved centuries, if not a millennium, before the Greek Bronze Age.

Botta had unearthed objects that had not been seen for thousands of years, among them, two figures, nearly 9 feet high, one of a winged personage with the head of a bird and the other a bearded king who held a trident terminated by three balls. Several bas-reliefs depicted attendants without beards. "They are not intended to represent women," Botta concluded, "but eunuchs."*

Within a month of his discoveries, he expressed growing alarm over the deterioration of his finds. The decay was so

---

* Botta was the first to draw this conclusion, and Assyriologists have been debating his conclusion ever since.

rapid in the air that, he said, "I fear nothing can possibly be rescued."

After his first letter, Botta's reports streamed to Paris. The more he dug, the more he found. And the more he found, the more mystified he was. Who were the artists? What civilization did they represent?

He continued to worry about decay. "These monuments must necessarily perish forever," he warned, "unless the enlightened munificence of the French government provides me with the means of rescuing the most interesting portions."

Fortunately, however, he made two spectacular finds of an imperishable nature, immense statues of a winged bull and a bird-headed man carved from a solid block of stone. "[As] everything else falls to pieces," he said triumphantly, "these colossal figures will stand as silent witnesses to the ancient existence of the rest."

In Paris, Mohl was elated. His belief in the mounds was vindicated.

Mohl rushed to the Academy of Inscriptions and Belles-Lettres with Botta's first letter and characterized Botta's work as "a discovery destined to throw a great light on one of the most obscure and interesting portions of ancient history." He wrote Botta that the Academy displayed "the liveliest interest," and arranged for the publication of Botta's reports in the *Journal de Société Asiatique.*

Botta's discovery electrified Paris. On May 24, 1843, barely six weeks after Botta broke the news, the French cabinet authorized a 3,000-franc grant to Botta to continue the excavations. This was soon followed by other grants totaling 140,000 francs. Eugene Flandin, a volatile, young, Italian-born artist, was ordered to proceed to Mesopotamia to make drawings of Botta's finds.

Flandin was familiar with the Near East; he had accompanied Coste's French expedition to Persia some years earlier. He was a brilliant artist, and also an obnoxious personality, vain and conceited. In his book about the expedition, *Voyage de Perse*, published in 1851, Coste is scarcely mentioned. Without Flandin, the whole expedition would have collapsed, the reader is informed. Flandin also revealed himself as a despic-

able character. On one occasion he complained to Persian
officials that some of his art materials were missing, probably
stolen. They presented him with a man, his hands tied behind
his back. "I did not recognize him but that mattered little,"
Flandin wrote. What Flandin wanted was satisfaction for the
"aggression" against him. "I thus pretended that the prisoner
was the guilty one." The innocent man was brutally whipped.
"When I believed enough of an example had been made,"
Flandin wrote, "I stopped the blows."

But Flandin's journey to Khorsabad was to be postponed.
In July, as the Mesopotamian summer lengthened, with temperatures above 115 degrees Fahrenheit, Botta wrote, "[I] am
now desperately ill." He was down with "a sort of cholera"
and, in delirious condition, was carried by litter to Mosul. He
no sooner recovered than he was mired in political problems.

Botta's difficulties started when rumors spread that he had
either found buried treasure or that the inscriptions he busily
copied were ciphers which revealed the location of the treasure. Wilder stories circulated among the less credulous. The
most fantastic claim was that the inscribed bricks were ancient
land deeds and that by acquiring them, the Franks would lay
claim to the whole of Mesopotamia. Still another tale was that
Botta built secret fortifications at Khorsabad.

In October 1843 the governor of Mosul, backed by Constantinople, prohibited Botta from continuing his excavations. In
the Turkish capital the French ambassador labored for months
before he could dispel these wild stories and obtain a firman
permitting Botta to resume the dig and Flandin to join him.
As a result of these political idiocies, Flandin did not reach
Mosul until May 4, 1844, almost a year to the day he was
commissioned to rush to Botta's assistance. During that interval much of what Botta had unearthed had dissolved as a
result of desert winds, searing heat, and harsh winter.

For the next six months the detached Botta and the flam-
mable Flandin engaged in a remarkable collaboration, remarkable given the conflicting nature of their characters.
Flandin made copies of the sculptures; Botta, the cuneiform
inscriptions. On October 31 they completed their work and
abandoned Khorsabad to the weather.

Nine days later Flandin left for Paris, via Constantinople, with their precious collection of drawings. The following year, on May 16, the French Academy authorized a grant of 400,000 francs for the publication of their masterwork. The result was a dazzling set of five folio volumes, measuring 1½ by 2 feet, entitled *Monument de Ninive Découvert dé Decrit*. The volumes were issued piecemeal, in ninety sections at 20 francs each. Critics complained that "few persons possess sufficient means to purchase the magnificent work." And magnificent it was—and is. Flandin's drawings of Assyrian art have never been surpassed—or, for that matter, equaled.

The title *Monuments of Nineveh* was not Botta's choice. He never claimed that he discovered the city. Surprisingly, many members of the Assyrian archaeological establishment, such as the late Sir Wallis Budge, have quoted Botta as writing Mohl, "I have found Nineveh!" There is no evidence to support this.* Botta's only claim was that the objects he uncovered at Khorsabad "probably" belonged to the Ninevite period. "As those who are better informed than myself will probably undertake to determine the age of this monument," Botta wrote, "I shall avoid all discussion on the subject." Unknown to Botta, he was right and the experts who insisted on Nineveh were wrong. Khorsabad was *not* the site of Nineveh; it was Dur Sharrukin, the Fortress of Sargon.

Before their departure from Khorsabad, Botta had selected several pieces of sculpture to be shipped to the Louvre. Working alone after Flandin's homeward passage, Botta prepared the objects for the journey to Paris. Several sculptures weighed as much as three tons, and he sawed them into manageable blocks. Yet transportation was so primitive that Botta spent six weeks forging axle trees strong enough to support the loads. Even so, he was compelled to abandon many pieces of sculpture along the way. He also had to build special keleks to carry the objects downstream to Baghdad. During the loading of one raft, a worker was crushed to death and several others injured. It was not until June 1845, eight

---

* According to Budge and other scholars, Botta's phrase "Ninive était retrouvée" appeared in his first letter to Mohl. I have read the letter; it does not appear there nor in any known writings of Botta.

months after he abandoned Khorsabad, that the sculptures arrived at Baghdad, where they sat on the riverbank until a French man-of-war picked them up for the voyage to France.

If Botta's discoveries excited Paris, they caused a sensation in Constantinople's diplomatic community especially among the Russians and British. The Russians were suspicious. They questioned the activities of the French and gave credence to the rumors that Botta was throwing up earthworks in an area long coveted by the Muscovites in search of a warm-water port on the Indian Ocean. The Russians even dispatched a mission to Khorsabad to inspect Botta's "trenches." Botta must have been amused. To allay Russian suspicions, he conducted an excavation in their presence. The Russians appeared satisfied and returned to Constantinople.

The British embassy was agitated for different reasons. Botta had instructed Cadalvene at Constantinople to show his letters to his young English friend, Henry Austen Layard, before sending them onto Paris. "During the entire period of his excavations," Layard reported, "M. Botta regularly sent me not only his dispatches but copies of the inscriptions."

Layard's admiration for Botta's selflessness was boundless. "There are few who would have acted this liberally," he said. Like Botta, Layard was not jealous by nature. But he would not have been human if he was not flecked by envy. Publicly, he hailed Botta's discovery. "To him is due the honor of having found the first Assyrian monument," Layard said. Privately, he wrote his mother, "Botta's great discovery makes one despair a little."

But Layard was not discouraged.

"The success of M. Botta," he said, "had increased my anxiety to explore the ruins of Assyria."

Layard, of course, had hurried to Canning with receipt of Botta's first letter announcing the discovery. He was aware that he was baiting the hook. At that very moment the Great Elchi was engaged in seemingly interminable negotiations with the Sublime Porte for the removal to the British Museum of bas-reliefs that had been accidentally discovered at Budrum, Turkey, the site of ancient Halicarnassus. It was there that Artemisia—not the Artemisia who was the mistress of Xerxes, but Artemisia the inconsolable widow of Mausolus—constructed in 353 B.C. a tomb in memory of her late husband. The edifice was the sixth of the Seven Wonders of the Ancient World and gave his name to its style—mausoleum. Canning was determined to rescue the sculptures from neglect and decay, and at his own expense, if necessary.

In a letter to his wife, who had just returned to England with their children, Canning told of his efforts to retrieve the Halicarnassus Marbles, as they are called today. The letter provides insight into Canning's character and explains why Layard was confident he could enlist Canning's support of his plan to excavate the mounds of Nimrod and Kouyunjik.

"I have at last surmounted all my difficulties about the Marbles at Budrum," Canning wrote his wife. "The letters [firman] are prepared ... [and I am ready] to secure the whole prize—thirteen inestimable blocks of marble, sculptured by the four greatest artists of the best days of Greece, mentioned in Herodotus and immortalized by the sentiment to which they owed their creation no less than by the genius which has shaped them into perfection. ... Oh! if they should founder on the way to England! Think of my venturing all at [our] own expense! ... Indeed, my own Artemisia, I shall be much disappointed if the new ministry and the Corn Laws be not thrown into the shade by these celebrated marbles, which it has cost me nearly three years of patient perseverance to obtain."

Today the Halicarnassus Marbles reside securely in the British Museum

Thus, Botta's letters excited Canning almost as much as they did Layard. Major Rawlinson, assigned to Baghdad as Taylor's successor, was also agitated by Botta's discovery. He wrote Layard to urge Sir Stratford "to take an interest in the antiquities of this country. It pains me grievously," Rawlinson said, "to see the French monopolize the field, for the fruits of Botta's labor, already achieved and still in progress, are not things to pass away in a day but will constitute a nation's glory in future ages."

Alexander Hector, the Baghdad merchant whom Layard interested in financing the excavations of the mounds, wrote in a similar vein from Mosul April 20, 1845. "I should like very much to have a dig in some of the mounds here. If I had the money I would do it at once."*

Indeed, earlier, Canning was made aware of the possibilities of archaeological treasure in Mesopotamia not only by Layard and Rawlinson but also by Christian Rassam's father-in-law, the Reverend Badger. En route to England via Malta, Badger stopped over at Constantinople and urged Canning to dig up the mounds.

Canning asked Badger to prepare a report for London, which he did. Writing from Malta, October 26, 1844, the Reverend ended his report: "It has occurred to me whether [I] might not tend to induce the government to undertake the excavation of this interesting mound." The "interesting mound," surprisingly enough, was not Kouyunjik. It was Nimrod. He asked Canning for a letter of introduction to Lord Aberdeen. Obviously, Badger planned to take up the matter directly with the foreign office on his arrival in London. But the Great Elchi, who frowned on missionary activity, felt no particular warmth for him and he never wrote the letter.

Badger's interest in the mounds was in their Biblical context. He was convinced—correctly it later developed—that cuneiform contained records bearing "upon the historical facts handed down in Holy Writ." The arrow-headed characters, he surmised, "will supply important testimony to the genuineness and authenticity of Old Testament scriptures."

Badger was a member of the burgeoning Evangelical movement which later characterized the Victorian period. It was Puritanism in new dress, and Puritanism with a vengeance against the French Revolution, the Age of Reason, the Industrial Revolution, and, above all, the libertine permissiveness which accompanied them. Evangelicalism represented a reaction to freethinking and, in the words of Ian Bradley, the contemporary British historian, was "one of the most important forces at work shaping the character of the Victorians." The movement gave rise to a cult of prudery, conformity, and

---

* The use of the term "dig" is worthy of historical footnote; it was its first entry into the archaeological lexicon and is the word now commonly employed by archaeologists to describe on-site excavations.

respectibility that John Stuart Mill and other social critics of the day loudly denounced.

While Badger, Layard, and Rawlinson vied for Canning's support, Flandin appeared on the Constantinople scene like icing on a cake and triumphantly showed Layard his drawings. Layard promptly reported the matter to Canning. The French had pulled the archaeological coup of the year. The Halicarnassus Marbles paled in comparison to the art uncovered at Khorsabad.

If Layard was bitter, it was not toward Botta and Flandin, but toward his compatriots. British capital, private and public, was available for industrial expansion, new trade routes, and colonial acquisitions. Digging up worlds of the past? These unprofitable fantasies hardly merited discussion.

But the more Layard thought about Botta's discoveries, the more he was convinced, as Botta suspected, that he had not discovered Nineveh. The site was too far from the Tigris and did not conform with historical accounts of its location. The extent of the ruins was also limited, yet Nineveh was a "great city." Nineveh still awaited the pick and shovel.

Layard was surprised that Botta did not launch an assault on Nimrod or other mounds. "Surely," Layard theorized, "other buildings of a vaster and more magnificent character must exist nearer the seat of government, on the banks of the Tigris."

Botta, however, believed that the lost cities of Assyria had decayed within the mounds over the millenniums just as many of the objects he found at Khorsabad had dissolved in front of his eyes on contact with the air.

"It is possible," Layard admitted. Yet he could not shake the feeling that Botta had only scratched the surface.

It is against this background, in the summer of 1845, as Canning packed his bags and made ready to join his wife and children on home leave in England, that Layard proposed to the ambassador that, with a couple of months to kill until Sir Stratford won over Aberdeen to Layard's appointment as an attaché, that he proceed to Mesopotamia and continue the explorations Botta had abandoned.

Layard estimated that the job of excavating Nimrod—he thought the traditional name of the mound itself a significant clue—would cost about £150 ($750), a figure based on Botta's pay scale of 4½ piasters (20¢) a day per worker. "Sir Stratford not only approved my proposal," Layard said jubilantly, "but offered to share in the expenses which would be incurred in making tentative excavations."

Initially, Canning contributed £60 to the project; later, he doubled it. Layard put up the difference (£30).

Canning and Layard also drew up a compact, dated October 15, 1845. Under its terms, Layard was "to inform Sir Stratford Canning of his operations and to give him a full account of any objects worthy of curiosity which he might see or discover ... to abstain carefully from meddling with anything of a political or religious character ... to avoid confidential or frequent intercourse with missionaries [Badger], whatever might be their country or religion ... to show respect and deference to the Turkish authorities and to lose no opportunity of cultivating their goodwill ... to maintain the character of a traveller fond of antiquities, of picturesque scenery, and of Asiatic manners ... not to leave without communication ... and to do his best to obtain permission on the spot for the removal of the objects discovered."

Both Layard and Canning thought the excavations would be completed in two months. "Should he [Layard] have reasons for adding another ten days or fortnight," Canning's *aide-mémoire* said, "he is at liberty to follow his own discretion."

As it developed, Layard was to spend the next seven years among the mounds of Assyria.

On the solitary pastures where our sheep [are] half
asleep . . .
was the site of a city great and gay (or so they say).
—BROWNING

XVIII

Canning, concerned lest Layard's sudden return arouse the French to resume their excavations, deemed it "most prudent" that Layard leave for Mosul furtively. Layard was unhappy with the deception. After all, the French had graciously kept the English informed of their work at Khorsabad. "The enlightened and liberal spirit shown by M. Botta is unfortunately not generally shared," Layard said with embarrassment.

Prior to his departure, Layard took a crash course in map-making from an English officer in the Turkish service. His plan was to make surveys "of any ruins I may discover and of the many ruins on the banks of the Tigris which are believed to represent the site of Ninoveh." Clearly, his search would center on "that great city," as the prophet Jonah described it.

Once again, as was his style, Layard traveled alone. He also traveled lightly. He crammed his effects into two leather saddlebags—some linen, a change of clothes, a few books, maps, surveyor's instruments, and a coverlet for sleeping. With only two months' leave, he traveled in breathless tatar-style and arrived at Mosul October 27, covering 900 miles in twelve days. The weather was miserable along the way, raining almost constantly, and he rode "usually wet to the skin."

Christian Rassam and his English wife, the Reverend Badger's daughter, were surprised to see him back in Mosul and greeted him warmly. It was good to see a friendly face.

From Mosul, he wrote his mother November 3, explaining his change of plans and his secret mission. "I have not yet commenced work, but intend doing so in three or four days," he said. "I have every reason to hope that I shall be to a certain degree successful."

The first order of business was to present himself to the local governor, Mohammed Pasha, a native of Crete who was known as Keritli Oglu, "the son of the Cretan." Cretin would have been a better word. He possessed one eye and one ear; he was short and fat; his face was pitted by the ravages of smallpox; he croaked when he spoke. "Nature had placed hypocrisy beyond his reach," Layard said.

At the time of Layard's arrival, the Keritli Oglu had Mosul and the surrounding territory in a state of terror and despair. When he took office the previous year, he commemorated his installation by strangling the three most important merchants in town and appropriating their money and property. When he traveled through the outlying districts of the Mosul pashalik or province in search of new revenue—modern bureaucrats, please copy—the governor insisted on "tooth-money," a tax levied on the village where he was entertained. The tax was compensation for the wear and tear on his teeth while partaking in the feasts hastily prepared in his honor.

The governor treated young Layard, who played the role of innocent tourist, civilly, however, and the audience went smoothly.

On November 8, with Rassam's help, Layard secretly procured several picks and shovels, engaged a mason, a *cawass*, and a servant, and floated down the Tigris to Nimrod on a small kelek. Henry Ross, a Baghdad merchant who arrived in Mosul the day before Layard set out, joined the expedition. It took six hours to float downriver to Nimrod.

The group arrived at dusk and took shelter in the miserable nearby village of Naifa, putting up at the hovel of the local sheik, Awad Abd-Allah, whose tribe had been plundered by the governor and was now scattered over the desertscape. Awad spoke a little Turkish and was "intelligent and active." Layard hired him on the spot as "superintendent of the workmen." That night Awad regaled the party with the traditions connected with the ruins of the Nimrod mound. Truly, he said, the mound was the site of a palace built by Ashur, the lieutenant of Nimrod, "the mighty hunter." This was the place where Abraham—peace be with him!—cast down down and broke into pieces the idols worshiped by unbelievers.

Layard slept little that first night as he dreamed of underground palaces. "I fancied myself wandering in a maze of chambers from which I could find no outlet," he said. When Awad summoned him to breakfast, the sun was just breaking. "The lofty cone and broad mound of Nimroud broke like a distant mountain on the morning sky," Layard recorded. The great mound, shaped like a parallelogram, stretched 1,800 feet in length, 900 in breadth, and about 65 feet in height.

Awad had augmented Layard's group with a work party of six Arabs. In stupefaction, they watched as Layard crawled around the mound collecting fragments of bricks and other rubbish. With a shrug, they joined in the search and were amazed as Layard jumped joyously when one of the workers brought him the fragment of a bas-relief. Awad pointed to a piece of alabaster which appeared sticking above the soil. Layard ordered the men to dig it up. They put their spades to the earth. It proved to be a huge slab covered with cuneiform inscriptions. At Layard's command, they dug deeper and faster, uncovering one slab after another. "[Then] we came almost immediately to a wall, bearing inscriptions," Layard said. Parts of the wall were seared, evidently scorched in antiquity. As night fell, Layard was convinced that something immense was buried within the mound, but precisely what it was or what he was looking for he did not know.

The following morning, November 10, Layard's work force was increased by five new workers. Before the day was out, Layard found himself in a room built of slabs. In the bottom of the chamber, amid the rubbish, he said, "I found several ivory ornaments" (they are now part of the collection of famed Nimrod Ivories, among the world's greatest archaeological treasures).

The surface of some of the ivories contained traces of gold and in the rubbish of the chamber, Awad recovered several fragments of gold leaf. "O Bey," he said, "Wallah! your books are right, and the Franks know that which is hid from the true believer. Here is the gold!"

Awad was convinced that Layard's real purpose at Nimrod was treasure. The sheik was nonplussed when Layard presented him with the gold leaf he found. Awad was now more confused than ever.

That night, in the glow of a campfire, in a mood of triumph, Layard wrote his skeptical godparents, Aunt Sara and Uncle Ben. He dated the letter, Nimroud, 10th November, 1845, and gave it to Ross to dispatch from Baghdad. "As yet no figures, but, from fragments discovered in the rubbish, I have no doubt they will come," he wrote. "[The mound] appears to be one great palace, principally of marble, which has been plundered, destroyed as far as possible by fire and has remained ever since under the accumulated dust of ages."

Interestingly, for reasons which he failed to explain, he somehow guessed the site was not Nineveh but another city of the Assyrians. It was to be some time, however, before he knew its true identity. "I believe the city to be Resen," he said, the Resen of Genesis, the great city built by Ashur. He also thought it might be the Larissa mentioned by Xenophon and his Ten Thousand Greeks in *Anabasis* during their reconnaisance of the Persian empire.

He continued to excavate the mound, and he continued to find walls and chambers, but by the third day he still had found no sculpture, his "chief aim."

On the fourth day, at Ross's insistence, Layard was compelled to call a halt and return to Mosul. His body was racked by fever and chills. Ross considered his physical condition dangerous. He had seen too many Europeans fall by the wayside, victims of ague.

In Mosul, while recovering from this latest attack of malaria, Layard wrote Canning his first report on their joint "speculation." The report filled twelve pages. "As yet I have not found sculptures, but from several fragments, which I discovered in the rubbish of the mound, I have every reason to think that figures exist," he said. "Indeed, I have found an old man here who pretends to have buried, fifty years ago, slabs similar to those of Khorsabad which he discovered when digging for building-bricks. He has promised to show me the spot."

But, he assured Canning, "should I not find sculptures, I trust the rich collection of inscriptions which have already been discovered and which cannot but form a very small portion of those contained in the whole building will repay the expenses of the experiment."

He wrote that "the ruins of Nimroud are very extensive," and that it would take "at least a month" to explore them. "Should I be fortunate enough to discover sculptures worth transporting," he continued, "Nimroud would be particularly adapted for the work as it is within three-quarters of a mile of the river."

Canning replied with a letter of encouragement. "What I would not give to be with you ... ," the ambassador said. "My curiosity is not only on tiptoe, but on stilts."

More bouyant than ever, Layard returned to Nimrod on November 19 and moved his headquarters to a new village, Selamiye, which was encircled with a mud brick wall and afforded protection should Bedouins hear of treasure and stage a night raid on his camp. He moved into the largest hovel in the village. It was little more than a barn. He occupied one half and the other half was inhabitated by cows, bullocks, and mules. A second hovel was occupied by the wives, children, and poultry of his laborers. A third served as mess hall and workers' quarters. The fourth building was turned into a stall for Layard's horses. The roofs of these buildings leaked badly when it rained, and Layard frequently passed a wet night under a rude table which he had himself constructed. His cawass, who was from sophisticated Constantinople, "complained bitterly of the hardships he was compelled to endure," Layard wrote, and he had difficulty prevailing upon him to remain.

The work at Nimrod proceeded apace. His Christian workers, Chaldeans he called them, were strong and hardy and manned the picks. The Arabs carried off the debris in baskets and threw it over the side of the mound, including, unknown to Layard, potsherds of inestimable archaeological value.

On November 28, Layard hit his first jackpot. The first stroke of the pick that morning revealed the top of a bas-relief. The workers were caught up by Layard's infectious enthusiasm. Despite a violent rainstorm, they worked until dark to bring the sculpture to light. One slab depicted the siege of a walled city; the second slab, a battle scene.

Layard, trained as an art connoisseur by his father, was overwhelmed by the artistic excellence of the relief. "I observed with surprise the elegance and richness of the ornaments, the faithful and delicate delineation of the limbs and muscles, both in the men and horses, and the knowledge of art displayed in the grouping of the figures, and the general composition," he wrote. "In all these respects . . . this sculpture appeared to me not only to differ, but to surpass the bas-reliefs of Khorsabad."

On December 1 he wrote Canning, "I am happy to inform your excellency that on Friday last I was sufficiently fortunate to find sculptures at Nimroud." And he added more good news: "The marbles sent by M. Botta are stuck at Baghdad waiting for a ship." Clearly, like Canning, Layard also had visions of the British beating the French to Europe with the first "Assyrian marbles." That same day he wrote his mother, "Some day you will have the pleasure of seeing some of the fruits of my labor in the British Museum."

In the midst of this elation, the governor at Mosul accused him of digging up a Moslem burying ground and ordered him to cease all excavations. The governor's aide, Daoud Agha, who had ridden to the mound with the pasha's decree, confessed secretly to Layard that during one of Layard's absences from the mound, the governor ordered him and his men to steal graveyard stones from a Moslem cemetery and plant them at Nimrod. "We have destroyed more real tombs of the true Believers," the conscience-stricken aide said, ". . . than you can have defiled [in all Mesopotamia] . . . We have killed our horses and ourselves in carrying those accursed stones."

Layard encountered little difficulty in circumventing the order. "I came to an understanding on the subject with Daoud Agha," he dryly reported. He simply bribed the governor's aide and resumed digging.

Astride the elongated mound, Layard arbitrarily selected a new spot to dig. His workers put their picks to the soil, and to their amazement, as well as Layard's, they immediately struck a piece of sculpted granite. They had stumbled on a pair of fantastic winged bulls and winged lions, 14 feet in height, forming the entrance to a huge chamber. The walls of the chamber were covered with carved human figures, each 9 feet tall.

Layard's reports to Canning thereafter flowed like the torrents of spring. A twelve-page letter, December 4, included a sketch of the figures. It was followed by a ten-page report December 15, a six-page report four days later, and so on. Canning was delighted. On December 27 the ambassador wrote: "It is too late to wish you a Merry Xmas and indeed would be like mockery in the midst of your burrowing on the banks of the Tigris. I . . . congratulate you on all you have done." Across the bottom of the letter, in large block letters, the Great Elchi wrote: HAPPY NEW YEAR.

Layard returned to Mosul shortly before Christmas and found the town in joyous ferment. A *tatar* had just brought the welcome news that the Sublime Porte had dismissed the governor and named a young major general of the reformist school, Ismail Pasha, to take charge of the pashalik. Layard found the Keritli Oglu sitting in a dilapidated room in his former residence. Rain dripped down upon him from a crack in the room. "Thus it is with God's creatures," the dismissed governor philosophized. "Yesterday all those dogs were kissing my feet; to-day every one, and every thing, falls upon me, even the rain!"

A letter from Rawlinson awaited Layard. "I can come to no other conclusion than that Nimroud is the original Nineveh," he wrote, and he invited Layard down to Baghdad to deliver a firsthand account of the discoveries. Layard readily accepted. He was anxious to make arrangements with the East India Company's representative for transporting the winged bulls to England. He also felt he deserved a night on the town, and what could be a better place than Baghdad?

Layard arrived in the fabled city of Haroun Al-Rashid and the thousand and one nights on Christmas Eve.

> I saw the visions of God . . .
> the face of a man, the face of the lion . . .
> and when they went, I heard the noise of wings.
>
> —EZEKIEL

XIX

Layard spent Christmas week at Rawlinson's imposing residence. The red carpet was unrolled in his honor. After the vermin-infested hovels and dirty tents of Nimrod, Layard luxuriated in a spotless room, neatly made bed, freshly laundered clothes, and an air-conditioned study. Rawlinson's library was a curious feat of local engineering: a waterwheel, turned by the on-rushing waters of the Tigris, poured a continuous stream of fresh water over the roof of the library. The temperature within the study hovered at a relatively cool 90 degrees Fahrenheit. Outside the thermometer soared to 120.

The East India Company's political agent was then thirty-five years old, seven years Layard's senior, and a bachelor. His passions were trying to decipher cuneiform and taming wild animals.

A pet mongoose had free rein of the house and made itself useful by killing snakes. A tame black panther sat curled at Rawlinson's legs. The menagerie was rounded out by a full-grown Mesopotamian lioness which, as a cub, was found along the banks of the Tigris. The beast served as Rawlinson's personal bodyguard (nobody else was permitted to feed her) and tracked after him in house and garden, like a favorite dog.

Although they had corresponded frequently, this was the first meeting between Layard, the founder of Assyrian archaeology, and Rawlinson, the Assyriologist, among the first to decipher Assyrian inscriptions. "It was a happy chance which brought together two such men," Rawlinson's older brother George, Canon of Canterbury and professor of ancient history at Oxford, later remarked. "Each [was] strongest where the other was weakest."

Layard was the excavator, robust, determined, active, energetic, inured to hardship by travel in remote areas. Rawlinson, who had joined the East India Company at the age of seventeen, who, like Layard, had never attended college, was scholarly by nature, a self-taught classicist and linguist who was fluent in modern and ancient Persian, in Hindi, Hebrew, and lesser-known tongues, a man of wide reading and deep insight.

Rawlinson's fixation was cuneiform. He was as determined to decode the nail-headed characters as Layard was to probe the core of the mound at Nimrod. Rawlinson thought of archaeology in terms of unearthing lost literature. He considered recovery of art a happy by-product, nothing more. In a paper on Assyrian inscriptions, published in the *Journal of the Royal Asiatic Society*, he fumed, "[The] discovery of an historical inscription appears to me to be of far more importance than the mere laying bare of sculptured slabs which, however interesting the design, neither furnish us with new ideas, nor convey any great historical truth."

This blind spot infuriated Layard and others who argued that one picture is worth a thousand words. The conflict came to a boil some years later when both sides tried to establish a chronology for the Assyrian empire.

"It is of course with extreme diffidence that I differ from one so well qualified to give an opinion on such a subject as he [Rawlinson] is," James Fergusson, the brilliant architect and friend of Layard and Rawlinson wrote some years later in an essay on the subject of chronology, "but, with all due deference, I think he overlooks and despises by far the most important element for deciding the question. For he scarcely admits the style of art to be evidence at all, but relies wholly on the inscriptions . . . as the only means we have of determining the question.

"Layard, on the other hand, who has an intuitive perception of the smallest shades of difference in expression, joins in a familiarity with the forms of Assyrian art as great as that of Rawlinson with the inscriptions.

"Documentary evidence may be altered in a thousand ways," Fergusson continued, pointing out that inscriptions may be added and altered long after the period to which they apparently belong. An absolute monarch, for example, may knowingly inscribe a falsehood on the walls of his palace; similarity of names may mislead, and mistranslation deceive, besides numerous other sources of error. But, Fergusson contended, "buildings always are, if I may use such an expression, contemporaneous with themselves, and always have a purpose, which never is to deceive." Art too is always the expression of some contemporary idea and conveys it unaltered to the latest times. "No monarch, however absolute," Fergusson said, "can make the art of his time other than the expression of the feelings of that age; nor can he make it better than the advancement of his people at that time will afford."

Then Fergusson stated the obvious: what is needed is a judicious understanding and appreciation of both—art and inscriptions.

The spirited debate between the merits of Assyrian art and inscriptions was never resolved. Layard was flexible and imaginative enough to see both sides. But Rawlinson, perhaps as a result of his military training, was obstinate and unbending. Having assumed a redoubt, he refused to surrender. Yet, as George Rawlinson recalled in a memoir about his brother, "The two men mutually esteemed and respected each other," adding, "[they] were ready to assist each other to the utmost of their power; and, if occasionally they clashed in opinion and maintained opposing views on the subject of antiquarian research, their differences led to no rancour or jealousy, but rather to an increasing regard as time went on."

December 25, 1845, was the most pleasant Christmas Layard had spent since his childhood in Italy. Rawlinson's residence was festooned with decorations, the table crowded with roast lamb and stuffed birds. Arak was plentiful.

Layard's ability to keep up with Rawlinson in the matter of

cuneiform impressed Rawlinson and was a tribute to Layard's scholarship, although as a man of action Layard's natural habitat was the field, not the armchair. That week Rawlinson and Layard identified together the arrow-headed characters for god, king, and city. In a letter to his mother, Layard boldly expressed confidence that "with the assistance of the materials furnished by the joint stock of Rawlinson and myself, I hope very shortly to have the alphabet." Rawlinson was less sanguine. In his diary, he wrote that he expected to crack cuneiform in "another two or three years." Was cuneiform Chaldean? Some dialect, long forgotten, of an existing language? Some unknown language? Endlessly, or so it seemed, both men discussed these questions. At the time neither realized that the Assyrian language possessed no alphabet.

Early in January, before returning to Mosul, Layard and Rawlinson entered into a pact. Layard promised to tranship his finds through Baghdad so Rawlinson could personally inspect each new cuneiform inscription. In return, Rawlinson promised to send a steam-driven vessel upriver to collect the art treasures and transfer them at Baghdad aboard a homeward-bound East Indiaman. Botta's collection was still sitting on a Baghdad wharf waiting for a French ship. Rawlinson—like Canning and Layard—relished the idea of the British Museum's beating the Louvre to it with the world's first exhibition of Assyrian relics.

His batteries recharged, on January 17, 1846, Layard returned to Nimrod.

Dramatic change had taken place in the countryside. It had rained incessantly since December, and the mound had sprung to life. "The mound was no longer an arid and barren heap," he said. "Its surface and its sides were equally covered with verdure."

Encouraged by the favorable behavior of the newly appointed pasha, Arab tribes had recrossed the Tigris and returned to their former camping grounds around Nimrod. They had pitched their tents and resumed cultivating the soil. "Even on the mound," Layard said, "the plough opened its furrows, and corn was sown over the palaces of the Assyrian kings."

During his absence, Hormuzd Rassam, the seventeen-year-old younger brother of the British vice-consul, had taken charge at Nimrod and had established a new base of operations atop the mound itself. Layard was given the most luxurious of the new dwelling places. "A few rude chairs, a table, and a wooden bedstead, formed the whole of my furniture," he said. Layard admired the young Hormuzd's eagerness and industriousness and appointed Hormuzd his agent at Nimrod, inviting him to share his primitive quarters.

The Nimrod mound covered 60 acres. Lest the vein he worked ran out—Botta's experience at Khorsabad—Layard thought it prudent to make some fresh experiments elsewhere on the mound.

Once again, luck, that fickle goddess, was his outrider. Arbitrarily, he pointed to a new spot and ordered another trench dug. With the first shovel of debris, his men struck a wall covered with bas-reliefs. But Layard was puzzled. Just as he could distinguish at the age of twelve the different styles of the Venetian school of painters, he promptly recognized that the artistic style of the new reliefs belonged to a period other than his earlier discoveries.

The new figures were 3 feet 8 inches high and were superbly executed. They appeared to have stepped from a nightmare— winged creatures with human bodies and the heads of either vultures or eagles. The curved beak of one was half open and displayed a pointed tongue covered with red paint. Clearly, he had discovered another Assyrian period.

Early the following morning, Layard rode off to parley with a local sheik, a feature of his continual shuttle diplomacy aimed at maintaining friendly relations with the various tribes in Nimrod's vicinity. As a matter of policy, he regularly presented gifts to local chieftains—a piece of silk or embroidered material, a pair of boots. The Arabs were delighted; among them, the compliment "my house is your house" was often meant literally, "more literally," Layard said, "than I had intended and I was seldom free from a large addition to my establishment." It was not uncommon for a sheik to appear suddenly in Layard's doorway with a dozen followers and expect to break bread with the strange Frank.

Returning to Nimrod from the parley late that morning,

Layard spied two Arab horsemen flying from the mound at full speed. Abruptly, they pulled up as they approached. "Hasten, O Bey!" exclaimed one panting rider. "Hasten to the diggers, for they have found Nimrod himself!" Off they galloped to spread the word, leaving Layard open-mouthed.

At the mound, Layard found a commotion. Awad, his foreman, stepped forward and proudly announced that they had unearthed the mighty hunter himself, the father of Ashur. Layard hastened to the spot. Protruding from the bottom of the pit was an alabaster head, 8 feet in height, which he promptly recognized as belonging to a gigantic, human-headed, winged lion. "The expression was calm, yet majestic, and the outline of the features showed a freedom and knowledge of art, scarcely to be looked for in the works of so remote a period," Layard said. Inwardly, Layard's computer hastily revised the Victorian conception of art. In his day, Greek sculpture was universally acclaimed the most perfect. Yet he was looking at sculpture of equal artistic merit, works of art that had preceded Periclean Greece by centuries, if not millenniums.

Layard's credulous Arab workers were terrified by the apparition. "It required no stretch of imagination [for them] to conjure up the most strange fancies," Layard wrote. In the tradition of the countryside, the head conjured up a visitation from the lower depths, from hell itself.

As Layard studied the head, the sheik with whom he had conferred earlier in the morning rode up with his warriors to view the wonder. "This is not the work of men's hands but of those infidel giants of whom the Prophet, peace be with him! has said, that they were higher than the tallest date tree!" he exclaimed. "This is one of the idols which Noah, peace be with him! cursed before the Flood."

Mosul was thrown into bedlam by the news. The Cadi, or titular orthodox religious leader of the pashalik, protested to the governor that Layard's activities ran counter to the teachings of the Koran, although the Cadi was hard put to explain precisely in what way. Nonetheless, with Mosul in agitation, the governor summoned Layard and advised him to quietly suspend his activities until the sensation subsided.

Canning was delighted with the latest news. "By your will,"

he wrote Layard, "give my best thanks to the gentleman who popped his head out of the mound and spoke words of encouragement to you!"

The discovery put Layard in a reflective mood. He pondered the meaning of meaning. "For twenty-five centuries [these sculptures] had been hidden from the eye of man, and they now stand forth once more in their ancient majesty," he wrote. "But how changed is the scene around them! The luxury and civilization of a mighty nation has given place to the wretchedness and ignorance of a few half-barbarous tribes. The wealth of temples, and the riches of great cities, have been succeeded by ruins and shapeless heaps of earth. Above the spacious hall in which they stood, the plough has passed and the corn now waves."

On April 21, 1846, while still waiting for the uproar in Mosul to subside, he wrote his mother a lengthy letter and singled out his winged, human-headed lions as "the most magnificent specimens of Assyrian sculpture that could be found above or under the ground." The sculpture of Nimrod, he wrote triumphantly, far exceeded that of Khorsabad. "The lions . . . for instance, are admirably drawn and the muscles, bones and veins quite true to nature and portrayed with great spirit," he said. "There is also great *mouvement*—as the French well term it—in the attitude of the animal."

The words of the Hebrew prophet Ezekiel haunted him. "Ezekiel appears continuously to have had the sculptures of the Assyrians or Chaldeans in his eye when he wrote his prophecies," Layard wrote home. "His [words] are exact descriptions of the bas-reliefs of Nimroud."

These conclusions, which spread rapidly through his reports to Canning, Rawlinson, and others, caused an uproar in Europe and America. An American churchman wrote a letter of encouragement. "You may scarcely dream of the importance which your solitary labors may have upon the right understanding of the historical and prophetical parts of the Holy Word," he said. The irascible Allison, Layard's embassy companion in drinking bouts and amorous adventures in Constantinople, wrote in a lighter vein and suggested he exploit the burgeoning Evangelicalism of the era. "The interest

about your stones is very great . . . ," he reported. "If you can
. . . attach a Biblical importance to your discoveries, you will
come the complete dodge over this world of fools and dream-
ers. . . ."

Mosul, meanwhile, refused to calm down. Layard became
increasingly restless. He appealed to Canning for a firman
permitting him to resume the excavations and remove the
finds. He also took the opportunity to touch on that hardy
perennial, money. In a letter to Canning dated April 21, 1846,
Layard pointed out that after almost six months of work, "the
entire excavating expenses amounted to 8,644 piastres [$400]."
He was running low on funds, he added, and drawing on his
own meager resources in the hope that, "should the government carry on the excavations, I shall be refunded."

Canning appreciated Layard's difficulties and replied: "I
shall do my best to come to your aid."

But even the Great Elchi could not wave a magic wand and
produce a firman and funds. It had taken him almost three
years to extract permission from the Sultan for the removal of
the Halicarnassus Marbles—Allison had just arranged for their
shipment to the British Museum—and Canning, quite rightly,
felt it would be gross to press so quickly for another firman.
The Sultan, at the top of a tottering empire that stretched from
Egypt to the Persian frontier, had other matters on his mind.

Canning was also worried about finances. Layard's two-
month sojourn among the mounds had lengthened into half
a year and, literally, he had barely scratched the surface. The
Cannings, after all, had three teenage daughters and, *ipso
facto*, three hope chests to fill. "I am quite proud of my public
spirit in the cause of antiquity . . . ," Canning wrote his wife,
who was now in England still waiting for his arrival, "but I
must not ruin either you or the children."

Lady Canning took a dim view of her husband's expensive
hobby and apparently sometimes described antiquities as
"trifles." This conclusion is implied in several of Sir Stratford's
letters as he felt compelled to justify his frivolousness in the
matter of archaeology. "Perhaps," he wrote her, "you think
me crazy for caring about such trifles but they are trifles for
which colleges, universities and nations would take each other

by the ears." And, appealing to her Evangelical sentiment, he crowned his case with the argument that Rawlinson tells me the inscriptions are likely to throw much light upon Scripture history."

But Layard was particularly anxious about acquiring a firman, since the French had dispatched a new vice-consul to fill the vacancy left the year before by Botta's departure. The new consul, M. Guillois, shocked Layard by disclosing his intention to reopen Botta's dig at Kouyunjik and announcing that the French were already in the midst of negotiations at Constantinople for a firman. Layard considered these moves a threat to British interests and wrote Canning, "I am very anxious to dig a few trenches at Kouyunjik before he obtains his permission."

Layard decided to take matters into his own hands. He felt the need to prod the governor into lifting the ban against digging at Nimrod. The situation demanded a dramatic diplomatic gesture. Accordingly, he decided to throw a monster bash. He issued a general invitation to all and sundry to attend the gala: the governor and his Turkish staff, Arab sheiks, Kurdish chieftains, leaders of the Christian minority, members of Mosul's old-line Jewish families, and the diplomatic community (the Rassams and Guilloises). Fourteen sheep were roasted and boiled. Musicians and dancers were hired. The party lasted three days. Madame Guillois, a radiant Parisian beauty, was a center of attraction. A sheik, in the midst of the festivities, whispered to Layard, "She is the sister of the sun!" and in flowery Arabic he continued: "Had I a thousand purses, I would give them all for such a wife. Her eyes are like the eyes of my mare, her hair is as bitumen, and her complexion resembles the finest Busrah dates. One would die for a *houri* like that."

Layard, who was never unmindful of beauty, commented in an aside, "The sheikh was almost justified in his admiration."

The party paid dividends. Layard's reputation, already high, acquired new stature throughout the pashalik. He was the talk of the bazaars and coffee shops. Impressed by Layard's popularity, the pasha concluded that "the dust had settled" and that Layard could resume his digging at Nimrod.

The governor no sooner flashed the green light than an official authorization, in Layard's name, arrived from Constantinople. Canning was finally ready to embark on home leave. He realized that there was insufficient time to obtain a firman and, in desperation, had approached the grand vizier, his intimate friend, for the next best thing, a vizierial letter. It was immediately forthcoming. The original copy of the document, dated May 5, 1846, together with Christian Rassam's translation, is in the British Museum. It is an impressive document, about the size of a tabloid newspaper, written in bold, cursive Turkish script and adorned with colorful seals. Rassam's translation is in the diplomatic French of the day, complex and archaic.

"In the vicinity of Mosul there are quantities of stones and ancient remains," the vizierial letter addressed to the governor of Mosul, began. "There is also an English gentleman who has come to the area to look for stones of this kind. ... The British ambassador has prayed that there be no obstacles placed in the way of the above-mentioned gentleman's taking some stones which can be of use to him, such as those which he may be able to discover in the midst of the excavations he will make in places believed to enclose stones of this type, and to his putting them on shipboard in order to transport them to England."

Neither Canning's nor Layard's name actually appears in the document. No need. In 1846 there was only one British ambassador in Constantinople and only one Englishman in Mosul collecting "stones." Nevertheless, much later the latter became a bone over which lawyers and academicians endlessly scrapped. Did the "stones" belong to Canning, who financed the expedition and extracted the vizierial authorization from Constantinople? Or to Layard, who labored in Mesopotamia and dug them up? If Layard, did he act on his own? Or as an agent of Canning?

And so it has gone ever since.

This sort of nitpicking is, in the spirit of the winged-bulls of Assyria, largely bullspit. That's how lawyers, academicians, and paper-shufflers in general earn a living. Debate over moot points provides them with work. The central truth is that the relationship between Layard and Canning was similar to the relationship between Layard and Rawlinson. One complemented the other. Each was strongest where the other was weakest. Layard's immediate reaction to the vizierial order and his and Canning's subsequent behavior attest to the fact that neither one thought about personal gain.

"I read by the light of a small camel-dung fire the document which secured to the British nation . . . the earliest monuments of Assyrian art," Layard wrote.

In a note accompanying the authorization, Canning urged Layard to exploit the letter to the fullest, to dig, shotgun style, into every mound that might contain Assyrian antiquities so that Britain could secure a prior claim to excavation. Even in this formative period of archaeology, a rule was generally accepted that whoever dug at a site first exercised a prior claim to it unless he relinquished it to another. But Canning also urged him to act circumspectly, not to be "too greedy" and to respect the claims and jealousies of others. "I need not tell you," he said, "that our Gallic neighbors are particularly in my thoughts."

They were also in Layard's. Guillois was surprised by the vizierial directive. The damn Anglo-Saxons had beaten the French to it again. Nonetheless, he warned Layard, France held a prior right to Kouyunjik in the light of Botta's earlier excavations, even though he had found nothing at the site.

Layard considered the French claim without merit. Botta, he argued, abandoned Kouyunjik. Moreover, he pointed out, the mound was nearly a mile in circumference. Surely there was enough room for both France and England? Guided by Canning's instructions, Layard invited Guillois to join in a joint Anglo-French excavation of the mound, but the Frenchman rejected the olive branch.

Like petulant children, the two Europeans rushed to the mound and began to dig in opposite directions. Layard had distinct advantages over his rival. He was a keen observer, connoisseur of art, and, by now, a relatively experienced digger. He was learning to read a mound the way a fisherman reads the ocean. For example, he had noticed that each mound appeared to have a pyramidal-shaped high point, and although he did not know what it meant, he suspected that by clearing the debris from around that spot he was likely to increase his chances of making a significant discovery. Today the high point is known as the ziggurat, or temple tower; in a sense, the Assyrian and Babylonian stairway to heaven. Accordingly, in the race to dig up Kouyunjik, Layard staked out a claim to the high ground. "I think I have commenced in the best place," Layard wrote Canning. "If M. Guillois continues his researches where he has begun them I have not much to fear."

The race, however, ended in a dead heat. "We both continued our research for about a month without success," Layard reported. He was baffled. Of all the Mesopotamian mounds, Kouyunjik, known to travelers from Xenophon to Rabbi Benjamin to Claudius Rich as a possible site of Nineveh, should have contained the richest lode. Yet, like Botta before them, they found only a few potsherds, kiln-baked bricks, and chips of sculptures.

As his frustration deepened, something happened which almost brought Layard's probe of the mounds to a dead end.

Although it was recorded in the secret official dispatches of the Turkish and British governments, Layard himself publicly suppressed knowledge of the affair for forty years. In his autobiography, for the first time, he gave his version of events.

When the Tigris flowed at its regular level, Layard crossed the river between Mosul and Kouyunjik over the famous bridge of boats. But when the river flooded, as in spring when the snows melted in the Armenian mountains, the bridge was replaced by a ferry.

One evening, when the river was at flood stage, Layard and several workers arrived at the river's edge after a particularly defeating day at Kouyunjik and found ferry service suspended for the night. Only one boat remained on the left bank, and Layard quickly engaged it. As they were about to push off, two Albanian irregulars in the Turkish army appeared and asked for a lift. Layard, in his customary outgoing fashion, obliged them. They shoved off, but in the distance they saw a group of men hurrying to the bank. Layard mistook them for travelers and thought they would have to spend the night on the bank. A scarred traveler himself, he ordered the boatman to return and wait for them. When the party arrived, he discovered it was led by the Cadi, the chief religious figurehead of Mosul, who was returning with his attendants from a prayer meeting at the tomb of Jonah. The Cadi, a bigot who was still fighting the Crusades, detested infidels, especially Franks. Layard offered to take him aboard and, according to Layard, "he eagerly accepted my offer and embarked with his people."

The open boat was now extremely crowded. Layard perched himself on the poop deck alongside the steersman, an area aft which could barely support two men. The other passengers crowded into the bilges. The Cadi stood just below Layard.

As the boat made its way across the turbulent waters, with the current sweeping along at better than five knots, the Cadi said in a loud voice, "Shall the dogs occupy the high places while the true believers stand below?"

Exhausted and irritable after twelve hours of fruitless digging in the searing heat, and angered by the Cadi's ingratitude, Layard lost his temper. He struck the Cadi on the head with a short-hooked swagger stick, such as the Bedouins used when racing their camels and which he usually carried with him.

Layard apparently felt the blow would have slight impact effect, since the Cadi wore a thick turban. "I was surprised," he said, "to see the blood stream down his face." Layard had almost split the Cadi's skull open. The Cadi's followers drew their swords and pistols as the boat tossed wildly in the current. The two Albanian mercenaries, better trained and armed, rushed to Layard's defense. Layard, in his swashbuckling manner, leaped from the poop deck and grabbed the Cadi by the throat, threatening to throw him into the river if his followers attacked.

The stalemate held until they reached the right bank. The Cadi, his face smeared with blood, rushed through the streets of Mosul shouting that he had been beaten by an infidel, that the Prophet had been insulted. Mosul was stirred, and Layard suddenly realized that the Christian minority (himself included) might be massacred. He hurried to the serai of the new governor and explained his case. "I called upon him to take sufficient precautions for my safety," Layard disclosed, "and warned him that he would be held responsible by the

British government and by the Great Elchi at Constantinople for anything that might happen to me."

Fortunately, the Cadi had a bad reputation. He was corrupt and unpopular. He also led the pashalik's opposition to Constantinople's belated attempt to introduce reforms to save the empire. The governor took Layard's side. In accordance with the vizierial letter, he denounced the Cadi for insulting a guest of Turkey, and the Sultan's Christian subjects who, under the new Turkish constitution, shared equal citizenship rights with their Moslem compatriots. The governor, however, begged Layard to take sanctuary in the serai and not venture out until the tension eased.

Layard felt that if he accepted the pasha's invitation, it would be interpreted by the Cadi and his followers as a sign of weakness and that he would never again command the respect of the peoples of the region. Without their support, his work among the mounds would come to an end.

Followed by his two Albanian irregulars, who were spoiling for a fight and were determined to see their benefactor safely through the incident, Layard took his leave of the governor, rode to the home of Christian Rassam, and, as a British citizen, officially reported the episode to the consul.

Mosul was tense for several days. The Christian community was in hiding; the governor had his forces on stand-by alert.

Rawlinson, his personal fondness for Layard notwithstanding, was shaken by the incident. The gratuitous insult of the Cadi, he wrote Layard, did not warrant risking a massacre and jeopardizing British interests in Mesopotamia. If the embassy at Constantinople did not support him, Rawlinson said, Layard must pack up and get out of Mosul forthwith.

Canning was equally distressed. Although he felt the Cadi got what he deserved, he bluntly informed Layard that he must learn to control himself or abandon any hope of entering the diplomatic service. The incident was another black mark against Layard in the book of Lord Aberdeen and the foreign ministry.

Fortunately for Layard, like a sandstorm, the incident blew over.

It was now summer, and a lesser individual would have put

off work until autumn, given the almost intolerable heat in Mesopotamia in the middle of the year. Not Layard. He had his authorization and he was determined to continue his explorations. Judiciously, however, he shifted his operations from Kouyunjik, the Cadi's bailiwick, to his beloved and productive Nimrod, where he could work in complete freedom.

But back at Nimrod, even Layard had to make concessions to the sun. The rickety dwellings Rassam had erected atop Nimrod were stifling, and life in an Arab tent was no improvement. Layard ordered caves cut into the Tigris's bank, and he converted one of these recesses into summer headquarters. "I was much troubled, however, with scorpions and other reptiles which issued from the earth forming the walls of my apartment," he said, "and later in the summer by the gnats and sandflies which hovered on a calm night over the river." But the apartment had a consolation: It was between 30 and 40 degrees cooler than outside.

As the summer lengthened, the heat took its unmerciful toll. Corn stalks buckled, flowers withered, sheep meadows turned the color of burnt sienna. Searing desert winds blackened the sky and swirled across the desert, accompanied by flights of locusts. Whenever a whirlwind approached, activities at Nimrod came to a complete halt. Layard watched in fascination as the column of sand swirled toward him. If the tornado struck while he was working on the mound, his favorite refuge was beneath a fallen lion. His workers huddled in trenches, blinded by the sand and almost on the verge of suffocation.

In these terrifying conditions, Layard pressed ahead. His hardships were compensated. His finds were spectacular. The mound was honeycombed with chambers and blackened walls. There were accumulations of ashes in places where wooden beams had been inserted to support a roof or wall. The city or palace, or whatever it was, had been put to the torch in antiquity.

Each day brought forth new wonders, deeper mysteries.

Gods, kings, warriors, and captives emerged from the depths of the mound, a fantasia of elaborately sculpted and richly ornamented figures, some 8 feet in height. Under a broken slab, for example, he discovered a magnificent yellow limestone human-headed ox or bull with wings. "I lifted the body with difficulty," he recorded, "and to my surprise I discovered under it sixteen copper lions, admirably designed, and forming a regular series, diminishing in size from the largest, which was above one foot, to the smallest, which scarcely exceeded an inch."

Daily, Layard filled his green, leather-bound notebooks, with their distinctive ruled, violet-tinted pages, with sketches, cuneiform inscriptions, architectural plans. His notes were terse, often cryptic one-liners: "M. 20 Nimroud."

The origin of the mound continued to baffle him, and he referred to the objects he unearthed as "Assyrian or Chaldean." Despite Rawlinson's heady conclusion earlier that Layard had rediscovered Nineveh, Layard—like Botta before him at Khorsabad—was reluctant to claim that he had found "that great city" of Genesis. To Miner Kellogg, an American painter friend who worked in Italy, he wrote that he had "set seriously to excavate among some ruins called "Nimroud" and modestly added, "They may be the ruins of Nineveh." Kellogg couldn't care less—Nineveh or no. After reading Layard's ecstatic descriptions of his finds, he dashed off a letter to Mosul and expressed "great joy . . . over the great success you have had in bringing to light long hidden wonders of ancient art."

While Nimrod's original name was uncertain, there was no doubt that Layard had found himself. "I live among the ruins," he wrote Aunt Sara, "and dream of little else. For the time being, my hopes and fears and joys center in them."

Although he did not know it, he was finding not only himself but also a place in history.

> I crossed rivers . . . I climbed mountains.
> —SHALMANESER III

XX While Layard was rummaging through Nimrod, Rawlinson made arrangements for the *Nitocris,* a steam-driven coaster of the East India Company named for a mythical queen of Babylon, to sail upriver "to assist in the conveyance of Mr. Layard's sculpture and other antiquities from that site to Baghdad." Layard's good friend Lieutenant Jones, who had fished him from the Tigris two years earlier, commanded the vessel. Rawlinson, Layard, and Jones considered the journey routine. Some years earlier, in an experiment, the *Nitocris's* sister ship made an almost effortless run upstream to a point within a few miles below Nimrod.

But the *Nitocris's* voyage was a complete failure. The river's ebbing current that year was exceptionally strong, and the vessel did well to maintain headway. Worse, engine break downs were frequent. Employing auxiliary sail was useless. When *Nitocris* got halfway to Nimrod, she was compelled to put about and return with empty holds to Baghdad. Layard was now confronted with the awesome problem of how to remove the immense winged lions and bas-reliefs, each weighing several tons, in the absence of transportation. Some of the blocks of sculpture were 9 feet square and 1 foot thick. The few ropes Layard procured were of such poor quality that they snapped like threads. And the carts used by the Arabs could "scarcely be used for carrying a load of hay."

He solved the problem as Botta had. Importing several Mosul stonecutters, he ordered them to saw the sculpture into manageable portions. Damage was unavoidable. "The inscriptions being mere [sic] repetitions," Layard said, "I did not consider it necessary to preserve them as they added to the weight." Two stonemasons broke them off and tossed them aside.

The blocks were packed in felt and straw and transported in twelve cases to the river's edge on rude buffalo carts. Special keleks, rafts of skins similar to the raft he and Mitford had floated down the Tigris on, were built. The crates of art, awash, were made fast. Down the Tigris the cargo went—at the mercy of currents and rapids. As much to Layard's surprise as Rawlinson's, the convoy landed safely at Baghad.

The British resident immediately took charge of the shipment and, after inspecting them (and no doubt lamenting the loss of the inscriptions), Rawlinson arranged for their transfer to a ship bound for England.

By now summer had lengthened and the heat at Nimrod had become so unbearable that even Layard complained. "The weather is so hot that for the next month I must give up hard work," he wrote the Austens at the end of July. "The Arabs can hardly stand the digging, though accustomed to the climate, and I am compelled to release them for three hours during the middle of the day. ... It is no joke, I can assure you, to draw with the thermometer at 115, and even 117, in the *shade*."

In the midst of these labors, the governor of Mosul and two hundred of his bodyguards and retainers descended on Nimrod to inspect the monsters Layard had unearthed. Layard was fond of the Turk and privately described him as a "gentleman, actuated by the best intentions, benevolent and anxious to do all in his power to increase the happiness and prosperity of the people." The human-headed lions, the bird-headed humans, and the other grotesque figures dumfounded the visitors. "These are the idols of the infidels," one of the pasha's aides solemnly declared. But the presence of Satan's works did not dull the appetites of the governor and his party. "They completely devoured the provisions intended for six months consumption and which an excess of frugality and economy had led me to lay up," Layard said.

The heat and low provisions forced Layard and his workers to abandon Nimrod and return to Mosul. The heat at Mosul was as intense, but at least one could spend the worst part of the day hiding in the *sardaubs,* the cellars of the more substantially built Mosul homes, including Christian Rassam's consular residence. But Layard was restless. The idea of "losing time" kept him awake at night.

Each morning he gazed across the Tigris and saw the great mound of Kouyunjik beckoning to him. He recalled Claudius Rich's words: "I doubt that but not many antiquities might be found in this mound."

Finally, he hit on a novel plan to defeat the sun. He decided to dig by lamplight from dusk to dawn.

The first weeks of nighttime digging at Kouyunjik were as unproductive as his earlier excavations and those of Botta and Guillois. Yet Layard was convinced that within this mound of mounds, the traditional site of Nineveh, there must be some clue to antiquity.

Once again, luck was with him. An aged Mosul stonecutter, whom Layard had employed at Nimrod, recounted how he was present when Rich found a bas-relief and that afterward, as a true believer, he had joined others in smashing the idol to pieces. "He offered to show me the spot," Layard reported, "and I opened a trench at once into a high mound which he pointed out in the northern line of ruins."

Layard's workers touched their shovels to the spot and promptly struck fragments of sculptured alabaster. For the next seventy-two hours, oblivious to the sun and moon, Layard worked around the clock to excavate the area.

The first major discovery was the entrance to a chamber guarded by two winged creatures, half-human, half-beast. They had been battered to pieces with hammers. The size of the sculpture—20 feet in height—astonished Layard, who thought he had grown accustomed to surprises. "The proportions were gigantic, and the relief higher than that of any sculpture hitherto discovered in Assyria," he recorded. The chamber was filled with broken pieces of sculpture, many bearing cuneiform inscriptions. A pavement of limestone led from the chamber into the interior of the mound. In high expectation, Layard followed it, but it petered out. Not another piece of sculpture was found. Once again, Kouyunjik kept its secret.

A modern archaeologist would be ecstatic over such a discovery, but Layard was dismayed. In this early period of archaeology, the success of a dig was measured by the amount of freestanding sculpture recovered. Potsherds meant nothing; inscriptions or designs were unintelligible curiosities except to a handful of people like Rawlinson; stratigraphy was unheard of; no detailed records of the dig were kept. This was one of the reasons Layard and his contemporaries were unable to put the Assyrian jigsaw puzzle together. They saved and studied only the big pieces and ignored or discarded the smaller ones. As a child knows, every piece of the puzzle, big or small, serves as a clue to completing the picture.

Layard's insistence that he work at the mounds in the middle of summer had taken a personal toll. He had lost considerable weight and was ravaged by recurring bouts of malaria. Christian Rassam and his wife Matilda were alarmed by the deterioration in his health and strongly advised him to emulate the Assyrian kings of antiquity and take to the hills, especially since a cholera epidemic had broken out at Baghdad and would probably spread to Mosul. He was in no condition to resist that dread disease. Disappointed over the meager results of his second assault on Kouyunjik, Layard bowed to their advice.

In September, accompanied by Rassam's younger brother Hormuzd, Layard left for the Tiyari Mountains, a district inhabited by the Nestorians or Chaldean Christians, who claimed to be the nearest descendants of the ancient Assyrians.

Yet Layard could hardly bring himself to a holiday without mixing in business. The mountains lay to the northeast, and he took a route that passed through Khorsabad in order to visit the French excavations. He scrambled over Botta's dig and found the mound's chambers and passages smaller and narrower than those at Nimrod.

In the two years since Botta had dug up the site, the

chambers he discovered had been partly filled in by collapsed trenches. The sculptures and the bas-reliefs which the French were compelled to abandon, were crumbling. "Shortly," Layard forecast, "little will remain of this remarkable monument."

Layard did not tarry at Khorsabad, because it was marshy and therefore "unhealthy." The marshes explained why so many of Botta's workers came down with "ague."

As the sun set, Layard and his party departed in haste. They moved on to another village, which turned out to be just as swampy, but Layard took the precaution of spending the night on a high platform. "I passed the night free from the attacks of the swarms of gnats which infested the stagnant water below," he wrote.

Of course, it was not the marshes which caused "ague." Nor were those insects gnats. They were anopheles mosquitos, the bearers of malaria, but almost half a century was yet to pass before an obscure French physician in northern Africa, Alphonse Laveran, discovered the malaria parasite.

The next several weeks served as a tonic for Layard. He traveled in the high mountains, whose scenery reminded him of Switzerland, and lingered among the Chaldeans, whom the Huguenot dubbed Protestants of the East.

But the excursion had its grisly moment. He was the first European to visit the area since a Turkish massacre three years earlier in which 10,000 Christians were slain. "In one spot," Layard wrote home, "I saw the bones of about 800 persons, men, women and children (the Nestorians say 2,000) still exposed, heaped up with the tresses of women, ragged garments and old shoes."

During his travels he maintained a lookout, as always, for traces of ruins, but the only remains he discovered were defaced bas-reliefs on a rock. They were so severely damaged that he could not copy the cuneiform characters. The highlight of the trip was a visit to Alkosh, and—according to local tradition—the tomb of the prophet Nahum. "This place is held in great reverence by Mahommedans and Christians, but especially by Jews, who keep the building in repair, and flock here in great numbers," Layard said. The tomb disappointed him, however. It was a simple plaster box covered with green cloth and "there are no inscriptions, nor fragments of any antiquity about the place," he said. Layard was unable to learn the origin of the tradition; according to St. Jerome, El Kosh (Alkosh?) was a village in Galilee.

Layard returned to Mosul at the end of September, found the heat still unbearable, and promptly came down with another bout of ague. His brow burned, his teeth chattered uncontrollably, and his bones ached.

The interlude among the Nestorians had attracted the notice of another repressed minority in Mesopotamia, the Yezidis or devil worshipers whom he and Mitford had brushed on their journey from Damascus to Mosul. The Yezidis sent a *cawal* or priest to Mosul to invite him to attend their annual October festival at which they propitiated Satan. The invitation was probably politically motivated. The name of the Great Elchi and of British activity at Baghdad was spreading along the Tigris and Euphrates. The minorities looked to the British presence for aid and comfort. Layard was considered an agent of the Great Elchi—all Englishmen were—and therefore a good man to befriend.

Among the Moslems and Christians of the region, the Yezidis were considered a mysterious sect founded by the nymphomaniacal Assyrian queen Semiramis. No European had ever witnessed Yezidi religious ceremonies, which were said to contain every excess of debauchery and lust, and Layard promptly accepted the invitation.

The religion of the devil worshipers, he discovered, was a potpourri of other beliefs. Indeed, the Yezidis reminded him of the Sabeans of Syria and Lebanon. The Yezidis recognized a Supreme Being. They believed in the cosmogony of Genesis—Creation and the Flood, for example. They considered Moses a prophet, as they did Mohammed. Jesus, they believed, was a great angel of the Lord who had taken the form of man, and they looked forward to his Second Coming. They baptized their children as Christians did; they circumcised their males as Jews and Moslems did; and, like ancient Egyptians, they revered the sun—they kissed the object upon which the first rays of the sun fell each morning.

What set the Yezidis apart from others was their reverence

for Satan. He was the mighty angel whom God punished for rebellion against divine will. Yet the devil was still a powerful force and must be assuaged, for he had the means of doing evil to mankind. One need only look at the human condition to recognize Satan's works.

The Yezidis went to great pains to avoid offending the Evil One. They never mentioned his name and exorcised from their language words which remotely resembled the Arabic word for the devil, *sheitan*. Thus, Layard was astonished to learn, the Yezidis refused to use the commonplace Arabic word *shat*, which means river, because it too closely resembled the first syllable in *sheitan*.

Among the Yezidis, Layard was careful to control his tongue, for he was in the habit of swearing freely in English or Arabic (as the occasion required). Only once did he slip among the Yezidis. A young boy shimmied up a tree and crawled out on a weak bough under which Layard and a group of Yezidi *cawals* were talking. Layard looked up and expected the bough to break under the boy's weight, boy and limb crashing down on their heads. In alarm, he pointed up at the bough and said, "If that young Sheit—" and immediately checked himself.

"Half the dreaded word had escaped," Layard later wrote. His companions were aghast. "I lamented that I had thus unwillingly wounded the feelings of my hosts," Layard said, "and was at a loss to know how I could make atonement for my indiscretion." Several awkward moments passed before the Yezidis regained their composure. They apparently accepted the slip as unintentional, and the crisis passed. Layard was relieved; the Yezidis were said to execute people who committed blasphemy.

Unrestrained by the presence of strangers at their festival, the Yezidi women forgot their timidity and removed their veils. "As I sat beneath the trees, laughing girls gathered around me, examined my dress and asked me of things to them strange and new," Layard said, obviously relishing the attention. "Some, more bold than the rest, would bring me the strings of beads and engraved stones hanging round their necks." Many of the stones were Assyrian in origin. Layard studied the relics as intently as the figures of the young devil-worshiping maidens.

About seven thousand Yezidis gathered for the festival, and he spent three consecutive midnights at their rituals, listening to their music and chants. But it was not what he had been led to believe. "There were no indecent gestures or unseemly ceremonies," he said. "Far from being the scene of orgies, the whole valley is held sacred and no acts, such as the Jewish law has declared to be impure, are permitted within the sacred precincts." Layard, however, did not attend the ceremony of the adoration of King Peacock—Satan himself. Only the initiated were admitted. Despite his warm relations with the Yezidis, he conceded, "I could not learn its nature."

Layard himself considered the Yezidis a "remarkable sect." In a letter to the Austens, whom he always enjoyed putting on, he jolted their Victorian smugness with the observation that "I never received more kindness than from these poor people," and he said that the Yezidis were of such good humor "I feel very much inclined to turn devil-worshipper myself."

Coincidentally, that same October, the governor of Mosul organized a good-will mission among the Yezidis, and although Layard was eager to get back to excavating Nimrod and Kouyunjik, he felt obliged to accept the pasha's invitation to accompany him in the hustings.

The governor undertook the journey with the pomp, circumstance, and show of force befitting an Ottoman governor. His column was headed by a regiment of regular infantry, followed by a company of artillery, and the governor and his aides, attired in the colors of a peacock and flying the pasha's personal standard, a green silk banner embroidered in gold with verses from the Holy Koran. The column was closed up by several companies of saber-rattling bash-bazouks or irregular cavalry.

"I was accompanied by my Cawass and my own servants," said Layard, "and rode as it best suited, and amused me, in different parts of the procession."

En route to the Yezidi country, the column passed a night at a hill station from which Layard commanded a sweeping view of the Assyrian plains stretching to the western horizon. "The ruins of ancient towns and villages rose on all sides; and, as the sun went down, I counted above one hundred mounds, throwing their dark and lengthening shadows across the plain," he said. "These were the remains of Assyrian civilization and prosperity. Centuries have elapsed since a settled population dwelt in this district of Mesopotamia. Now, not even the tent of the Bedouin could be seen. The whole was a barren, deserted waste."

Ezekiel's prophecy had been fulfilled.

Although the governor had come in peace, the Yezidis had suffered so grievously under his predecessor that no assurances could quiet their fear. The *cawals* served notice on the advancing column of their determination to resolutely defend their villages.

As the pasha's army approached the first village, with Layard riding up front, it was met by a round of fire and two Turkish soldiers fell dead at Layard's feet. The pasha was outraged by this unprovoked attack, and he ordered his irregulars to discipline the village. The *bash-bazouks*, who had been restless under the command of a good-natured governor who seemed genuinely interested in developing a good-neighbor policy, enthusiastically complied. The village was quickly overrun, but it was largely empty; most of the villagers had taken to the mountains, leaving behind a few old men and women, too infirm to leave with the rest. The irregulars rounded up the aged and infirm like lambs and, for good measure, lopped off their heads.

"In the evening the heads of the miserable old men and women . . . were paraded about the camp," a mortified Layard said, "and those who were fortunate enough to possess such trophies wandered from tent to tent, claiming a present as a reward for their prowess." Layard appealed to the pasha to have the heads buried, "but the troops were not willing to obey his orders, and it was late in the night before they were induced to resign their bloody spoils, which they had arranged in grim array, and lighted up with torches."

For the next several days the pasha's column tried, unsuccessfully, to dislodge the Yezidis from their mountain retreats. The governor's forces sustained heavy casualties. To encourage his men in their assault, the pasha placed his carpet under the Yezidi guns. He invited Layard to join him. The scene was out of Kipling.

"Here he [the governor] sat with the greatest apathy smoking his pipe, and carrying on a frivolous conversation with me, although he was the object of the aim of the Yezidis; several persons within a few feet of us falling dead, and the balls frequently throwing up the dirt into our faces," Layard recorded.

Layard had no recourse other than to match the governor's machismo or lose respect. He realized that a loss of face would impair his future operations at Nimrod and Kouyunjik.

By nightfall the Yezidis slipped off deeper into the mountain fastness, leaving behind a frustrated Turkish column. Layard was relieved to get back to Mosul and his mounds in a single piece.

In such bizarre situations, Assyrian archaeology was born.

New lamps for old! New lamps for old!
—ALADDIN

XXI While Layard was traveling in the mountains, Canning was in London bringing influence to bear to get the crown to underwrite a massive excavation of the mounds. He pressed the Prime Minister, pestered the Treasury and Foreign Office, put pressure on scholarly friends at his alma mater, Oxford, and visited the trustees of the British Museum.

The obstacles were considerable. However unfairly, Layard's reputation in London was suspect. Although Lord Palmerston had replaced Lord Aberdeen as foreign secretary, the Foreign Office remembered the incident involving the jealous British consul at Belgrade who falsely accused Layard of impersonating a British embassy official. The Treasury recalled the Coutts affair, although the bank had exonerated Layard and conceded it was their error. The Museum's trustees viewed Layard uneasily as a hotspur who would embroil them in all sorts of difficulties, and cited the Cadi affair as a case in point.

But in Canning, Layard had a forceful and respected spokesman. Sir Stratford was, as Tennyson put it, "the voice of England in the East." When Canning spoke, people—especially officials—listened.

In a letter to Sir Robert Peel, then the prime minister, Canning frankly explained his interest in Nimrod. "Botta's success at Nineveh [Khorsabad] induced me to adventure in the same lottery," he told Peel. "My ticket has turned up a prize."

Canning never referred to Layard by name but simply as "my agent," whose labors at "a gigantic mound called Nimroud" were rewarded by the discovery of "sculptures and a world of inscriptions." Just as Layard had played on Canning's patriotism to gain the vizierial letter, Canning played on Peel's to gain the necessary funds. "If the excavation keeps its promise to the end ... ," Canning said, "Montague House [the British Museum] will beat the Louvre hollow."

He also put pressure on the Treasury and on close friends, such as Sir R. H. Inglis, the Oxford classical scholar and a trustee of the Museum. In an age when the term "public relations" was yet to be invented, Canning's Nimrod campaign gathered irreversible momentum. When the Treasury and Museum waffled, Canning circulated Layard's private reports about the preliminary discoveries in the mound. The trustees were impressed and came down on Layard's side. With the perfection of a statesman, however, Canning made certain that his own role in the discoveries was secure in history. For the official record, a formal memorandum of the Museum made clear that "Sir Stratford Canning has very liberally offered the Trustees of the British Museum the results of the researches and excavations ... made by Mr. Layard under His Excellency's direction in Kurdistan [sic], and he has likewise signified his willingness to commit to the Trustees the promotion of that enterprise."

Perhaps the basic reason for Canning's difficulties in London was neither Layard's reputation nor the questionable thesis that objects of value lay in the mounds. Rather, it was a cut and dried matter of investing money in a project which promised no return interest. It was like offering new lamps for old. The niggardliness of the Museum's offer supports this conclusion. The Museum authorized an expenditure of £2,000 ($10,000) to meet the costs of excavating the mound and set a deadline of ten months, June 30, 1847, for its completion. The money was to be cut four ways—£400 for Canning, to repay him for his out-of-pocket outlay; £500 for Layard as compensation plus £100 in travel expenses for his return to England at the completion of the project; and £1,000 for the excavation itself.

The authorization was a joke. In effect, Layard was provided with £100 monthly to cover all his expenses at Nimrod. Out of this amount he was expected to hire and pay more than a hundred workers; superintend the dig; make drawings of bas-reliefs in duplicate (the Museum refused to send an artist, as the French had sent Flandin to Botta); copy all cuneiform inscriptions; make duplicate casts of sculptures and bas-reliefs which could not be removed; pack and move the sculptures; and arrange for the embarkation for London of "the spoils," as Canning referred to the treasures. By contrast, the French government had presented Botta and Flandin with £5,000 simply as a token of the nation's appreciation of their effort at Khorsabad, in addition to the thousands of pounds freely spent to produce the incomparable *Monuments of Nineveh.*

Canning was appalled by the British Museum's insensitivity to the problem. But as a skilled diplomat he sought to extract as much as he could from the situation. Now he put his talents to work to convince Layard of the wisdom of accepting the arrangement, however disappointing the amount involved. "The British Museum undertakes Nimroud in my stead," Canning wrote Layard, feigning enthusiasm. "You are the agent." That letter went out in September. It was closely followed by another, before Layard had time to reply. "I shall be disappointed," Canning said, applying subtle pressure on his protégé, "if you are not satisfied."

When Layard returned from the mountains with the pasha's battered troops, Canning's letters and a contract from the British Museum, dated September 21, 1846, awaited him. As he held the envelopes in his hand he was ecstatic. The great moment had arrived. When he read the contents, he was plunged into a state of deep depression. The amount of money for the operation was so small that he did not know whether to laugh or cry. Worse, the contract stated that it was "impossible" for the Museum "to provide in any way for Mr. Layard's further employment" at the conclusion of the dig. He had not even begun to work for them and he was out. When the excavation was completed Layard would find himself "again thrown upon the world at an age when I could no longer enter into a profession or hope for an honorable occupation." Engaging in uncharacteristic self-pity, he wrote Canning, "I have been so long unfortunate that I begin to despair."

Rawlinson, the only person other than Layard who fully recognized the enormity of the project ahead and the incredibly primitive conditions in which it would be carried out, was appalled by the Museum's parsimony. He labeled the trustees' offer "disgusting."

As far as Layard was concerned, the letter which accompanied the contract was equally disgusting. In it, the Reverend J. Forshall, the Museum's secretary, lectured Layard on his tasks at Nimrod. The first objective, he said gratuitously, must be "preservation of the monuments." Layard must be "extremely careful not to injure any sculptures, inscriptions, or other objects." Having just discovered the existence of the mounds, the Museum suddenly became the authority on the subject. The Museum was also greedy. "Mr. Layard should be induced to extend his operations beyond the mound of Nimroud," the letter instructed, and it warned him that "it is possible, though perhaps not likely, that he may meet with competition from the agents of the other European powers." Read: France.

The trustees also expressed unconcealed alarm over Layard's famous temper. As the operations would now be conducted on a larger scale, with more workers on the site, giving rise to "more frequent occasions for disputes and discontent, it will be necessary for Mr. Layard . . . if possible, to be more guarded and circumspect than heretofore."

Layard's first reaction was to reject the Museum's contract and the insulting Forshall letter out of hand. But then what? Clearly, he would forfeit his great dream of exploring the mounds. He would jeopardize his intimate relations with Canning and foreclose hope of entering the diplomatic service. In sum, it would mean returning to England a complete failure. From afar, Aunt Sara sensed that her unsettled godson had reached a watershed. "This is the crisis of your career," she wrote and implied that he take up the offer.

Sara Austen was not far from the mark. Layard struggled with the decision for days. But, gorging on his disappointment and hurt pride, he finally accepted the Museum's proposal. Nonetheless, his pride and desire for independence impelled him to strike back at the Museum. He told the trustees to keep his £600 salary and travel expenses. Better still, Layard wrote, he would add that sum to the amount they allocated for the excavation of the mound. He would spend it on equipment and manpower.

Layard's letter made the trustees look like small and unimaginative personnel directors and administrators. They were.

There was a time in which there existed nothing
but darkness and an abyss of waters, in which
resided hideous beings ... among them bulls with
human heads.

—BEROSUS

XXII

On November 1,
1846, Layard reopened excavations at Nimrod on a massive
scale.

The first order of business was to establish a permanent base
camp and recruit workers. For his headquarters, Layard erected
an elaborate house of mud bricks on the outskirts of Nimrod.
Ross, the Baghdad merchant who had joined Layard on his
first inspection of Nimrod, described it in a memoir: "It was
run up in a hurry, the bricks were not properly dried and it
rained before the roof was done, so when it was inhabited
inside walls were quickly clothed with sprouting barley which,
for want of light, grew longer and whiter every day and hung
down the walls in fantastic festoons."

Adjoining the Layard residence was a series of huts built
for his *cawass* and servants. A stable and a "guest house" for
important Arab visitors completed the complex.

In the course of construction, the builders made equidistant
holes in the walls of the buildings, in a style popularized on
the other side of the world in the same period by the Alamo
in Texas. The warlike appearance of the houses was designed
to frighten off Bedouin raiders. Although the bricklayers had
the best of intentions, Layard was horrified. He feared rumors
would get back to Constantinople that he was erecting fortifications at Nimrod—the problem Botta had had at Khorsabad.

(163)

"I immediately ordered the holes filled up," Layard said. But he did not neglect the need for defense in case of Bedouin attack.

Forty workers and their families were ordered to pitch their tents around Layard's camp. Forty more Arab families were instructed to erect their tents atop the mound itself, and the remainder of the Arab work force were directed to peg their tents along the banks of the Tigris, where they busied themselves building keleks for moving the Assyrian relics downstream to Baghdad. The Arab men were all armed.

In addition, with Turkish permission, Layard recruited the *bairakdar,* or standard-bearer of the Turkish irregular garrison at Mosul, "of whose courage I had seen . . . convincing proofs," Layard said. The *bairakdar* was authorized to keep the camp in a state of readiness against Bedouin marauders and to guard whatever art treasures were recovered from the depths of the mound. "He served me faithfully and honestly," Layard wrote years later.

On the mound itself, immediately above the colossal winged lions he had discovered earlier, Layard ordered a barracks built for his fifty Nestorian diggers and their families. He also directed the construction of a godown atop the mound for storing relics.

Quite literally, Layard's camp was a re-creation of the Tower of Babel. Arabs, Kurds, Turks, Christian Chaldeans (Nestorians) and, for good measure, a Jacobite (Syrian), who was a renowned Mosul marble-cutter, made up his work force.

The workers were paid abysmal wages. The wage scale ranged from three to five piasters daily—roughly 13 to 22 cents. But, as Ross put it, "The people about were very poor and only too glad to gain a few piastres by working for Layard." Within a matter of days, Layard recruited 130 workers and an extra couple of dozen guards and servants.

Hormuzd Rassam, now eighteen, Layard's chief of staff, lived in Layard's house and assisted in keeping the books. Layard had implicit faith in him, and among the young Rassam's responsibilities was meeting the weekly payroll. "He soon obtained an extraordinary influence amongst the Arabs," Layard said approvingly, "and his fame spread through the desert."

As an agent of the British Museum, and therefore the crown, Layard was responsible for the disbursement of public funds. His legal training came in handy, and he maintained meticulous ledgers. The cost of establishing the camp was 2,407.20 piasters ($108.31), including 590 piasters for his hovel and those of his workmen; 1,369 piasters for wages, tools, and supplies—wicker baskets, felt, wood, iron screws, mats, and so on.

Layard freely engaged in payola. His workers expected it, it was sound diplomatic policy, and he enjoyed the role of a Santa Claus. Thus, the first monthly financial statement he submitted to the Reverend Forshall and the trustees recorded disbursements such as these: "37.20 piastres for a present to Arab sheikh; 100 piastres for gift for shiekh's daughter; 103.20 piastres for a present to servants for cooking for staff." After having been put down by Layard, Forshall and his associates accepted these expenses without protest.

Layard divided his workers into gangs. Each party contained two to four Chaldean diggers—the strongest and most active men in camp—and between eight and ten Arabs who carted off the earth in baskets. The debris was either piled in fresh heaps atop the mound or flung over the side of the artificial mountain to the desert floor below.

Each team of workers was headed by an overseer, and in the British grand tradition of divide-and-rule, Layard put Arabs of hostile tribes in the same party. "By that means," he said, disarmingly, "I was always made acquainted with what was going on, could easily learn if there were plots brewing, and could detect those who might attempt to appropriate any relics discovered during the excavations."

At sunrise each day, except on Friday, the Moslem Sabbath, the workers gathered at the dig to begin their arduous work. When Layard first put a shovel in his own hand, he found his hands blistered and the work exhausting. But gradually his skin toughened, and in short order he was the equal in stamina and vigor of any of his diggers. At eleven o'clock each morning, dinner (breakfast really) was served on the mound by the children of the laborers. Few workers enjoyed more than a loaf of millet bread. Sometimes the wives of workers surprised their husbands by gathering a few herbs, which were boiled in water with a pinch of salt and dispatched to the dig in wooden bowls. Depending on the condition of their flocks, occasionally sour milk and curds bolstered the men's diet. "The little children, who carried their father's or brother's portion, came merrily along, and sat smiling on the edge of the trenches, or stood gazing in wonder at the sculptures, until they were sent back with the empty platters and bowls," Layard recorded.

Occasionally a Mosul peddler, driving before him a donkey laden with raisins or dried dates, appeared at the dig. "Buying up his store," Layard said, "I would distribute it amongst the men. This largess created immense satisfaction and enthusiasm, which any one, not acquainted with the character of the Arab, might have thought almost more than equivalent of the consideration."

In these pitiful conditions, Layard and his tattered workers assaulted the mound.

Layard attacked Nimrod on all sectors. He darted around the mound, issuing orders, boring holes here, digging trenches there. This, of course, was the era of the shovel and kerosene lamp, and he played the dig by ear. There were no infrared photographs, radioactive isotopes, carbon dating, bulldozers, or forklifts.

The Layard strategy was simple and direct: dig pits until walls were struck and then follow the walls with trenches. With his modest financial resources, Layard could never truly explore each uncovered area. His game plan was to dig around the walls in search of bas-reliefs and sculptures without removing the earth from the center of a chamber or building, a rather primitive manner of excavation. Moreover, he no sooner uncovered a chamber than he quickly explored it and hurriedly filled it in, moving on to a new pit. "Any small objects of great interest may have been left undiscovered," he conceded.* Layard was not entirely to blame, of course; the niggardly Museum was partly responsible for the shambles that ensued.

---

* In 1949, for example, a British expedition recovered thirty additional Nimrod Ivories amid Layard's rubble.

His method of digging left much to be desired. His techniques were not only primitive but crude. They never approached scientific methodology. In some respects Layard's work was disastrous; many inscriptions and art objects were either buried under new avalanches of debris, bypassed completely, or unnecessarily broken into unrecognizable pieces. But this assessment is hindsight. It is unfair commentary. Nonetheless, his helter-skelter *modus operandi* left him open later to the criticism of armchair archaeologists.

After a week into the dig, with rising spirits, November 7, 1846, Layard announced in a letter home: "I am now exploring Assyrian ruins in the neighborhood of Mosul on the Tigris."

Nimrod was about to yield its secrets.

XXIII

In the last century
Sir William Matthew Flinders Petrie, a founder of Egyptology,
complained that too many people exhibit quaint notions about
archaeology. As a case in point, he cited a London matron
who once asked him how she should excavate a ruined town—
should she begin to dig at the top or the side? Petrie winced.
A cake or raised pie was apparently in her mind, and the only
question was where to best reach inside it.

The young matron probably gained her impression about
archaeology from Layard's exploits. Layard simply put his
thumb into Nimrod and pulled out a plum.

His first six weeks of digging, November 1 to December 12,
produced a cornucopia of art. "Scarcely a day passes without
some new and important discovery," Layard wrote in his
journal. "The six weeks following the commencement of
excavations upon a large-scale were amongst [my] most pros-
perous," he said. "My Arabs entered with alacrity into the
work, and felt almost as much interested in its results as I did
myself."

Within that breathless period he discovered three palaces,
twenty-eight immense chambers and halls, thirteen pairs of
colossal man-headed winged bulls and lions, walls covered
with bas-reliefs, the renowned Black Obelisk, and enough
vases, weapons, cuneiform tablets, and Assyrian artifacts to

fill a museum—which he did. The results of his excavations stirred Europe and set in motion an irreversible curiosity about the worlds of the past. Single-handed, he brought to light the first direct link between Assyria and the Old Testament, incontestable evidence of the Bible's historical accuracy. But the deeper he plumbed the mound and the more he discovered, the less he knew.

He was unable to read the cuneiform tablets or the inscriptions on the monuments. He did not understand the symbolism of the Assyrian deities, half-man, half-beast. He did not know who fought whom in the battle scenes which adorned the palace walls. He did not know the names of the palaces or the names of the monarchs who inhabited them.

At one point his workers uncovered a bas-relief and "saw men portrayed upon the wall." A portion of the bas-relief retained its original color, flecks of vermilion. In the pictures, the Assyrians battled against some strange people. Layard's description has a scriptural ring. "The king stands gorgeously attired, in a chariot, drawn . . . by three horses richly caparisoned," Layard said. In the Book of Ezekiel, the sinful Samaria talks of "the Assyrians her neighbors, captains and rulers, clothed most gorgeously, horsemen riding upon horses, all of them desirable young men."

The battle scenes on the bas-reliefs depicted castles and battlements; warriors riding upon horses; the enemy on foot, some wounded, some dead, some in fetters; engineers undermining the walls of an adversary's fortress; engines of war spitting fire; and vultures hovering in the sky above the killing ground. "They are designed with great spirit," Layard marveled, "carefully executed."

Slab after slab was recovered, a nickelodeon in stone, in which a battle unfolded from the first shower of Assyrian arrows to the counting of the dead as an Assyrian scribe, stylus and ledger in hand, counted the number of severed enemy heads piled at his feet.

Not all the bas-reliefs were of battle. There was a scene of a victory banquet, showing butchers butchering a lamb and bakers baking bread. Assyrian boats were shown in rich detail, down to the construction of the vessel's rudder. Layard was amazed: "It is singular that this is precisely the mode adopted by the inhabitants of Mosul to this day when they cross the Tigris in barques, perhaps even more rude than those on the same river three thousand years ago."

As the workers strained to lift one slab from the bottom of a trench, Layard immediately recognized scales of armor. Each scale was separate and was of iron, from 2 to 3 inches in length, rounded at one end and squared at the other with an embossed line in the center, not unlike the mail employed by Crusaders in the Middle Ages.

"The iron was covered with rust," he reported, "and in so decomposed a state, that I had much difficulty in cleansing it from the soil." He collected three baskets of these relics.

Other portions of armor were also found in the pit, some of copper, some of iron, and others of an alloy of copper and iron. Unexpectedly, he came upon an Assyrian helmet in a perfect state of preservation. It was shaped precisely like the pointed helmet represented in the bas-reliefs. Layard touched it and the helmet crumbled before his eyes. Carefully, he collected the fragments. Soon other helmets were found, but they also fell apart on exposure to the fresh air. Helpless to prevent the decay, Layard was heartsickened by these losses. History was being lost as quickly as it was recovered.

Layard also stumbled across thousands of potsherds. Without realizing their value as time-prints of civilization, he and his workers cast them aside—" curious relics," is how Layard described them. On one occasion, however, he felt compelled to collect the fragments, not because he was interested in potsherds but because they bore cuneiform characters. He spent hours trying to match the pieces but found the task "impossible." He put them aside only to return to them again and again. Finally, one evening, under a hot and smoky kerosene lamp he completed the puzzle and, to his surprise, found that the characters were similar to those on some of the pottery Botta had found at Khorsabad. Like a ten-year-old child who remembers each and every stamp in his philatelic collection, Layard filed away in his memory vault every arrow-headed character he came across.

He speculated that the name inscribed on his and Botta's

pottery was the name of some king. And, it was later developed, it was—Sargon the Great.

On another occasion a worker came upon a perfect vase but unfortunately struck it with his pick and broke away the upper part of it. Layard shouted, "Stop!" and leaped into the trench and took the shovel. "Working cautiously myself," he reported, "I was rewarded by the discovery of two small vases, one in alabaster, the other in glass, both in the most perfect preservation, of elegant shape and admirable workmanship."

Whichever way Layard turned on the mound, he entered a new art gallery. Indeed, he grew so accustomed to finding bas-reliefs, sculptures, and cuneiform tablets that sometimes he was blasé. "The shape of this chamber was singular," he reported, adding, "It has two entrances ... nothing of *any* importance was discovered. The slabs were unsculptured, upon each of them was the *usual* inscription" (italics added).

While a party of workers cleared the debris from around the slabs, Layard rushed off to the center of the mound to superintend the excavation of the spot where, earlier, he had discovered his first pair of man-headed, winged bulls, the logo of the Assyrian empire. As he helped clear the rubbish from around the monsters, he discovered that the backs of the bulls were adorned with inscriptions in large and well-formed nail-headed characters. He suspected that the bulls were sentinels who guarded the entrance to a palace or chamber. Accordingly, he ordered a trench dug at right angles to the bulls in the hope of discovering what they protected. The work was hardly under way when his diggers struck a winged figure with a bird's head which towered 14 feet above them. Then they bumped into the beard and one of the five legs of another winged bull, this one carved from an immense block of yellow limestone. Layard was elated "These remains, imperfect as they are, promise better things," he recorded.

But the next several days produced nothing, the only dry spell he encountered during those first forty days of digging. By now the trench extended for 50 feet at a depth of 10 feet. Before abandoning it, Layard decided to continue in another direction. Only minutes after he made his decision, the workers uncovered the corner of a piece of polished black marble.

Tearing away the earth and rubble with shovels and hands, they uncovered a magnificent monolith, 6½ feet in height, lying on its side.

With the aid of ropes, and extra teams of workers, the obelisk was carefully raised from the bottom of the trench. It was sculptured on four sides. There were twenty small bas-reliefs and 210 lines of inscription, which Layard meticulously copied. The obelisk was in a superb state of preservation. "Scarcely a character of the inscription was wanting," Layard said, "and the figures were as sharp and well defined as if they had been carved but a few days before."

The monolith depicted a king, a prisoner at his feet, reviewing a procession of exotic animals—the elephant, the rhinoceros, the two-humped camel, the wild bull and lion, the stag, and various species of anthropoid apes. Layard concluded it had been erected to commemorate the "conquest of India or some country far to the east of Assyria."

The monolith's discovery encouraged Layard to dig deeper and to extend his trenches across the mound. Again his energy and enthusiasm were rewarded. The southeast corner of the mound was a horn of wonders, including a pair of winged lions about 5 feet high and 5 feet long. These lions, moreover, had the usual four legs, not the five legs he found on all the other Nimrod lions and bulls. They were carved from coarse limestone.

Behind the lions was a stone monster, with the head of a vulture, the body and arms of a man, and the tail of a fish. Layard recalled the Biblical description of the god Dagon of the Philistines, a figure with the torso and arms of a man and the head and tail of a fish, before whose altar the people "gathered together to offer a great sacrifice and rejoice [when Samson] bowed himself with all his might against the pillars and buried the lords and the people beneath the ruins of the temple."*

Between the two lions was a pair of crumbling sphinxes. "They differed from all Assyrian sculpture hitherto discovered," Layard said. "Nor could I form any conjecture as to

---

* Contemporary scholars identify the half-man, half-fish creature as the Mesopotamian god Oannes, a precursor of the Greeks' Prometheus.

their original use." They were not in relief, but freestanding. The human heads were beardless, but Layard could not determine whether they represented man or woman. The body of each sphinx, like the great Egyptian sphinx at Giza, on the outskirts of Cairo, was that of a lion. But unlike the Egyptian sphinx, the Assyrian version boasted a pair of graceful wings, forming a platform which Layard suspected was a sacrificial altar. The area around the altar was buried in charcoal, and the fire which obviously had destroyed the temple (he found traces of fire everywhere in the mound) "appears to have raged with extraordinary fury," he observed.

Of the two sphinxes, one was completely damaged and the other worthy of rescue. But both sphinxes proved evanescent.

"I endeavored to secure [the intact one] with rods of iron, and wooden planks; but the alabaster was too much decomposed to resist exposure to the atmosphere," Layard said. "I had scarcely time to make a careful drawing, before the whole fell to pieces; the fragments were too small to admit of their being collected, with a view to future restoration." In the charcoal debris, however, he recovered a small head of alabaster, and to his delight, the body of another winged sphinx— a miniature or model of the large ones that had decomposed.

A few days later workers reported a new find, this time in the northwest corner of the mound—bricks bearing the same cuneiform characters as those Layard had found earlier among the ruins of Kouyunjik opposite Mosul. This discovery linked the traditional site of Nineveh—Kouyunjik—with Nimrod, the suspected site of the real Nineveh. But the discovery left Layard confused.

He had little time to analyze his confusion. As he studied the problem, a cry went up from another part of the mound. Layard hurried off to find a huge slab with an inscription on it, probably the name of a monarch. "I ordered it to be raised with the intention of copying it," he said. Crowbars were employed, and amid the usual grunts, groans, and curses the stele shifted. Layard and his workers were dumfounded, and almost dropped it. Beneath the slab was a narrow earthen sarcophagus and in it a well-preserved skeleton. As they stared at the skeleton, it fell to pieces on exposure to the air.

The trench was lengthened and another earthen sarcophagus was discovered, lined with vessels baked in clay. It contained two skeletons. "Although the skulls were entire when first exposed to view," Layard said with disappointment, "they crumbled into dust as soon as touched, and I was unable to preserve either of them."

These finds baffled Layard completely. The burned walls, the skeletons, the Black Obelisk, the sphinxes—they told a story, but he could not fathom it.

Intuitively, however, he sensed, especially in the Black Obelisk, that he had uncovered one of the great prizes of archaeology. Only later, when the cuneiform code was cracked, would he learn that the monolith was erected in 841 B.C. by Shalmaneser III and showed the Assyrian monarch receiving tribute from five nations, including gifts from Jehu, the son of Omri, king of Judah. Thirteen Israelites were depicted on the stone bearing tribute to the king, including vessels of silver and gold, blocks of tin, and a platter of preserved fruit. In addition to the name Jehu, wonder of wonders, the obelisk also bore the name of Hazael.

In the Book of Kings, Jehu and Hazael were anointed by Elijah, who conveyed the news that they would rule over Israel and Syria. Through the obelisk, Layard had established the first hard link between the Old Testament and the mounds of Mesopotamia.

His discovery was to give new impetus to the gathering strength of the Evangelical movement during the mid-Victorian period. Indirectly, Layard exercised a great influence on the life and times of his age. Layard's discoveries in the bowels of the earth provided additional strength to those who preached the doctrines of man's sinful state and the desperate need for salvation and redemption through Christ. As a prominent Evangelicalist wrote in the aftermath of Layard's discoveries, "We have been confronted with innumerable proofs of the accuracy of Scripture, and the more we compare the records and learn their meaning, the more shall we be convinced that the Bible is indeed the inspired revelation which it claims to be."

But while Layard's discoveries strengthened the forces of

Evangelicalism, they buttressed anti-Catholicism in Victorian England. *Two Babylons,* by the Reverend Alexander Hislop, first published as a pamphlet in Edinburgh in 1853, shortly after Layard resurrected Nineveh, illustrates the point. Hislop quoted from *Nineveh and Its Remains* and *Babylon and Nineveh* to uphold his claim that "Papal worship [is] actually the worship of Nimroud" and that "almost all of the practices of the Roman cult have been brought over from paganism." Hislop is a hardy work; a second American edition was published in 1959.

When Rawlinson, with the help of others, made the initial break-through in deciphering cuneiform, the whole of Europe would be thrown into uproar and confusion. The inscriptions incontrovertibly revealed that Nimrod was Calah, the Calah of Genesis 10:11, and the first of the four cities built after the Flood. But if Nimrod was Calah, and it was, then where was Nineveh?

By means of toil man shall scale the height . . .
And who seeketh fame without toil and strife,
the impossible seeketh and wasteth life.
—THE ARABIAN NIGHTS

XXIV

Layard's work pattern at Nimrod would have exhausted the most indefatigable of explorers. Daily he rose with the sun and after a hasty breakfast spent the remainder of the day in the searing heat superintending the dig, making copies of inscriptions, preparing rubbings of bas-reliefs, arranging for the removal, packing, and shipment of finds. He jumped into freshly dug pits, struggled out of 15-foot trenches, handled the pick and shovel himself as the occasion demanded. Nightly he sat by a hot kerosene lamp comparing the inscriptions in his notes with the paper impressions he had made earlier in the day, finishing rough sketches, going over the camp's accounts with Hormuzd Rassam, ordering supplies from Mosul and Baghdad, handling correspondence with Forshall and the trustees, Canning and Rawlinson, and planning the next day's digging strategy. These tasks were rarely completed before midnight. Exhausted, he fell asleep in his rough-hewn bunk and slept soundly for five solid hours. As the sun's first rays touched down on the barren mound, Layard leaped from bed and embarked on another nineteen-hour work day.

Since Layard alone at Nimrod possessed even a superficial knowledge of "modern" medicine, he quickly acquired the role of country doctor. He himself was frequently downed by fever and chills; yet, the workers and their families had complete confidence in him. He treated them as best he could for trachoma, dysentery, and other chronic West Asian diseases.

He also found himself pressed into the role of justice of the peace whenever fights broke out between rival Arab worker factions or when domestic quarrels erupted. As an outsider, Layard was considered an impartial and a fair tribune. Best of all, perhaps, he did not charge a fee. Thus, it was cheaper to go to him to settle a dispute than appeal, in the usual manner, to the Cadi at Mosul, who exacted compensation for his arbitration.

Domestic fights accounted for most of the disputes. As soon as a worker saved a few piasters, his thoughts turned to the purchase of either new wife, new spear, or new cloak, usually in that order. "The old wife naturally enough raised objections," Layard said, "and picked a quarrel with the intended bride, which generally ended in an appeal to physical force."

Fathers and brothers of the bride-to-be were drawn into the affair to protect the family's honor. Their clan would soon join the fray to protect the tribe's honor. "I had almost nightly to settle such questions as these," Layard said. Rassam, who had obtained extraordinary influence over the Arabs as Layard's purser, sat at his elbow and provided the background to each dispute. "Only on one occasion," Layard said, "did either of the parties refuse to abide by my decision."

Free spirit himself, Layard also recognized that all work and no play would make his workers restless, if not dull. "I frequently feasted the workmen," he said, "and sometimes their wives and daughters were invited to separate entertainments, as they would not eat in public with the men." And the workers sometimes organized a party of their own. After the day's work, Kurdish musicians frequently strolled through the camp and spontaneous dances were the order of the night. The dances lasted through a greater part of the evening, and Layard often felt compelled to exhort his men to get rest and save energy for the next day's work. Occasionally, the sheik of a neighboring desert tribe visited Nimrod. Around campfires, the sheik and his lieutenants would pass the latest gossip, news of vendettas, plundering expeditions, and assorted tidbits. By nature the Arabs are great storytellers, and Layard listened with enthusiasm.

When the nomads moved on, they in turn spread tales about the great wonders disgorged daily from Nimrod and about the all-powerful Frank who had been befriended by a jinn and had learned the secrets of the mound. Like a windstorm, these stories swept across the desert, and Layard's "guest house" was almost perpetually occupied by visiting sheiks and others.

Often Layard's impoverished Arab workers entertained him at a "feast," a term pathetically misused in this instance. If a worker saved enough piasters to buy a handful of raisins or a piece of camel meat, or if he had a cow which occasionally yielded butter or sour milk, he would immediately summon his co-workers and Layard to share in the good fortune. "The whole dinner, perhaps, consisted of a half a dozen dates or raisins spread out wide, to make the best show, upon a corn-sack; a pat of butter upon a corner of a flat loaf; and a few cakes of dough baked in the ashes," Layard said, describing such an occasion. "And yet the repast was ushered in with every solemnity;—the host turned his dirty keffiah, or head-kerchief, and his cloak, in order to look clean and smart; and appeared both proud of the honor conferred upon him, and of his means to meet it in a proper fashion."

Layard knew and appreciated the meaning of poverty. His ability to empathize with downtrodden people largely accounted for his extraordinary acceptance in western Asia's melting pots. Although a Christian and a Frank, his workers spoke of him as "one of us."

"I endeavored, as far as it was in my power, to create a good feeling amongst all, and to obtain their willing co-operation in my work," Layard said. "I believe I was to some extent successful."

Canning, Rawlinson, and the British Museum were delighted with Layard's stream of play-by-play reports on his discoveries and urged him to ship the treasures with dispatch. Botta's relics were still at Baghdad awaiting a French sloop-of-war. The British could still beat the Louvre to the first exhibit in the Western world of the Ninevite treasures—if only

Layard would make haste in floating the objects down the Tigris to Baghdad.

These appeals coincided with the spread of Layard's fame through the desert and the increasingly wild tales that he had found gold at Nimrod. Several Bedouin tribes considered a raid against Layard's isolated encampment a potentially profitable enterprise. Layard got wind of the plans and kept his *bairakdar* on red alert.

By early December Nimrod's godown was bursting with so many sculptures, bas-reliefs, and other relics that Layard considered the moment propitious to send a convoy of treasures downstream. He rode to Mosul for supplies—mats, felts, and ropes. These were sent by raft to Nimrod while Layard returned to base by fresh horse to superintend the movement of the treasures to the bank of the river.

The supply convoy, however, never arrived. En route from Mosul, the rafts were attacked and plundered by Bedouin marauders. Layard appealed to Mosul's governor to track down the culprits and recover his property. The appeal was in vain. "The Arabs of the desert," the Turkish governor said, "are beyond our reach." Although the loss amounted to only a few pounds, Layard considered his situation precarious. "If this robbery passed unnoticed," he said later, "the remainder of my property, and even my person, might run some risk." He foresaw a Bedouin attack on Nimrod itself, and an end to the excavations.

Several days later, Layard learned the name and location of the band that had pillaged the convoy. Accompanied by the *bairakdar* and another irregular both heavily armed—Layard rode straight for the Bedouin encampment. The ensuing swashbuckling action belongs in Rafael Sabatini.

"We reached the encampment after a long ride," Layard said, "and found the number of the Arabs to be greater than I expected."

Layard's audacity stunned the Bedouins. No stranger, certainly no Frank, dare enter their turf.

"Peace be with you!" Layard signaled as he dismounted in front of the sheik's tent. "I know the laws of friendship; that

which is my property is your property, and the contrary."
Politely, he asked for the return of his stolen supplies. The
sheik feigned ignorance. "O Bey," he replied, "no such things
as mats, felts, or ropes, have ever been in my tents." As he
spoke, Layard noticed a new rope supporting the principal
pole in the sheik's tent.

At a prearranged signal, Layard, the *bairakdar*, and the
irregular drew cocked pistols, handcuffed the sheik, pointed
a gun at his temple, rushed out of the tent, mounted their
mares, and dragged the sheik after them at "an uncomfortable
pace," with guns trained on him.

Layard's impudence paralyzed the sheik's followers. The
sheik was taken to Nimrod, where he was given the option of
freely returning the supplies or being handed over to the
Turkish authorities at Mosul. With visions of the bastinado,
the sheik quickly acquiesced to Layard's demand. The following day all supplies were returned together with a lamb and
a kid as a good-will gesture. "I dismissed the Sheikh with a
lecture," Layard said, "and had afterwards no reason to
complain of his tribe—nor indeed of any tribes in the neighborhood."

Among the recovered supplies, he noted in a ledger entry
dated December 18, 1846, were three dozen pencils, one pound
of glue, ten sheets of double elephant paper, seven quires of
drawing paper, two "black lead rubbers," and four pieces of
India rubber together with a set of instructions from the British
Museum on how to make rubbings.

A week later, Christmas Day, he recorded the "satisfaction"
of seeing the twenty-three cases, including the obelisk, floating
downriver. As the treasures disappeared around a bend, he
was overcome by reverie.

"I could not forbear musing upon the strange destiny of
their burdens," he said. After adorning the palaces of Assyrian
kings, the obelisk and other works of art had been buried
unknown for centuries beneath a soil trodden by Persians
under Cyrus the Great, by Greeks under Alexander the Great,
and by Arabs under the first descendants of Mohammed, their
prophet. Now the treasures would cross the most distant seas
of the southern hemisphere and wind up in the austere halls

of the British Museum. "Who can venture to foretell how their strange career will end?" Layard mused. (Miraculously, the British Museum and its treasures would escape the horrors of the London Blitz.)

As the keleks vanished from sight, Layard mounted his mare and galloped off to Mosul to celebrate the Feast of the Nativity with the few Europeans "whom duty or business had collected in this remote corner of the globe." His hosts, Christian Rassam, the consul, and his wife Matilda, prepared a banquet for the occasion.

But Layard worked even through Christmas week. He completed notes, wrote up his account ledgers, redrew his map of Nimrod, and dispatched a lengthy report to London on his work.

The trustees were delighted with his work and directed their secretary, the Reverend Forshall, "to express to Mr. Layard the satisfaction of the Trustees with the progress he is making and to enquire as to the intentions of Mr. Layard respecting the manner and time of conveying these cases to England in order that the antiquities may be insured against sea risque."

The year before, Layard had spent Christmas with Rawlinson. Now with the Rassams. Perhaps he would spend next Christmas at Constantinople, or even London.

How long shall Ashur take you away?
—NUMBERS

XXV

On New Year's Day, 1847, Layard returned to Nimrod refreshed by the week's holiday at Mosul and eager to get on with the excavations. He dug with great expectations and was not disappointed. Indeed, in a two-volume account of the operation, he wrote, "I should weary the reader, were I to describe, step by step, the progress of the work. . . . The labors of one day resembled those of the preceding; [and] it would be difficult to convey to others an idea of the excitement which was produced by the constant discovery of objects." A day rarely passed that a *kakhaneh*, or work gang, did not summon Layard to gaze on a new wonder.

This assessment is supported by independent sources, including occasional visitors to the mound, such as the trader Ross and J. A. Longworth, the foreign correspondent of the London *Morning Journal* and Layard's companion during his Constantinople capers. It was also confirmed by the notes of the trustees of the British Museum.

Perhaps no stronger evidence of Layard's incredible successes may be found than in a letter to him from the Reverend Forshall. "[We] desire to compensate you upon your happy success," Forshall wrote, and announced that over Layard's objections about receiving payment for his work, the Museum had deposited £500 to his personal bank account as compensation for a job "well done."

Longworth's first dispatch from Nimrod, meanwhile, caused a sensation in London. Until then, the general public had the impression that Layard was excavating aboveground ruins, somewhat along the lines of Pompeii or the pyramids of Egypt. Except for a handful of insiders, nobody conceived of ruins hidden underground.

"I should begin by stating that the ruins are all under ground," Longworth wrote in his first dispatch datelined from Nimrod. To the amazement of his readers, he hastily explained that Layard was digging a complex of trenches and tunnels at a depth of 15 feet and more to reach the treasures. "The time of day when I first descended into these chambers happened to be towards evening; the shades of which, no doubt, added to the awe and mystery of the surrounding objects," he wrote. "It was of course with no little excitement that I suddenly found myself in the magnificent abode of the old Assyrian kings; where, moreover, it needed not the slightest effort of imagination to conjure up visions of their long departed power and greatness."

In detail, Longworth described the nature of the monsters who inhabited the core of the mound, the vulture-headed humans, with long dropping wings, winged bulls and lions with bearded, human faces. These were the idols of a religion long since dead and buried like the figures themselves. Now they suddenly raised their heads from the sleep of millenniums. "Certainly the feeling of awe which they inspired me with," Longworth conceded, "must have been something akin to that experienced by their heathen votaries of old."

Longworth's dispatches resulted in Layard's first fan mail. "How gaily you are getting on with your winged-lions," a friend wrote in admiration. Another letter writer hailed him "as an example of patriotism and archaeolgy."

When Layard's convoy of rafts, bearing the first shipment of sculptures and inscriptions, reached Baghdad safely, Rawlinson was overwhelmed. Since the "marbles" belonged to the British Museum, he hastily wrote Forshall on January 27, 1847, for permission to write up the discoveries for scholarly journals. "Naturally I am anxious to communicate this information to the world," he said.

The trustees were delighted. They directed Forshall to "acquaint Major Rawlinson that he is at liberty to make any use as he thinks proper of the information he derived from the Antiquities which passed through his hands and that it is gratifying to the Trustees to hope that by means of Major Rawlinson's search, these antiquities may be soon made to contribute to the increase of historical knowledge."

When Canning learned how hard Layard was driving himself, he expressed alarm. "There is nothing," he wrote Layard from London February 9, "like taking things in time." But Botta, in a *"mon cher* Layard" note, congratulated his English friend and encouraged him to press ahead.

And onward Layard pressed.

In the very first week of the new year he discovered eight new chambers with bas-reliefs. "They excel all those that had yet been discovered," Layard reported in his journal. Among the scenes were winged priestesses bearing garlands in one hand and raising the other hand as if in some act of adoration; lion and stag-hunting vignettes; strange creatures of various shapes and sizes, all equipped with wings; and figures of eagle-headed humans. As an art student, Layard was captivated by the bas-reliefs, especially those which still retained their original color—blues, reds, whites, yellows, and black. Green and purple, he noted with surprise, were completely lacking, although Assyrian painters, with their color wheels, must have known of their existence. The favorite colors of the Assyrians were blue and yellow.

During this second phase of the Nimrod dig, Layard made a remarkable discovery—a number of strange, white-yellow ornaments of "considerable beauty and interest." The objects, when uncovered, adhered firmly to the soil and were in so advanced a state of decomposition that Layard encountered great difficulty in extracting them, even in fragments. "I spent hours lying on the ground, separating them with a penknife, from the rubbish by which they were surrounded. . . . With all the care that I could devote to the collection of the fragments, many were lost, or remained unperceived, in the immense heap of rubbish under which they were buried."

After spending most of the day on his hands and knees in

a trench some 20 feet below the earth, gathering up these curiosities, Layard retired to his shack and spent the night trying to piece them together and to determine their composition. Ross made one of his irregular visits to Nimrod at this time and joined in the game. "We often sat up at night trying to piece bits of inscriptions together," Ross said in a memoir published posthumously by his wife Janet in 1902. "But the greatest puzzle we ever had were strange bits of what seemed to be brittle whitish stone or porcelain."

"In vain they were turned and twisted," Ross wrote, "until one night the light fell at an angle on a splinter I had in my hand, and I recognized the waving texture of ivory." These were the fabulous Nimrod Ivories. They rank today among the world's greatest archaeological treasures.

When the objects reached England, chemists at once saw that age had completely broken down the animal gluten, leaving nothing but the calcerous substance of the ivory. Museum officials boiled the fragments in a glutinous compound—a form of Jello—and restored what centuries of burial had exhausted. The work of restoration was so admirable that when Layard ultimately returned to England, he hardly believed his eyes.

The most important of the ivories contained Egyptian hieroglyphics, a royal cartouche, and the solar disk of Akhenaten, the heretic monotheist pharaoh who, before Moses, smashed the idols of Egypt and proclaimed the existence of one God. The hieroglyphics were inlaid with blue and opaque green pastes and were intended to imitate lapis lazuli and feldspar.

Layard also discovered in those first weeks of 1847 numerous clay-baked vessels containing human remains. The sarcophagi were generally bowl-shaped. "In nearly all were earthen vases, copper and silver ornaments, lachrymatories and small alabaster bottles," he said. He was able to preserve two skulls, although most of the remains crumbled on exposure to the air.

Among the coffins he found a well-constructed tomb, built of bricks and covered with a slab of alabaster, apparently the grave of a person of high rank. He sifted the human dust through his hands and found beads and small ornaments

belonging to a necklace. The beads consisted of agate, carnelian, amethyst, and opaque colored glass. The prize was a
magnificent lapis lazuli pendant shaped as a couchant lion.
He also found copper ornaments. "I carefully collected and
preserved these interesting remains," he said. Layard speculated that the remains were those of a woman. Who was she?
A queen? A princess? A priestess? Once again Layard felt
frustrated. "I wish I had read more before I started out," he
told Ross. "Half the value of my journey is lost through
ignorance. At what period were these tombs made?" he raged.

Another set of tombs equally mystified him. They were
discovered atop the ruins of one of the Nimrod palaces. On
top? How could tombs be located on the roof of a building?
It made no sense, nor would it for almost another generation—
until archaeologists came to appreciate that one of the curiosities of urban civilization is that cities are built on top of
cities, the present city rising on the dust and rubbish of the
previous generation, century, or millennium.

War, the most grisly of man's pursuits, also appeared to be
the inescapable handmaiden of civilization. Layard was fascinated by the modernity of the Assyrian war machine. They
were masters of block and tackle, and possessed a detailed
knowledge of leverage. These skills were demonstrated on
bas-reliefs showing the Assyrian engineering corps in action,
employing battering rams, flame throwers, wall-scaling ma-
chines, catapults, and the like.

Some of Layard's discoveries were breathtaking, among them
the large ceremonial hall to a palace whose entrance was
formed by gigantic winged bulls and lions. Between them
stood a pair of *double* sphinxes, something he had not found
before (nor has anyone since). The sphinxes were carved out
of coarse, gray limestone.

Every wall of the huge hall had been scorched by flames.
Clearly, the whole of Nimrod had been put to the torch in
antiquity. The smoke and cinders of the city's desctruction
spread over Mesopotamia like an ominous mushroom-shaped
cloud.

One evening, after a particularly exhausting day, an old
desert nomad arrived at the dig and spent the night with

Layard's workers. Nimrod's idols and jinns did not impress him. The Arab said he had seen the same thing at Khalah Sharghat years before. Layard, who had visited that mound two years earlier and returned to Mosul empty-handed, attributed his tale to "the fertile imagination of the Arabs." But the man persisted and wagered that he could show Layard the exact spot of one great piece of sculpture, carved in black stone.

Layard accepted the bet. Khalah Sharghat, he recalled from his first visit there, was infested by Bedouin marauders, notoriously dangerous. Nonetheless, he felt the marbles worth the game, especially since the latest reports indicated that a friendly and powerful sheik had pitched his tents near the mound. Accordingly, Layard sent ahead a small reconnaisance party while he led a well-armed column, including Rassam and his *bairakdar*, to the spot, several miles south of Nimrod.

En route they passed bitumen pits which dotted the desert. "They cover a considerable extent of ground," Layard said, "the bitumen bubbling up in springs from crevices in the earth." The area today marks one of the great oilfields of modern Iraq.

Layard's party found the friendly Arab encampment about 10 miles from Khalah Sharghat. The great mound was visible from this spot, rising high above the scrub jungle that clothes both banks of the Tigris in northern Mesopotamia.

The sheik warmly greeted the Frank and his party and showed the Englishman off to his harem and even to his sister, "whose beauty I had often heard extolled," Layard said. She was more than worthy of her reputation, and Layard recorded with surprise, "She is still unmarried."

In the afternoon of their arrival they rode to the mound. "Hares, wolves, foxes, jackals, and wild boars continually crossed our path," Layard wrote, "and game of all kinds seemed to abound." There were also tracks of lions, the area marking the northern limit of their habitat along the Tigris.

The old Arab storyteller won his bet. He directed Layard's workers to a particular spot, and after an hour's digging they uncovered a sitting figure in black basalt, the head and hands missing. It was a beautiful piece of sculpture. The square block of stone upon which the figure sat was covered on three sides with cuneiform. Layard did not know it at the time, but the figure was that of the Biblical king of Assyria, Shalmaneser II. It was novel in one respect. It was the first life-sized figure of an Assyrian Layard had ever seen. All the other figures were either miniatures or colossi.

Impressed by the discovery, Layard ordered trenches dug at right angles to the statue. His workers soon came upon walls, bits of basalt with small figures in reliefs, portions of cuneiform-covered slabs, and a series of now familiar tombs, shaped like dish covers.

In one coffin he found a superb copper cup, identical to one he saw held by a king in a bas-relief at Nimrod. The cup linked Nimrod and Khalah Sharghat.

Studying the mound with the eye of a seasoned excavator, Layard suddenly understood the general plan of these Assyrian complexes. "The principal ruin at Khalah Sherghat, as at Nimroud, Khorsabad, and on other ancient Assyrian sites, is a large square mound, surmounted by a cone or pyramid," he said.

Actually this was the terraced ziggurat, or temple tower, a distinctive feature of Assyrian and Babylonian temples, that Layard was to learn a great deal more about during the course of his excavations.

On the second night, Layard recorded, "a violent storm broke over us; the wind rose to a hurricane—the rain descended in torrents—the thunder rolled in one long peal—and the vivid streams of lightning, almost incessant, showed the surrounding landscape. When the storm had abated, I walked to a short distance from the tents to gaze upon the scene. The huge fire we had kindled, threw a lurid glare over the trees around our encampment. The great mound could be distinguished through the gloom, rising like a distant mountain against the dark sky. From all sides came the melancholy wail of the jackals—thousands of these animals having issued from their subterranean dwellings in the ruins, as soon as the last gleam of twilight was fading in the western horizon. The owl, perched on the old masonry, occasionally sent forth its mournful note. The shrill laugh of the Arabs would sometimes rise above the cry of the jackal. Then all earthly noises were buried in the deep roll of the distant thunder. It was desolation such as those alone who witnessed such scenes can know. . . ."

Layard was convinced that if he dug deeply he would make a spectacular discovery. But he lacked the manpower to do the job. He didn't even have the means of transporting the black basalt figure to Nimrod and had to leave it where he found it.

The sideshow at Khalah Sharghat had eaten up more of his limited financial resources. Yet, he rationalized, the excursion and expenditure was in line with Forshall's instructions that he establish Britain's prior claim to excavate at as many different sites as possible. If nothing else, he had at least short-circuited the French at Khalah Sharghat.

"I renounced the further examination of these ruins with regret," he said. "I have little doubt, from the fragments discovered, that many objects of interest, if not sculptured slabs, exist in the mound."

As he departed, he speculated about the mound's identity in antiquity. Judging by the fragments he found, as compared to those at Nimrod, he concluded—rightly—that the mound was "one of the most ancient cities of Assyria." He thought that it was either Calah or Ur, the lost Chaldean city of Abraham.

It would have boggled his mind to know the true name of the mound. Khalah Sharghat was Ashur, the first capital of the Assyrian empire.

Semiramis quarried out a stone . . .
and this she hauled . . .
to the river and there loaded it on a raft.
—DIODORUS

XXVI The spring of 1847
advanced rapidly across the land between the two rivers,
accompanied by severe drought. The water level of the Tigris
sank, and Bedouin raiders, driven from their waterholes deep
in the desert, encroached upon more permanent settlements,
including the villages near Nimrod. Not only were the Bedouins moving too close for comfort, but in the light of crop
failures, the peaceful Arab tribes, from among whom Layard
recruited most of his manual labor, planned to move north to
Mosul and beyond in search of water.

Once these tribes departed, Layard surmised, "the country
would not be only very unsafe but almost uninhabitable and
I should be compelled to leave Nimroud."

In this situation, Layard decided to terminate his excavations
and focus on shipping his treasures to England.

To their credit, Forshall and the trustees of the Museum did
not expect Layard to remove the winged bulls and lions from
the mound. Botta had tried to do so at Kharsabad, they were
aware, and the results were disastrous. Botta left one winged
bull abandoned on the road between the mound and the Tigris.
The other, which he had sawed into pieces, was still sitting
in the sun at Baghdad awaiting a French vessel. In any case,
the idea of sawing the winged colossi offended the British
Museum's artistic sensibilities, and Layard was instructed to
leave the fabulous creatures *in situ* and cover them with earth.

"I was loath, however, to leave all these fine specimens of

Assyrian sculpture behind me," Layard said. His credibility was at stake. If he returned to London without these grand prizes, he was afraid that people would be "half-inclined to believe that I have dreamed a dream, or have listened to some tale of Eastern romance."

But how could he get the gargantuan statuary to London? The answer, he felt, was in the classics. Specifically, in the writings of Diodorous. "Semiramis, the Assyrian queen," Diodorous wrote in 50 B.C., "quarried out a stone from the mountains of Armenia which was 135 feet long and 25 feet wide and thick; and this she hauled by means of many multitudes of yokes of mules and oxen to the river and there loaded it on a raft, on which she brought it down the stream to Babylonia."

If Semiramis could move the stones in antiquity, why couldn't Layard do the same some three thousand years later? "I resolved," he said, "upon attempting the removal and embarkation of two of [them]."

From among the thirteen pairs of human-headed winged bulls and lions, Layard selected one bull and one lion, the smallest and best preserved, each about 14 feet in height and weighing about ten tons.

A working party was sent into the mountains north of Mosul to fell mulberry trees, the same trees employed by the Assyrians in the construction of roof beams for their palaces and fortifications. Layard also acquired the rusty iron axles Botta had used in transporting his sawn blocks to the Tigris. Each wheel was constructed from three solid pieces of wood, nearly a foot thick, and bound together, like a beer barrel, with iron hoops. Beams were laid across the axles and, in turn, cross-beams above them.

"Simple as this cart was," Layard said, "it became an object of wonder in the town." Like Lilliputians, crowds of Mosul residents gathered daily to inspect the gargantuan cart. When the cart, drawn by a team of bulls, was ready to leave the city, a local holiday was proclaimed. The governor's indolent aides lifted themselves from their divans; guards abandoned posts; bazaars were emptied; and half the population of the town assembled at the gates of Mosul to witness the spectacle.

Layard ordered the digging of a trench some 200 feet long and 15 to 20 feet wide from the base of the colossi to the plain below. He also directed the construction of a miniature railroad bed of greased roller ties over which to move the sculptures through the massive trench to the waiting cart. Incredibly, the Nimrod mound was so rich in archaeological treasure that in the midst of this new flurry of digging, Layard discovered another chamber and new slabs of magnificent bas-reliefs.

From Baghdad, with the compliments of Lieutenant Jones and the Royal Indian Navy, Rawlinson shipped Layard naval spares, including hawsers, jackscrews, blocks, and tackle. While waiting for the shipment to arrive overland, Layard superintended the packaging of the colossi. They were mummy-wrapped in felt and mats to protect them as far as possible from injury during transport.

By mid-March all was in readiness. The bull was the first to be moved. The earth and debris around the foundation were scooped away; thick beams were placed against the bull to support it; and a myriad of ropes were made fast around its waist. Layard's three-hundred-man work force was now augmented by large numbers of Arab horsemen who descended, out of curiosity, to lend a hand.

Layard took a position on a high pile of earth overlooking the pit containing the bull, from where he planned to orchestrate the operation. "It was a moment of great anxiety," Layard said. And also of great din. There was so much noise that Layard could not be heard above the tumult and, in desperation, threw bricks and clods of earth at the working parties to draw their attention. "But," he conceded, "it was to no avail."

As the operation got under way, the drums and shrill pipes of the Kurds sounded like the advance of Scottish infantry; Arab workers, stripped to the waist in the broiling sun and half frantic with excitement, raised chilling war cries; women and children congregated on the sidelines shouting encouragement to the men.

The wedges were knocked away from the bull and the Arab workers strained to hold the ropes as it began to tilt over. Frantically, the Chaldeans threw water on the ropes to ease the strain, but the hawsers snapped like kite string and the workers holding the ends were catapulted backwards, like acrobats. The bull toppled from its foundation, and a cloud of dust swirled up from the bottom of the trench. "I rushed into the trenches," Layard said, "prepared to find the bull in many pieces."

The gods of Assyria, however, hovered over the dig: the bull was not damaged. "I saw it lying precisely where I had wished to place it," Layard said, "and uninjured!"

The Kurdish pipes and drums started up again, the women shouted and clapped hands, and the workers danced with joy. The sun was going down and the occasion demanded a party. Several lambs and cows were slaughtered, boiled, and roasted. Despite Layard's exhortations, the workers danced until dawn as if to demonstrate their ability to resist fatigue.

The following morning the bull was skillfully moved over the greased rollers and, as the stone monster reached the bottom of the mound, lowered safely onto the waiting cart. The oxen harnessed to the yoke, however, felt the enormous weight behind them and refused to budge. They were replaced by several hundred men, who proceeded to haul the great cart across the scrub desert.

With the *bairakdar* at his side, Layard rode at the head of the colorful procession. Then came the Kurdish pipers and drummers, followed by the cart itself. Tracking behind the vehicle were the women and children, shouting encouragement. The procession was closed by a troop of Arab horsemen who executed daring field maneuvers, raising swirls of sand as they raced up and down the column, their tufted spears held high, simulating cavalry charges.

Abruptly, the procession came to a dead halt. Two cart wheels sank in a rut, and every effort to dislodge them failed. Ropes snapped, men cursed. The sun set. Layard called it a day and left behind his *bairakdar* and a company of armed Arabs as custodians lest some Bedouin raiders make an effort in the middle of the night to steal the ropes, mats, and felts.

"My suspicions did not prove unfounded," Layard later reminisced. Scarcely had he returned to the base camp when rifle fire crackled across the desert wasteland. Hastening back to the mired bull, Layard discovered that a band of Bedouins had been driven off after a sharp exchange of musketry. One ball passed through the matting and felt and left its mark on the side of the bull.*

The following morning after hours of backing and filling, the cart finally resumed its journey to the Tigris—and made it. It was a prodigious accomplishment.

In a letter to his mother, Layard expressed satisfaction with his work. "I have just moved one of my great winged bulls to the river and he is now ready to be embarked. I have succeeded in my attempt," he gloated, "while the French bull is still sticking half-way between the river and Khorsabad."

Next he set to work on the lion. To avoid a second spill, he doubled the number of ropes. Again, while clearing the rubble from around the base of the lion, he made a new discovery, inscribed slabs. Two days later the lion was sitting on the bank of the Tigris as complacently as the lions of Trafalgar Square.

While these activities were in progress, Layard directed another party of workers to build two enormous rafts, each consisting of six hundred inflated goat and sheep skins, for the more than 500-mile journey downstream from Nimrod to Basra, at the mouth of the Tigris. Layard estimated it would take about ten days for the rafts to negotiate the rapids and currents to Baghdad and another two weeks or more to complete the second leg of the journey from Baghdad to Basra, largely because the last 60 miles was a tidal current, ebbing and flowing alternately every six hours.

On April 20 there was a slight rise in the level of the river, and Layard rushed to exploit it. Very much in the style of launching a boat on a well-greased slipway, the bull and lion were slid onto the rafts as hundreds of workers held back their rapid descent with ropes. Two days later the keleks were

---

* In London, at the British Museum, I was amused to notice, while inspecting the Museum's Nimrod Gallery, that the bullet scar is still clearly visible on the bull. Almost a century later, in 1934, Seton Lloyd, a British archaeologist, conducted a similar operation in connection with the transport to Baghdad of the last two bulls discovered at Khorsabad (they were discovered by a University of Chicago expedition). Lloyd had at his disposal considerable horsepower, including twenty-ton earth-moving vehicles. Even so, it was a massive undertaking and in his account of the operation, in quiet admiration, Lloyd described Layard's feat as "formidable."

pushed offshore and sent on their way—at the mercy of the gods.

"I beg to inform you," Layard wrote Canning on May 3, "that the two large sculptures, the bull and the lion, were safely placed on rafts and floated down the river." Six weeks later he submitted an expense account to the British Museum. The operation had cost 9,560 piasters (less than $500), including 1,156 piasters for wood, 335 piasters for guards to accompany the rafts, and 45 piasters for steersmen.

For all practical purposes, the work at Nimrod was completed. Not too soon, either. Thereafter, almost daily, Bedouin raiding parties were reported near the mound. "We were still too strong to fear the Bedouins," Layard said, "but I was compelled to put my house into a complete state of defense and to keep patrols round my premises during the night to avoid surprise." A small settlement within sight of the mound was attacked by a band of Bedouins at the end of May, and several villagers were killed.

In May, Layard brought the Nimrod excavations to an end when, in accordance with the instructions of the Museum's trustees, he began to fill in the trenches and pits and cover up the winged figures and bas-reliefs he was compelled to leave behind. The precaution was necessary to preserve the sculptures not only from the weather but also from the clubs of Bedouin marauders and other Moslem zealots who were always quick to smash the idols of unbelievers. He also leveled his huts and fortifications. When the trenches were filled, the mound reverted to its former appearance, a barren, windswept escarpment.

"Some, who may hereafter tread on the spot when the grass again grows over the ruins of the Assyrian palaces," Layard wrote, "may indeed suspect that I have been relating a vision."

He was unhappy about leaving Nimrod. The ruins, he felt, had been "very inadequately" explored, he wrote in his diary. "[I] left a great part of the mound of Nimroud to be explored by those who may hereafter succeed me in the examination of the ruins of Assyria."*

* A century later the British School of Archaeology in Iraq, headed by M. E. L. Mallowan, resumed the work left behind by Layard, and dug up anew the objects he had buried.

Closing down the camp gave Layard and those around him a time for reflection. The shiek whom he had visited at Khalah Sharghat confessed that he was mystified. "In the name of the Most High, tell me, O Bey," he asked Layard, "what are you going to do with those stones? So many thousands of purses spent upon such things! Can it be, as you say, that your people learn wisdom from them; or is it, as his reverence the Cadi declares, that they are to go to the palace of your Queen, who, with the rest of the unbelievers, worships these idols?

"As for wisdom," the sheik continued, "these figures will not teach you to make any better knives, or scissors, or chintzes, and it is in the making of those things that the English show their wisdom."

But something far deeper disturbed the sheik.

"Here are stones which have been buried ever since the time of the holy Noah,—peace be with him!" the sheik said. "Perhaps they were under ground before the Deluge. I have lived on these lands for years. My father, and the father of my father, pitched their tents here before me; but they never heard of these figures. . . . Lo! here comes a Frank from many days' journey off, and he walks up to the very place, and he takes a stick and makes a line here, and makes a line there. Here, says he, is the palace; there, says he, is the gate; and he shows us what has been all our lives beneath our feet, without our having known anything about it. Wonderful! wonderful! Is it by books, is it by magic, is it by your prophets, that you have learnt these things? Speak, O Bey; tell me the secret of wisdom!"

Halfway to Mosul the road crossed a low hill, and from its crest both the town and the ruins were clearly visible. The long, dark and brooding line of mounds moved Layard deeply. He reined up his horse and looked upon them for the last time.

Then, never glancing backwards for fear he would awake from his dream, he galloped toward Mosul.

The men of Nineveh will arise.
—ST. LUKE

XXVII Back in Mosul, however, the mounds on the left bank continued to fascinate Layard. So thrifty had he been at Nimrod that he still had a little money left from the Museum's meager funds. "I proposed, therefore, to devote my last piasters to an examination of the ruins opposite Mosul," he said, "particularly the great mound of Kouyunjik."

After more than a year of digging, Layard still had not discovered the true site of Nineveh. Now, though he would not know it for some time to come, he was about to realize a lifelong dream. Kouyunjik had proved elusive to everyone who had dug there. When Guillois, the French consul, had heard of Layard's incredible successes at Nimrod, he had resumed digging at Kouyunjik, but, like Botta and Layard before him, he turned up nothing. He would dig a few feet at one spot, find nothing, and then go off in another direction and dig another hole. By the time Layard reappeared in Mosul, Kouyunjik resembled a Swiss cheese.

But the discovery of the "pyramid" or ziggurat at Nimrod and Khalah Sharghat had provided Layard with the ultimate clue. When he retackled Kouyunjik in June, he was convinced more than ever that great treasures were locked within the mound, palaces and sculptures that had eluded the spade because no one understood how the Assyrians built their acropoli.

Poking around the "pyramid" at Nimrod, Layard had learned the secret of digging up a Mesopotamian mound, a secret exploited to this day by contemporary archaeologists. Whenever the Assyrians erected a palace or temple complex they first constructed a platform of sun-dried bricks 30 to 40 feet above sea level. When the Assyrian acropoli were overrun and destroyed, the ruins remained on top of the platform and in time were covered by wind-blown sand and dust, forming great artificial mounds. "Consequently," Layard reasoned, "in digging for remains, the first step is to search for the platform of sun-dried bricks. When this is discovered, the trenches must be opened to the level of it, and no deeper."

At Kouyunjik, Layard put his men to work in search of the platform rather than sculptures and inscriptions. He was becoming a sophisticated excavator. After several days of digging he struck pay dirt, a platform of unbaked bricks some 20 feet below the crest of the mound. Guillois, who had fruitlessly combed the mound for almost eight months, was incensed.

While the dig was in progress, Layard returned to Mosul to write up his reports to Canning and Forshall. Before departing, however, he left standing orders that if sculptures were found, the first person to reach him with the news would be rewarded.

"One morning, as I was in Mosul," he said later, "two Arab women came to me and announced that sculptures had been discovered." As Layard paid the reward, one of his principal overseers, a corpulent Arab, came panting into the house with the same news. "I rode immediately to the ruins," Layard said.

By the time he got there his workers had reached the entrance to a chamber and had uncovered a sculptured slab which had been almost completely destroyed by fire. Layard directed the men to follow the burnt wall. Soon they stumbled across a foyer formed by enormous winged bulls, the largest Layard had ever seen, almost 17 feet in height. By mid-June, Layard had opened nine chambers, each fire-damaged. Many of the sculptures and reliefs had been defaced, apparently hacked by an enraged mob or a revengeful adversary. The architecture and sculptures closely resembled those found in the palaces of Khorsabad and Nimrod. But there was a notable difference. Everything at Kouyunjik was on a grander scale. The figures in the bas-reliefs, for example, stood fully 10 feet high. "Kouyunjik yields to no other known monument in Assyria," Layard declared.

Whichever direction he dug, new sculptures emerged, among them, four pairs of fantastic man-headed winged bulls. The chambers were strewn with earthen vases and fragments of pottery, bottles and pieces of broken glass, and curious oblong tablets of dark unbaked clay covered with nail-shaped characters. The tablets looked like leaves of a book. As it turned out, they were.

The scenes depicted in the bas-reliefs were gruesome— foreign cities put to the torch by victorious Assyrian armies, lines of prisoners with their hands bound, people and cattle driven before their conquerors with rawhide whips, long linon of captive women cradling children in their arms, the severed heads of the vanquished tabulated by Assyrian scribes. The scenes recalled the Old Testament's admonition about the Assyrians: "All who see ye shall flee." As at Nimrod and Khalah Sharghat, Layard was confused as to the true origin of Kouyunjik.

Unknown to him, he had found the exact site of Nineveh! The ruins were those of Sennacherib's palace, the Sennacherib of the Books of Kings, Chronicles, and Isaiah.

Earlier, influenced by Rawlinson, Layard had considered Nimrod to be Nineveh. Then he revised his scheme of things to make Nineveh an immense city, in conformity with Jonah's description of it as an "exceedingly great city of three days' journey." Now he wrote, "The position of the ruins [of Kouyunjik] proves that at one time this was one of the most important parts of Nineveh; and the magnificence of the remains shows that the edifices must have been founded by one of the greatest of the Assyrian monarchs."

Layard now considered Kouyunjik a "part of Nineveh," and he viewed the latter as encompassing an area stretching from Nimrod to Kouyunjik.

But still he was not sure, even of this latest speculation. For example, in a letter to Cecilia Berkeley, dated June 14, he wrote, "Besides the palace at Nimroud, I have lately discovered a building on the left bank of the Tigris, opposite Mosul. This may have been the palace of one of the Assyrian kings mentioned in the Old Testament—Sennacherib, Esarhaddon or Tiglath Pileser." Yet, he observed, the palace at Kouyunjik seemed to be of more recent vintage than the Nimrod palace, and therefore, falling back on Rawlinson's mistaken scholarship, he concluded that Nimrod "appears to be the true site of Nineveh."

Layard was desperately trying to unravel the obvious links between the Bible and his discoveries. But neither he nor anyone else could yet read cuneiform. "If we succeed in deciphering the character and reading the inscription in which good progress has already been made," he wrote Cecilia, "important illustrations of Scripture history will probably be attained."

Of one thing he was certain: his funds were being rapidly depleted, his staff was inadequate for the task that lay ahead, and he had barely scratched the mound. Yet he was more than satisfied by his new discoveries. "The discovery of this building and the extent to which the excavations have been carried out," he wrote the British Museum in June, "I conclude establishes our claim to the future examination of the mound should the trustees be desirous to continue research in this country."

Drained physically, mentally, and financially, Layard noted, "My labors in Assyria are now drawn to a close." (How many times had he thought his soujourn at an end, only to be drawn back inexorably to the land of the *Arabian Nights?*)

It only remained for him to wind up his affairs at Mosul. The winged colossi had safely reached Basra on the first leg of their journey to England.

England. He had not seen the white cliffs of Dover in almost eight years. If he was ever able to capitalize on his discoveries and land a diplomatic post, this was the moment to be in London. He even had money for the trip home. As another reward for his labor, the trustees of the British Museum, much to his surprise, had deposited an additional £500 to his personal account. It was a reward for moving the bull and lion. Yes, the moment was ripe to return to England.

Fittingly, before his departure from Mosul, he organized an enormous farewll party for his workers, friends, and acquaintances. Even the Cadi and the French consul were invited. Indeed, so many people were on the guest list that he had to hire a village for the occasion. Tents were pitched at the site, and it looked like a garden party on the grounds of Buckingham Palace—well, not quite.

Layard's invitation was daring. Both men *and* women were invited. Even the Christian women, who ostensibly enjoyed greater freedom than their Moslem counterparts in Turkish Asia, were impressed. "The quiet Christian ladies of Mosul, who had scarcely before this occasion ventured beyond the walls of the town, gazed with wonder and delight on the scene," Layard wrote, "lamenting, no doubt, that the domestic arrangements of their husbands did not permit more frequent indulgence in such gayeties."

Platters of boiled rice and roasted lambs, bowls of garlic and sour milk, and other Arabic culinary delights abounded. Music, dancing, and laughter prevailed until dusk. Layard made a short farewell speech, thanked his workers, distributed small presents to his superintendents, and their wives, and invited anyone who felt he or she had been wronged to come forward for redress of grievances. Sheik Khalaf, who often acted as spokesman at these gatherings, stepped forward from the crowd. They had lived, he said, under Layard's shadow, and, "God be praised! no one has cause to complain." But every worker requested one favor, he continued, a *teskerè*, or note, to certify that they had been in his employ. This would not only be of some protection in dealing with repressive officialdom, but, he explained, it would also serve as a souvenir which they could show to their children and their children's children when they told tales of the great wonders unearthed at Nimrod.

Layard was honored and touched, and he spent the next several days writing notes, acquiring a stiff wrist in the process.

On June 24, 1847, Layard abandoned Mosul, accompanied by the bright-eyed, eighteen-year-old Hormuzd Rassam. Layard had proposed to Christian, the vice-consul, that he take the boy with him to Britain for a "proper education," the very same phrase the Austens used in discussing his own childhood. Christian Rassam readily accepted the generous offer.

Almost the whole town rode out with him to some distance from Mosul as a farewell gesture. His workers followed on foot, and as he passed through the gates of Mosul their wives and daughters, in an emotional outburst, clung to his horse, kissed his hand, and wailed their grief at his departure.

As he and the young Rassam galloped westward, Layard reflected on his labors in Assyria. Scarcely a year before, with the exception of the ruins discovered by Botta, not one Assyrian monument was known.

Layard was neither deeply religious nor unusually superstitious. Yet his luck at Nineveh troubled him. For thousands of years the Assyrian cities had laid hidden under the Mesopotamian plains, awaiting a deliverer. Why him? "It had often occurred to me during my labors," he later confessed, "that the time of the discovery of these remains was so opportune that a person inclined to be superstitious might look upon it as something more than accidental."

In any event, Layard had produced convincing evidence in an age of increasing skepticism that the magnificence and puissance of the Assyrian empire, which had made Nineveh the envy of the ancient world and her fall the theme of prophets and poets, was not a myth.

The Assyrian shall come into our land.
—MICAH

XXVIII On a hot and
humid July 31, 1847, an exhausted Layard rode up to the
ornate gate of the British chancery in Constantinople and
dismounted. Fleetingly, he recalled his first reception there
five years earlier. This time he was not coldly turned out of
the anteroom. On the contrary, Lord Cowley, chargé d'affaires
in Canning's absence, greeted him personally "with the greatest kindness."

Over a cup of tea, Cowley handed him a sealed envelope
from Canning. "I am happy to inform you," Canning wrote,
"that Lord Palmerston* has obligingly consented to your being
attached to the embassy at Constantinople."

Then Canning dropped the other shoe. The job paid nothing.
He intimated, however, that Layard would be named to the
Anglo-Russian boundary commission then being formed to
resolve the Turco-Persian frontier dispute, a job that paid £250
a year. "It is certainly not much," Canning admitted candidly,
"but your period of service commences with it."

Layard read the letter with mixed emotions. Not only was
the appointment without pay, but it blocked his desire to
return to England. Yet he had no alternative but to accept. He
was thirty years old and had no other career on the horizon.

Canning explained that he planned to return to Turkey later

* Palmerston had replaced Lord Aberdeen as foreign secretary.

(203)

in the year and expected Layard to assist him in preliminary work on the Turco-Persian question. As a member of the diplomatic service, Layard had now lost freedom of movement. He could not proceed to London—or anywhere else—without the foreign office's permission.

Cowley sympathized with Layard's situation and suggested that he take a holiday while waiting for Canning's return. A sea voyage would do him wonders and would help restore his strength and spirit. Cowley proposed that Layard join him on a cruise of the Aegean aboard a British gunboat, which was departing in a fortnight.

Layard accepted Cowley's offer. In the course of the sail, the party anchored off the Troad, a marshy plain in northwestern Turkey. The swampy area was so infected at night by "bad air"—anopheles mosquitos, of course—that, Layard recorded, "the result was that most of the party on their return to Constantinople suffered from intermittent fever." In Layard's case, however, the fever was not intermittent, and the embassy's physician warned Cowley that unless Layard returned to England immediately "I will not answer for his life."

Early in October, with a roll of 250 drawings of Assyrian sculptures and inscriptions tucked under his arm, and with Rassam trailing behind with their bags, Layard boarded a French ship bound for home. During the voyage he could not shake the fever and spent most of the time in his cabin, but when the vessel put into Italy, he and Rassam disembarked. He felt the Italian air would improve his condition. He was also homesick for Florence, the city of his childhood.

While he was in Italy he learned that a French sloop, Le Commorant, had docked at Le Harve after a difficult passage from Basra, her holds filled with the sawed-up pieces of Botta's bulls. French peasants were amazed to see the great blocks floated down the Seine to Paris on barges. The blocks were unloaded alongside the Louvre and reassembled. The Assyrian bulls caused a sensation, and Canning, among others, was chagrined. "The French have beat the English hollow," he complained.

During his brief stopover in Florence, Layard hobnobbed with the cream of the British diplomatic service, including

such imperial figures as Lords Minto and Napier. The bulls
and lions of Assyria had won him entry into the inner power
circle of the British empire. Other doors opened for him. Pope
Pio Nono invited him to an audience. Layard described His
Holiness as "one of the great objects of my curiosity." Raymond
of Toulouse would have been astonished by the ecumenical
spirit of the nineteenth century. But on the day Layard was
scheduled to meet the Pope, he came down with another
attack of malaria and was forced to cancel the visit.

At Leghorn, Layard embarked for Marseilles, and after
several bowls of steaming bouillabaisse to ease the chill in his
aching bones, he headed for Paris. The French had still not
built a rail link across France, and the journey between the
two cities took four days and three nights in a comfortless
diligence.

In Paris Layard was eager to visit the Louvre and to inspect,
firsthand, Botta's discoveries. He also sought to renew his
friendship with Botta, who was living on the right bank and
was completing work on his Monuments de Ninive. Layard
admitted that he knocked on Botta's door with some trepi-
dation. Since his finds were incomparably more important than
those of Botta, he feared that his friend would display envy
and view him as an upstart English rival who had upstaged
him.

Layard should have been ashamed of these thoughts. Above
all, he should have known Botta better.

True to character, the selfless Botta threw his arms around
Layard and embraced him warmly. In a letter to Henry Ross,
whom Layard had left at Mosul in charge of his affairs, Layard
described Botta's treatment of him as "exceedingly kind and
attentive." But he found him in "indifferent health," the price
Botta paid in part for his residence at Mosul and in part for
his addiction to a Chinese pipe.

The appearance of an equally sick Layard at his door acted
as a tonic on the debilitated Botta. In a burst of energy, Botta
rushed off to the Institute Français to announce Layard's
arrival, set up an appointment for him with Jules Mohl—the
German-born pioneer of Assyriology—and other French savants, and arranged for Layard to attend the December 17

meeting of the prestigious Académie d'Inscriptions et Belles-Lettres.

With pride, Botta also dragged him to the newly opened Salle de Ninive at the Louvre. Layard marveled at the ingenuity of French engineers in putting together Botta's winged bulls, but beyond the bulls, Layard found the collection disappointing. "[Botta's] work on Khorsabad is splendid," he reported in a letter to Ross at Mosul, "but the museum of Nineveh in the Louvre, with the exception of the two bulls (which have been admirably restored), and the two giants strangling the lion, are most miserable."

Rushing around Paris with Rassam and Botta brought on another severe malarial attack, and when Friday, December 17, rolled around, Layard was still confined to bed. But he was determined not to miss the meeting with the French savants. Wrapped in a great afghan, his face drawn, leaning on Rassam for support, Layard took a coach to the academy's ornate building. Botta had played the role of advance man with perfection, and Layard was mobbed on his arrival at the meeting.

A scholar-lawyer was scheduled to speak that evening, and he was politely asked to cut his prepared remarks since Layard was ill, only passing through Paris, and his presence presented French scholarship with a unique opportunity to question the explorer of Nimrod. For an hour the bored audience put up with the lawyer's mumblings and ramblings. Suddenly, when he said he would now divide the subject into five parts, the group's patience was exhausted. There were hoots from the audience and calls for "l'homme Nimroud!" Tumult ensued, and the president of the academy interrupted the indignant speaker and turned the lectern over to Layard.

"I was still suffering from my attack of fever, and those who have had the advantage of experience in these matters know that one of the results of fever is a considerable excitement of the brain, consequent audacity, and no small additional loquacity, only controlled by physical debility," Layard said.

In a phrase, Layard was high. And rightly so. This was his first public recognition, the moment that made up for the years of vermin, filth, malaria, and other hardships he had suffered in the East.

Layard unrolled his portfolio of drawings, and the audience gasped. Clearly, his discoveries transcended those of Botta. Layard then launched into a discussion about his discoveries—in superb French, much to the delight of the audience. He demonstrated that many of the refinements in sculpture attributed to the Greeks had their origins centuries, perhaps millenniums, earlier in ancient Assyria. The Ionic column, for example, was clearly of Assyrian design. His conclusions jarred some listeners, pleased others.

An uproar ensued as the scholars argued back and forth. The group's enthusiasm crystallized a project that had been taking shape within Layard for months—a published account of his adventures and discoveries in Assyria. "If the results of the Nimroud excavations create half as favorable an impression in London as they have done in Paris," he wrote, "I may hope that something may be done towards publishing them."

By the end of the meeting it was plain that Layard's talk had generated more questions than answers, and it was unanimously agreed to hold an "extraordinary meeting" the following night, including a dinner in Layard's honor. To Layard's surprise, and gratification, the most influential members of the academy conferred hastily among themselves and announced that they would propose Layard as a Corresponding Member of the Académie, an honor coveted by scholars throughout Europe.

At the Saturday night gala, M. Lenormand, one of France's leading academicians, summed up the results of Layard's impact on European thinking: "Hereafter, no one could venture to enter upon the subject of Greek art or mythology without being thoroughly acquainted with the details of Nimroud."

For all their vaunted chauvinism, the French savants abandoned their rivalry with the Anglo-Saxons and impressed on Layard that immediately upon his arrival in London he must arrange for the publication of his drawings and inscriptions. The French also promised him the special typeface that they had cast for Botta's volumes.

Layard laughed as he thought of his penny-squeezing compatriots. "I confess," he told the French, "I cannot see how that is to be."

These were troubled times in France, and Botta, a royalist

and supporter of King Louis Philippe, privately forecast the fall of the monarchy. He was eager for his friend to meet the King, but Louis Philippe was not expected back in Paris until Christmas Eve. If the choice was between an audience with the French monarch and Christmas at home after years abroad, there was no choice. "I . . . sacrificed His Majesty to a Christmas dinner in England," Layard said.

On December 19 Layard left for Calais and Britain. He and Botta parted warmly. It was the last time they would ever meet. Botta, the supreme gentleman, would be caught up in the French Revolution of 1848, the abdication of the King, and the founding of the Second Republic. Although Botta had been planning to return to Mosul and reopen his Khorsabad excavations, he was shipped in disgrace to a minor post in Syria and died many years later in obscurity.

Botta was to Layard what Toscanelli was to Columbus and Wallace to Darwin, a catalytic agent whose name is lost in history. G. J. Gadd, a former member of the British Museum's department of Assyriology, summed up Botta's character as that of an able, brave, and resourceful scholar whose outstanding and most attractive quality was generosity. Gadd put it beautifully: "It is a pity we do not know more about him."

Bundled in a heavy coat and a thick scarf, with Hormuzd Rassam at his side, Layard crossed the cold and angry English Channel on December 21. Layard must have been in a highly emotional state, but with a reserve uncharacteristic of him, he repressed his feelings with a veneer of Victorian insouciance: "I arrived in London the 22nd of December," he noted, "after being absent from England for nearly eight-and-a-half years."

> Weary and worn,
> all his toil he engraved on a stone.
> —GILGAMESH

XXIX

Fittingly, Layard reached London during the most joyous season of the year. He took a brougham directly to the stately Austen house at Montague Place, in Bloomsbury, a pebble's throw from the British Museum.

The city's festive air brightened an otherwise windless, overcast day. Jenny Lind and Donizetti's *Figlia del Regimento* were packing them in at the Surrey Theatre. A new Brazilian steam frigate, named after Alfonso, the late son of the Emperor of Brazil, was the talk along the docks of Limehouse Reach. Pursell's boasted the "largest assortment of Christmas cakes in London," from five to fifty shillings apiece. Scotch New Year buns were cheaper and more popular. Stout sold at four shillings for a case of twelve one quart bottles. Amontillado cost sixty shillings a case, although sherry of lesser quality could be had at half the price. *Mrs. Russell's Cookery*, which was on the best-seller list when Layard left England, was still up there. A letter in the *Times* chided the nobility and gentry for putting off the payment of holiday bills until after Christmas, imposing a severe strain on merchants.

The news from abroad that week focused on the Ottoman empire. The Turks announced the "pacification" of the Albanians—again. An outbreak of cholera at Constantinople was reportedly being held in check. Merry Old England, however, was her stable self. "The Queen and Prince Albert with the royal family," the Court Circular said, "arrived from Osborne at [Windsor] castle." In their company, according to dispatches, was Lady Canning, who had served as lady-in-waiting to the Queen.

At Christmas dinner, over roast beef and Yorkshire pudding, Layard regaled his family with tales of adventure and discovery among the lost cities of Assyria. The Austens beamed. He was no longer their idle, drifter nephew. He was their godson again, and they took pride that he bore their name.

Layard had changed outwardly as well as inwardly. Although weary and worn, his slender frame had filled out. A portrait of him by G. F. Watts, after Layard had recovered his health and had shaven off his beard, revealed a chubby face with aristocratic aquiline nose, dark and heavy brows, Byronesque locks, and the firm lips of a man in command. Only his eyes remained the same as in his youth, clear and blue and possessing the faraway look of the visionary, the romantic, the adventurer.

Layard not only talked of Assyria that day but also of another love, foreign affairs. He warned his listeners about Russian designs in the Near East and the need for speedy reform if the Ottomans were to save their empire, and he forecast impending revolution in France. His views on France shocked the Austens, who thought the royalists were in firm control.

Layard's fame extended beyond Montague Street. Oxford University, where he had placed Hormuzd Rassam for schooling, bestowed a Doctor of Canon Laws upon him, an honor he especially relished when he recalled his days at the Reverend Bewsher's school. He was also elected a member of the Athenaeum, a society founded some twenty-odd years earlier by Sir Walter Scott and Thomas Moore. Layard's name had also crossed the Atlantic. Miner Kellogg, his American painter friend, wrote from New York: "The Ethnological Society here have a deep interest in your discoveries and your letters to me have been read before it."

Sir Stratford Canning, returning to his post, wrote a note of encouragement from Switzerland dated January 2. "You must make the most of the Assyrian antiquities," Canning counseled. "Do them justice and yourself credit, and make the public understand that they got a prize."

His enthusiastic receptions in Paris and London, coupled with Canning's letter, suddenly made him acutely aware of the possibilities of using Assyria for leverage in ascending the diplomatic ladder.

New Year's Eve he wrote Viscount Palmerston, the new foreign secretary, and requested a personal interview—which he promptly got. Admittedly, the letter was obsequious. "Although I have not had the honor of receiving your lordship's dispatch appointing me an attache to Her Majesty's Embassy at Constantinople," Layard wrote, "an account which I have received at the Foreign Service will, I trust, be sufficient to authorize me to express my sincere thanks to your lordship not only for the appointment but for my nomination."

He also dropped by the British Museum and introduced himself to the secretary, the Reverend Forshall, who greeted him warmly and arranged immediately for a formal meeting between Layard and the trustees January 8. The meeting was chaired by no less a figure than the Duke of Cambridge, Victoria's first cousin and one of the Queen's favorites, who, behind his back, was called "Royal George." Others present were the Marquess of Northampton, the Viscount Mahon, Sir Inglis Bar, and the Dean of Westminster. Layard was moving in high circles. A record of the meeting, reports that Royal George conveyed to Layard the "best thanks of the Trustees for his zealous, successful and in every respect satisfactory services. . . ." Thereupon Layard unrolled his collection of Assyrian drawings and launched into a description of his discoveries. The trustees were fascinated.

At that moment, however, the "Nimroud marbles" were encountering the same obstacles that earlier had confronted Botta. Layard's winged bull and lion were stuck at Basra with no ship on the horizon. So were the Black Obelisk, the Nimrod Ivories, and the lion-hunting scenes. Layard estimated there were "from 70 to 80 marbles and from 30 to 40 smaller objects." He appealed to the trustees to put pressure on the Admiralty to give the transport of the relics to England a naval priority.

With the French pleas of only a fortnight ago still reverberating in his ears, Layard also appealed to the trustees to publish his drawings "without delay as cheaply executed as is consistent with accuracy in order to give the engravings as wide a circulation as possible." To his surprise, the trustees proved agreeable and established a "special committee" headed by Royal George to explore the matter. But nothing came of it. The Peel government was against spending £4,000 on the project, and it was not until 1850 that the drawings were published.

Layard left the meeting exhilarated, although one aspect of the session troubled him. The Duke of Cambridge had referred to the Assyrian discoveries as the joint effort of Canning, the Museum, and Layard. Be that as it may, after his input of sweat and tears among the mounds, Layard looked on the Assyrian relics as *his* marbles. In a letter to Ross following his warm reception in London, he wrote, "I am told a wing will be built expressly for *my* antiquities" (italics added).

Whatever the case, four days later, in a lengthy report to the Museum, Layard outlined a grandiose plan for a major British expedition to excavate the whole of Assyria. Such a project, he estimated, would take a minimum of three years and cost upwards of £5,000 per annum. He described the moment as "peculiarly favorable" and explained that the Turks planned to build their first museum at Constantinople and that governors throughout the empire had been ordered to excavate and transport "marbles" from their pashaliks. Villages were already being formed into work gangs and, without compensation, were being ordered to dig up sculptures. As a result, the peasants often destroyed the antiquities they found to evade forced labor.

"The work of destruction has already commenced," Layard warned, basing his information on private reports from Rawlinson, Ross, Christian Rassam, and others.

Obviously, Layard was not yet done with the mounds of Mesopotamia.

His plan kicked around several departments for weeks and was finally dropped by the Peel government as a frivolous waste of public money. But the root cause for the project's abandonment went deeper. It was a matter of politics. Peel knew he could not sell the plan to the public. Louis Philippe of France had abdicated, setting in motion the Revolution of 1848, and Layard conceded in a letter to Ross, "events in France have driven Nineveh and all other antiquities out of people's heads. I am inclined to think that nothing will be done." And nothing was.

Another cloud partially darkened his otherwise bright homecoming: repeated malarial attacks. The disease now affected his liver and forced him to give up social drinking. It also forced him to postpone plans to return to Constantinople.

Although the state of his health improved over the next few months, Harley Street physicians insisted that he was still not strong enough to join a boundary commission in the wilds of the Turco-Persian frontier. Finally, in May, on the advice of his doctors, the foreign office extended his home leave six months. The extension dovetailed beautifully with his plans to write a book on his adventures and cash in on the excitement created by his discoveries.

Lord Aberdare, who, as William N. Bruce, edited a portion of the Layard Papers in 1903, noted: "Layard spent the greater part of the year 1848 in England, preparing his well-known book, Nineveh and Its Remains. . . ." Layard still was not sure of the exact site of Nineveh, nor even whether it was a single ruin or a vast complex encompassing several. But the focus of the book is on Nimrod and his excavations there. In attributing the origins to Nimrod, he was undoubtedly influenced by Rawlinson's preliminary and inaccurate reading of cuneiform.

During the writing of the book, he spent most of his time at Canford Manor, Dorsetshire, near Bournemouth, the home of a cousin, Lady Charlotte Guest, and her husband, Sir John, both of whom he had recently met in London.

Sir John and Lady Charlotte were good friends of the Disraelis and the Cannings. In December, the month Layard returned to England, Canning had shown Lady Charlotte some of the drawings Layard made at Nimrod, and she had found them fascinating and "curious," as she noted in her diary. In February, Charlotte and her husband, who was a member of

Parliament, paid a short visit to London "to vote on the admission of Jews to Parliament," and in the course of their stay, Charlotte met her first cousin for the first time. She was immediately taken with "the Eastern explorer," as she described him, and Layard was soon ensconced at Canford Manor as a member of the family circle.

Layard was thirty-one at the time, Charlotte five years his senior, and her husband, Sir John, was sixty-three years old and ailing.

When Charlotte had married him in 1833, at the age of nineteen, Guest was a vigorous, forty-nine-year-old widower and ironmonger—and a commoner. He had never got beyond grammar school, but he was alive to the ongoing Industrial Revolution and at Dowlais experimented with substituting raw coal for coke in the manufacture of steel. He was the first ironmaster to roll rails, a feat which was scoffed at in his day as impractical.

Charlotte's wedding had shocked the nobility and gentry. She had married "into trade," as it was quaintly expressed in those days, and the couple was ostracized by society. But soon the whole of England was riding on Guest's rails and he, in turn, rode those tracks to enormous wealth and respectability. By 1838 the aristocracy had come to terms with England's emergent new class; trades people had became "captains of industry," and Guest was created a baronet.

Charlotte was as remarkable an individual as her husband. She was not only vivacious, attractive, and independent-minded, but also talented. Chaucer was her favorite author, with Virgil and Byron close seconds. She read the classics in Greek and Latin, and was familiar with Persian and Hebrew. After her marriage to John Guest, she took up Welsh and translated into English *Mabinogion*, a project that took eight years and required her to master the early medieval text in which the Welsh tales were composed. Her translation of *Mabingion* was published in three volumes in 1846, two years before Layard arrived on the scene at Canford, and it was these tales that inspired Alfred Lord Tennyson to write *The Idylls of the King*.

Charlotte Guest was a remarkable woman in other ways. In

fifteen years of marriage, she bore ten children, five boys and five girls. A portrait of her in this period by Watts, the same artist who sketched Layard's picture, shows a singularly youthful face.

As a wedding present for his young bride, Guest had acquired and rebuilt Canford Manor, a medieval ruin fit for archaeological research. In the ensuing years the manor was reborn on a grand scale in the popular neo-Gothic style of the Victorian period, complete with its own cricket field.

It was at Canford Manor that Lord Aberdare first met Layard in 1848. In a memoir forty-six years later, Aberdare recalled: "I have vividly before me the scene of our first acquaintance, when, being on a visit to his relations, Sir John and Lady Charlotte Guest, he described to the Dowlais workmen in vigorous and graphic language his wonderful discoveries of buried monuments, with—what specially interested them—their close bearing on Biblical history and their illustrations of Bible language and imagery."

Layard regaled not only the Dowlais workers and their families with stories of Nineveh and the Bible but also Charlotte's children. He spun tales from the Arabian Nights, recounted his own adventures in the East, and enthralled them with stories about the stone monsters he found buried in the earth—lions with wings, bulls with human heads.

Among the children, one in particular took a special fancy to "Uncle Henry," five-year-old Mary Enid Evelyn, whom he bounced on his knee and who bore a striking resemblance to her mother. Enid, as she was called, fell madly in love with her mother's Ninevite.

Though Layard's move to Canford Manor raised some Victorian eyebrows, there is no reason to believe that his relationship with Charlotte went further than an endearing friendship. Through Charlotte, he renewed his acquaintance with Disraeli, and he found his stay there pleasant and comfortable.

As he wrote to Ross, back in Mosul: "The pleasure of English country life spoils one for the adventures and privations of the East."

I sent him back to his post.
—ASHURBANIPAL

In truth, however,
Assyria was rarely out of Layard's thoughts. At Canford he
worked steadily and happily, almost effortlessly, on his two-
volume epic, *Nineveh and Its Remains.*

Sara Austen, who had helped Disraeli with his first novel—
some critics suspected she rewrote *Vivian Grey* for him—and
cousin Charlotte, an author in her own right, vied over who
deserved credit for his subsequent literary successes. At least,
that is the impression gained from the records of his publisher,
John Murray, and from Charlotte Guest's diaries. Both women
were natural rivals and enjoyed stage center.

Aunt Sara, then fifty-two, was a whilom beauty who still
loved to play the Egeria to clever young men at her salon.
According to George Paston, Murray's biographer, "Now she
took the affairs of her nephew into her very capable hands."

Paston implied that she interested Murray in Layard's
manuscript and Paston produced evidence to show that she
at least offered editorial advice. Based on her talks with Sir
Stratford Canning during his home leave, Sara wrote Murray,
"It would be most impolitic to enter into minute details of the
discoveries," and quoted Canning as expressing alarm that
too detailed a book on Nineveh might "provoke French rivalry
and French intrigues.

"Therefore," she advised Murray, "he [Canning] thinks it

highly essential not to particularize the most precious articles discovered—the Obelisk, Bronzes, Ivories, for instance."

An entry in Charlotte Guest's diary, April 7, 1848, however, observed that Layard had brought Murray to meet her at Canford. "I had promised to see him about the publishing of the drawings Henry had made at Nineveh." Apparently she was prepared to subsidize the publication.

Murray came away from Canford impressed by Layard's manuscript and expressed great interest in publishing it. "I like your narrative very much and I think it will be successful," Murray later wrote Layard. "I will most readily undertake the publication at my own cost and risque, and will give you one-half of the net profits of every edition."

Charlotte's influence was also felt. "I am prepared to embark a considerable sum in illustrations." And, independently of *Nineveh and Its Remains*, Layard did produce a companion piece, *The Monuments of Nineveh: From Drawings Made on the Spot*, which contained one hundred plates and which was probably partly financed by the Guests.

Thus, it seems, Sara and Charlotte jointly influenced Murray and the course of Layard's literary efforts, although Layard disregarded Sara's editorial advice and gave a detailed account of the discovery of the Obelisk, Ivories, and the rest.

While working on *Nineveh* and *Monuments*, Layard worked simultaneously on a third book, *Inscriptions in the Cuneiform Character*, a collection of the texts he had copied at Nimrod, Kouyunjik, and elsewhere. Any one of these three projects would have been more than enough for a professional writer to handle—and Layard was working on all three projects while recovering his health.

In a note to Forshall, he described the Nineveh manuscript as "a popular description of the objects discovered in the operations in Assyria." As usual, Layard's modesty failed to do him justice. His account of Nineveh was more than another travel book. Layard was creating a new genre in literature, the book on archaeology, in narrative form, which interwove scholarship, travel, romance, and high adventure. His impact on the literature of archaeology is as deep today as that of Edgar Allan Poe on the development of the detective story.

Since Layard, many of the finest books on archaeology have been patterned on his model, from Heinrich Schliemann's masterwork, *Troy and Its Remains,* published in 1870, which imitated Layard's style, through Howard Carter and his discovery of the tomb and treasures of Tutankhamen in the Roaring Twenties, to M. E. L. Mallowan's *Nimrud and Its Remains* in 1964.

Mallowan, one of the great living Assyrian archaeologists, who reopened Layard's dig with his wife, the late Agatha Christie, the mystery writer, at his side, unabashedly conceded in his own two-volume work: "The form and scheme of this book is in a sense archaic, a continuation of Layard's memoirs."

As evidence of Layard's literary skill even today, Victorian literature anthologies such as *Victorian Prose 1830–1880* include excerpts from Layard along with those of William Makepeace Thackeray, George Eliot, Charles Dickens, Thomas Hardy, and Emily and Charlotte Brontë as stunning examples of the period.

While Layard maintained an incredibly tight writing schedule at Canford Manor, he still found time to orchestrate further excavations in Assyria by remote control. Through Ross, Layard arranged for the reopening of the Kouyunjik excavations and the removal of the headless statue of Shalmaneser II from Khalah Sharghat (Ashur). He also maintained unremitting pressure on the British Museum to reconsider his grandiose scheme for a massive assault on Mesopotamia.

The extent of Layard's involvement with the mounds during this period is reflected in the exchange of letters and reports between Layard at Canford and Ross in Mosul.

On January 24, after inquiring about Layard's health, Ross wrote: "The excavations are much more promising than they have been for a long time past. I am digging in the S.W. corner, and half tablets of chariots and horsemen are coming out in regular series, and apparently leading to something good. But the depth of the trench is tremendous; and with the few men I have the work proceeds slowly."

The report ended on a familiar note. "I am at the last gasp for funds."

In March, Ross dispatched a work gang with mats and ropes to Khalah Sharghat to retrieve the headless statue. Layard had hoped to complete the job for under 2,000 piasters ($92). But Ross complained that "the Khalah Shirgut [sic] stone will cost a good deal more than you thought." He did not give the cost figure, but it probably cost another $15 or $25 to excavate and transport to Mosul.

Meanwhile, Ross, in high excitement, reported that he had struck another mother lode at Kouyunjik. "The ground is so deep that we are digging in tunnels, breaking a hole here and there to give light," he said. "The roof is six or seven feet thick." Ominously, he reported that the frustrated French vice-consul had resumed digging at Botta's old stamping ground, Khorsabad, and that "Guillois has found a bull with an eagle-headed figure in one of the little mounds near Khorsabad."

By May 20 Ross was working so deeply underground that he could have used a Newcastle minor's lamp. "The excavations are regular catacombs," he said, "and in spite of the perforated skylights, I have to examine some of the slabs by candle light." The bas-reliefs were covered with scenes of sieges, with the Assyrians scaling ladders, and "headless corpses falling to the ground. The scenes," Ross wrote, "[are] in fact, just like the Nimrood ones, but completely charred."

On a lighter note, Layard inquired about his girlfriends. Bachelor Ross reported back that he was having so much trouble with the free and easy ladies of Mosul that he had barred his room to them and pledged "not another woman shall put her foot within my door."

Summer descended rapidly on the Mesopotamian plain, and the temperature soared. In June Ross was forced to quit the dig—not because of the heat; like Layard, he would have carried on through hell—but his father needed him at the Malta branch of their trading company. Ross left for Malta overland, via Constantinople, and in his first letter from the Mediterranean island, he wrote Layard, "Fancy at Kouyunjik, on the last day I was there, fragments of what must have been a barrel-formed terra-cotta cylinder with very small and beautiful inscriptions turned up." This was one of the Assyrian cylinders, among the most fabulous treasures in archaeology.

Ross also reported that en route he had had a hilarious visit with Canning at Constantinople.

"Sir Stratford Canning," Ross recounted, "received me very

politely, but was evidently much preoccupied, and moreover had forgotten me so entirely that he thought I was dead! He said, 'I was sorry to hear that the young gentleman who went to Mosul some years ago and dined with me here had died there.' I was puzzled as you may suppose, and said I was not aware than that any young Englishman had died anywhere near Mosul, but H. E. [His Excellency] insisted that he had talked to him and liked him, and knew he had died. It then flashed across me that it was myself, and I told him I had been near dying but had stopped short of actual death."

At Canford Manor, in the comfortable surroundings of Lady Charlotte and her children, summer slipped gently into autumn. Layard's health was restored and his manuscripts completed. The malarial bouts ceased, and he put on weight. Although he would have preferred to remain at Canford through Christmas, he could no longer delay his return to Constantinople. Canning was impatient.

As Layard prepared for his departure, the brig H.M.S. *Jumna* docked in October at Chatham, on the right bank of the Medway, 10 miles above its confluence with the Thames and about 30 miles from London, a principal Royal Navy station since the reign of Henry VIII. Her holds were packed with fifty-five cases of Nimrod treasures. They had almost wound up at the bottom of the Indian Ocean.

The Assyrian relics had been shipped by sloop from Basra to Bombay and, after considerable delay, transferred to *Jumna*. After leaving Bombay, the brig was enveloped by violent monsoon weather, blown off course, and dismasted. Instead of sailing westward for East Africa, she was compelled to run southeastward and wound up in Ceylon—ironically, Layard's objective when he and Mitford set out for the East in 1839. Aboard the vessel was the most precious Biblical treasure unearthed at Nimrod, the Black Obelisk.

Layard rushed to Chatham to arrange personally for the transfer of the cargo to the British Museum.

At the Museum, on a fog-shrouded October 12, Forshall, the trustees, and other officials gathered around Layard as he pried open the cases. But when Layard looked inside, his temper flared. The treasures had been carelessly packed, the order in which he had crated them scrambled, and several pieces were missing! Suddenly he recalled a letter Ross had written from Mosul which had puzzled him at the time and which he had laughed off as bad reporting. According to the *Bombay Monthly Times,* Ross said, the local branch of the Royal Asiatic Society had conducted a seminar on "the remains found by Major Rawlinson [sic] at Nimroud" and that a rubbing of the Black Obelisk showed the inscriptions were probably Egyptian hieroglyphics. "So much for learned societies," Ross, the businessman, said.

As Layard stood in the basement of the British Museum in the midst of the opened crates, he realized that they had been opened and pilfered in Bombay on their way from Basra to London. The trustees were upset and addressed a formal query to the Court of Directors of the East India Company, demanding an explanation. An official inquiry was launched by the Bombay government and the East India Company.

The board of inquiry concluded that many crates had not only been opened but placed on exhibition on the Bombay docks. Several Assyrian relics were stolen, probably as souvenirs. Apologies were sent to the Museum. The furor had a salutory effect, however. The Bombay authorities thereafter placed every Assyrian relic shipped from Basra under tight naval security. There were no more thefts.

Pilferage aside, the trustees were delighted by the contents of the shipment (the winged bull and lion were still to come). In a letter to Foreign Secretary Palmerston, the Museum described Layard's collection as "one of the most important contributions to . . . archaeological science . . . in recent times." And it was.

At this juncture, the situation regarding Layard's appointment to the Turco-Persian border commission became roiled. Canning and Layard were under the impression that Layard would be placed jointly in charge of the commission with Colonel Fenwick Williams, who later, as a general, became one of the national heroes of the Victorian period. But, it suddenly developed, Layard would serve only as a junior member of the commission, little more than a glorified clerk despite his intimate knowledge of the disputed frontier areas.

Canning, whose temper outmatched Layard's, was furious with this coarse treatment of his protégé.

"I do not like the idea," he wrote Layard, "of your going on this trumpery frontier work."

Canning advised him to resign from the commission. Layard, equally angry, agreed. In a letter to Palmerston, Layard asked to be taken off the commission and said he preferred to work directly under Canning as an attaché at the Constantinople embassy. The foreign office accepted Layard's letter of resignation and assigned him to the embassy but, in the process, took a cheap shot. The posts of paid attachés at Constantinople were filled, the foreign office said, and "Lord Palmerston sees no sufficient reason to increase that establishment." Accordingly, Layard lost the £250 per annum that he was to receive as a member of the border commission.

Layard was furious. But at least it was a job, albeit, as he put it, that of "an unpaid attache without a sixpence."

In November he sailed for Turkey and on Christmas Day dined with the Cannings at the embassy.

The name of Nineveh will last to the latest ages;
and now the name of him who laid bare,
who brought to light its treasures,
will be handed down with it.

—WALPOLE

 In Constantino-
ple, as Canning's indefatigable aide, Layard quickly returned
to familiar routine. At 6:00 A.M., sometimes an hour earlier,
he and Canning shared a pot of tea and went over a daily
mound of dispatches. On occasion they postponed lunch until
it was almost time for dinner. Nightly, Lady Canning retired
at 10:00 P.M., but Sir Stafford often worked through the night.
"It was no uncommon thing for an attache to enter his
excellency's room in the early morning," a friend of the
ambassador recalled, "and find him still in his evening dress.
... Few men could toil as he did."

Few, except Layard.

Incredible stamina and unrelenting drive were among the
bonds between Canning and his protégé. Canning also respected Layard's political judgment and increasingly relied
on him to check his own impulsiveness. At the close of his
lenghty career, Canning remarked that Macaulay and Layard
were "the two most brilliant men I ever met."

Canning went out of his way to develop Layard's diplomatic
contacts. For example, he arranged for Layard to be presented
to the Sublime Porte, Sultan Abdul Mejid, in the ornate setting
of the fabulous Seraglio. The audience had an amusing twist.
Canning delivered an eloquent discourse on the illustrations
of history furnished by Layard's discoveries and the moral to
be derived from the fall of great cities. The official interpreter

pithily summed up the oration. "This is the man who dug up the old stones." The Sultan nodded sleepily.

But it seemed questionable how long the strange relationship between the headstrong ambassador and the unpaid attaché would continue. Layard gave the impression of the independent dollar-a-year man, but he lived uncomfortably on handouts from Canning. Layard, now "middle-aged"—he was thirty-two—descended into increasingly frequent periods of melancholy over his inability to get a regular paying job, the nightmare that had haunted him since his days as an apprentice law clerk.

Suddenly and unexpectedly, the years of struggle and sacrifice paid dividends. In early 1849 Murray published Layard's *Nineveh and Its Remains*. The book was such a brilliant success that even Murray was surprised. Nearly 8,000 copies were sold the first year, making it a runaway best seller.

"It is rarely once or twice—it may be in a century—that a book of this high character is brought before us," *Bentley's Magazine* said. The London *Times* was ecstatic. "The most extraordinary work of the present age," the reviewer said. "We question whether a more enlightened and enterprising traveller than Mr. Layard is to be met with in the annals of modern history." And the *Tribune* added, "The book has a rare amount of graphic, vivid and interesting narrative."

"No one speaks of any other book," Aunt Sara wrote from Montague Place. ". . . your course, my dear Henry, is now clear. *Nothing can stop you.*" The Royal Geographic Society honored Layard with the Gold Medal, and Uncle Ben accepted the award on behalf of the absent Layard. Benjamin Austen, who had spoken despairingly of his godson as a shiftless romantic, now saw him differently. "When he left England, he had no letters of introduction, and no patronage or assistance of any sort," Uncle Ben proudly told the Society's dinner. "But . . . he combined an indomitable and enterprising spirit . . . with courage."

Henry Crabb Robinson was amused. "His uncle had accused me of misleading him," Robinson said, but now Layard's discovery of Nineveh assured him "a place in the future history of art."

The foreign office was also impressed. "Nobody asks: 'Have you read it?' " a colleague in the department wrote Layard. "That is taken for granted."

Coincidentally, with the publication of Nineveh, the schooner Apprentice docked at Chatham with seventeen more cases of Assyrian sculptures aboard, including the headless figure of Shalmaneser from Khalah Sharghat, the Ashur of Genesis. The relics were immediately placed on display at the British Museum. Book sales spurted.

Even Victoria's interest was whetted, and she dispatched Prince Albert to the Museum to inspect the newly opened Nineveh Room. Edward Hawkins, who had replaced the Reverend Forshall as secretary, served as the Prince Consort's guide. "These things are without price," he told Albert. "No thousands could buy them and they have cost the country nothing."

Serious journals such as Quarterly Review, in a forty-six-page review of Nineveh, apologized to its readers that "our limited space forces us to compress into a brief summary our account." Layard, in his unpretentious style, taught people more about the Near East and the Ottoman and Assyrian empires than a shelf of scholarly tomes and Ph.D. theses, the reviewer, H. H. Milman, historian and dean at St. Paul's, said. "We cannot close," he concluded, "without once more congratulating Mr. Layard on his success as a writer, as well as a discoverer."

In that same issue of the Review, immediately following Milman's commentary, two other reviews bore by their position testimony more eloquent than words about Layard's impact on Victorian literature. The other two books? Vanity Fair and Jane Eyre.

Nineveh was enthusiastically received abroad, especially in Paris. In Russia an eccentric millionaire with a passion for Homer read Layard with amazement. If Layard could find fabled Nineveh, he could find mythical Troy. His name was Heinrich Schliemann.

Most reviewers were impressed by Layard's modesty, a humility that carried over in his private letters as well as public writing. Layard never took himself seriously. He subscribed to the Biblical admonition, "Woe unto you when all men shall speak well of you."

Layard planned to dedicate the book to Canning. But he apparently feared it would be misinterpreted at the Foreign Office—especially among his critics of the Aberdeen era—as a blatant effort to honey his diplomatic career. With wry humor, he "affectionately dedicated" the book to Benjamin Austen, Esq. In the American edition later that year, in an 1859 popularized British edition, and in Saggs's edited reprint in 1970, the dedication page is conspicuously absent.

Layard paid Canning a higher tribute: he incorporated him into the narrative and referred to him on several occasions as instrumental in his success. In the pages of Nineveh, Canning and Layard are inseparably enshrined for all time.

By mid-year, Nineveh had run through four printings and Murray tore up his contract with Layard. He had agreed to publish the book on the usual terms of half profits. After the sale of the first edition, he wrote Layard that the sale had so far exceeded his expectations that he considered it right to give Layard two-thirds instead of half the profits. (This was in an age before the literary meadow turned into the literary jungle.)

Murray also sold the American rights to George Putnam, who dropped everything at New York and rushed into print with it. Dr. Edward Robinson, who taught at the Union Theological Seminary in New York, wrote the introductory note and likened Layard's narrative to a romance. "In its incidents and descriptions," Robinson said, "it does indeed remind one continually of an Arabian tale of wonders and genii." This insight is profound, for Robinson was unaware of Layard's obsession with the Arabian Nights.

As the adulation filtered down to Constantinople, Layard was embarrassed. "I am inclined to feel ashamed of myself," he wrote home, "as if I were humbugging the public, when I read the flattering notices in the press." The lengthy, flattering review in the London Times was especially upsetting. "I blushed on reading it," he said, "and have been ashamed to show it here."

He would have been mortified to know it was written by Aunt Sara.

The adulation also embarrassed the government and the British Museum, both of which had treated Layard shabbily. Lord Palmerston, the foreign secretary, now described Layard glowingly as "extraordinary ... enterprising ... accomplished" and announced that he had been promoted, effective April 1, to the rank of *paid* attaché—still only £250 better than an unpaid attaché. Lord John Russell, the prime minister, was so overwhelmed by the Museum's exhibit that he ordered the first lord of the admiralty to dispatch a naval vessel to Basra immediately to pick up the winged lion and bull. And the Museum, with the government's endorsement, proposed that Layard lead a second expedition into Assyria, complete with staff artist, assistants, and medical officer.

Layard and Canning were elated by the news, especially the government's decision to underwrite a second expedition. Details were still forthcoming, but letters from Layard's relatives and Canning's foreign office sources indicated that the Russell ministry was pulling out the stops. There was talk that £20,000, and more, would be made available for a two- or three-year Assyrian campaign.

Hormuzd Rassam was instructed to return to Constantinople and assist Layard in organizing the expedition. Rassam had been studying at Magdalen College, Oxford (his academic record was not particularly distinguished), and was being lionized by British society as the companion of "the remarkable Mr. Layard." The nineteen-year-old lad was reluctant to return to the East. "I cannot bear to leave," he wrote Layard. "I would rather be a chimney-swooper in England than become a pasha in Turkey." But, he said, with a dramatic flair reminiscent of a Layard, "I will sacrifice myself for England," and announced his immediate departure for the East.

On the voyage to Constantinople, Rassam was accompanied by Frederick Charles Cooper, twenty-eight and newly married, who had been hired by the Museum as the expedition's artist at £200 per season. (Their vessel no sooner gathered headway than Cooper began to pine for his bride.)

These developments elated Layard and Canning and restored their faith and confidence in Britain's national concern about art and archaeology. By God, who said the English were no match for the French when it came to spending money on culture? Here was the proof. The British lion held high its head not only as a military and economic power but also as a cultural force in world affairs.

Then the sky came tumbling down.

On April 1 the Museum sent Layard a copy of the expedition's proposed budget for two years. For the first season's dig, September 1849 to April 1850—the "cool" months—the government authorized and appropriated an expenditure of £1,500. The sum was to cover outfitting the expedition with new guns, spades, pickaxes, saddles, notebooks, transport animals, food, medical and other supplies; the salaries of Cooper, Rassam, and a physician, still to be selected; the wages of 150 workers; and the costs of packing, crating, and shipping the finds downriver to Basra.

Canning lost his diplomatic aplomb. "Incredible," he roared.

Layard wrote the Museum: "Utterly impossible."

In Baghdad, Rawlinson heard the news, and could not believe it.

Layard and Canning sat up through the night working on the figures. After paying for general expenses, they estimated that the expedition would have left between £300 and £400 for workers' wages, and about half that amount would go to the cost of building rafts. The budget was utterly ridiculous.

The Museum sought to ease the tension. Sir Henry Ellis, the principal librarian, noted that the £1,500 would only be the first payment and that a similar amount would be appropriated for the second season, 1850–51. Layard thought Sir Henry was putting him on. But, in a private letter, Hawkins, the Museum's new secretary, cautioned Layard that the Museum was besieged by so many requests for funds that failure to accept the offer meant the money would be quickly diverted elsewhere.

Layard wavered for weeks. While he vacillated, Nineveh went into several new editions, and Layard suddenly had an unexpected source of income. (Layard was to earn £1,500 a year in royalties for many years—ironically, the very same amount the Museum proposed for the expedition's operations.)

On August 20, as the summer's heat waned on the Assyrian plain, Layard made up his mind. He would use the royalties to underwrite the expedition. Just as he made the trustees look small once before when he told them they could keep his salary, he again held a mirror up to their faces. "My private resources are far from considerable," Layard wrote, "but such as they are they shall be devoted to the undertaking." The trustees and the government climbed back in their hole.

In public, however, Layard practiced diplomacy. In *Nineveh and Babylon*, published four years later, Layard observed: "Arrangements were hastily, and of course inadequately, made in England," but he said nothing more.

A week later, Layard and his party bade farewell to Canning and prepared to embark on the journey to Mosul.

In addition to Cooper and Rassam, Layard had acquired the services of Dr. Humphrey Sandwith as the expedition's medical officer. Sandwith, it developed, was a bumbling, good-natured Dr. Watson, more interested in shooting parties than medicine. He reveled in his opportunities of shooting cranes, bustard, and other game unknown in England and he described Mesopotamia as an "ornithological Babel." For Sandwith, the expedition was the central event in his life and was stamped so vividly upon his memory that in later years his family and friends laughingly charged him with beginning half his stories with the words, "When I was in Mesopotamia."

In addition to Sandwith and Cooper, four others completed the party: Layard's faithful *bairakdar*, who rode shotgun; his old *cawass*; and two new faces, a Catholic Syrian and an Armenian, as servants. Layard felt that after the hardships of the past decade, he was entitled to travel in a bit of style.

As the last moment five armed Yezidi *cawals*, or high priests, joined the group. While Layard was in England, they had journeyed to Constantinople with letters of introduction from Layard to Canning, and through the ambassador, the *cawals* had secured an audience with the Sultan. The devil worshipers extracted from the Sublime Porte a firman guaranteeing their sect freedom of religion within the Ottoman empire. Until then, Yezidis were the subject of fearful Turkish pogroms and their women could be legally abducted and sold into Turkish harems. Understandably, the Yezidis looked upon Layard as a savior.

The British Museum's instructions to Layard were direct

and simple. He was to "return to the site of Nineveh" and ship "selected specimens" of Assyrian sculptures and inscriptions to the Museum on Great Russell Street. Everything the party discovered and all the drawings made by members of the expedition were the property of the Museum.

Despite the expeditions' minibudget, Layard planned a breath-taking series of excavations and explorations. In the course of the expedition he would reopen the mound at Kouyunjik and pursue the new leads uncovered by Ross before his departure for Malta. He would reexcavate Nimrod and Khalah Sharghat. He would travel south into Babylonia, resurrect ancient Babylon, and expose to light the Tower of Babel. Somehow, in the midst of these shotgun operations, he would find time to search for Assyrian relics in Susiana, the shadowy zone where the Turkish and Persian empires overlapped. These activities were to occupy the autumn, winter, and spring.

During the terrible heat of summer he would lead excursions into the Kurdish and Armenian mountains north of Mosul and trace the northern limits of the Assyrian empire. In between, of course, he would maintain a daily journal, with a view to writing a new book, carry on a heavy correspondence with relatives and friends, and, naturally, file secret reports to Canning on political conditions in the areas he visited.

On August 28, 1849, the second Assyrian expedition boarded a British vessel in the Golden Horn and set out for Mosul in an unusual manner—by sea. For four days the party steamed through the Black Sea, along the northern coast of Turkey. The voyage was restful and refreshing. At the port city of Trebizon, not too far from the Russo-Turkish frontier, Layard organized a caravan and plunged south through eastern Armenia and Kurdistan. "The novelty of the route," he said, "appealed to my adventurous nature."

In his journal and notes, however, it is plain that one of his ulterior motives was to retrace the march of Xenophon and his Ten Thousand Greeks through this wild country. And he carried in his saddlebag a worn copy of Xenophon's celebrated *Anabasis*. He succeeded admirably, to the delight of Greek scholars and other classicists. Layard was putting into practice the *modus operandi* he learned when, in his youth, he accompanied William Brockenden in search of Hannibal's route across the Alps.

After an uneventful journey through the Kurdish and Armenian settlements along the edge of the great escarpment of Central Asia, Layard's caravan descended onto the Assyrian plains. He was back in Mesopotamia.

News of his impending arrival reached Mosul on the wind, in the mysterious manner in which news travels across deserts, jungles and ice floes.

When the party was within 40 miles of Mosul, Layard's *cawass* saw a horseman, closely pursued by a Bedouin, racing toward the caravan for protection. When the Bedouin spotted Layard's armed group, he turned back and disappeared on the horizon, and the pursued horseman reached Layard almost speechless with terror. He was a Yezidi, and he reported that the Bedouins had butchered a nearby village.

"I urged on the caravan and took such precautions as were necessary," Layard said. "Suddenly, a large body of horsemen appeared on a rising ground to the east of us. We could scarcely expect Arabs from that quarter; however, all our party made ready for an attack."

Cooper, the artist, was paralyzed with fear. Sandwith looked forward to the fire-fight as a bit of grouse shooting. Layard felt the best defense was offense. He and a *cawal* cocked their long rifles and rode out toward the war party to reconnoiter while the caravan drew up the wagons.

"Then one or two horsemen advanced warily from the opposite party," Layard recalled. It was a tense moment.

Suddenly, the *cawal* let out a shout of joy. "In a moment we were surrounded," Layard said, "and in the embrace of friends." A large, armed party of horsemen had ridden through the night to meet and escort Layard, as needed, to Mosul. "Their delight at seeing us knew no bounds," Layard said. "Nor was I less touched by a display of gratitude and good feeling, equally unexpected and sincere."

The following day, Sunday, September 30, as Layard crossed a hillock on the outskirts of Mosul, he saw the walls, towers, minarets, and domes of raunchy Mosul rising along the right bank of the Tigris, "cheating us into the belief, too soon to be dispelled, that Mosul is still a not unworthy representative of the great Nineveh." On the left bank, Layard's clear blue eyes settled on the vast mound of Kouyunjik and, nearby, on the adjoining mound, the white dome which marked the tomb of the prophet Jonah.

With Layard riding point-man and the large band of warriors serving as outriders, the caravan galloped through the crowded bazaar as Turks, Arabs, Kurds, Yezidis, Chaldeans, and Jews waved their hands and shouted welcome. Layard alighted at his old house. Uninstructed, his former servants had reoccupied their familiar places and pursued their regular occupations as if he had never left.

Layard felt he was home again.

"Indeed, it seemed as if we had but returned from a summer's ride," he confessed later. "Two years had passed away like a dream."

Not open, but half revealed,
thou shalt be hid.
　　　　—NAHUM

XXXII As the sunlight
flooded the Assyrian plain on the morning after his arrival in
Mosul, Layard rode to Kouyunjik and reopened the dig. "Little
change had taken place in the great mound since I had last
seen it," he wrote in his journal. "It was yellow and bare, as
it always is at this time of year." Heaps of earth were scattered
across the mound, some accumulations rising 30 feet above
the ruins.

After Ross's departure, the digging had progressed under
the direction of Hormuzd Rassam's brother Christian, largely
to retain the British right to excavation, pending Layard's
return. The elder Rassam, however, had hit upon a novel
scheme for extending the operation and skirting the problem
of removing thousands of tons of earth and debris. He tunneled
along the walls, sinking shafts at intervals to admit light and
air. The tough soil, mixed with potsherds, bricks, and the
remains of buildings erected atop the Assyrian ruins, rendered
the technique simple and safe. When Layard visited the site,
he marveled at Rassam's ingenuity. He felt he was in a Welsh
coal mine. "The subterraneous passages were narrow, and
were propped up when necessary either by leaving columns
of earth, as in mines, or by wooden beams," he observed.

The galleries were dimly lighted and lined with Assyrian
art. Broken urns projected from the walls. Potsherds were

strewn along the palace corridors. Strange statues occupied recesses and corners. Layard strolled through a unique underground museum. His heart throbbed with excitement.

"I lost no time in making arrangements for continuing the excavations," he said. He considered Rassam's method so effective that he imitated it. "I determined to continue the tunneling," he said, "removing only as much earth as necessary to show the sculptured walls."

Unannounced, his former work crews reassembled on the mound that morning and Layard soon put his old gangs to work in the bowels of the stifling mound, one hundred men divided into a dozen work parties. The emaciated Arabs removed the earth and rubbish; the heavier labor with pick was left to hardier Chaldean mountaineers.

Layard's luck at Kouyunjik continued to hold. Work no sooner resumed than he ran into a fantastic series of bas-reliefs in which "the history of an Assyrian conquest was more fully portrayed than in any other yet discovered." The king, accompanied by chariots, cavalry, and infantry, marched through forests and across mountains, storming enemy castles, occupying towns, carrying the war into the heart of the enemy countryside. The heads of the slain were piled up in pyramid fashion. The wounded fell under the feet of advancing cavalry. The bas-reliefs showed long columns of prisoners: men chained together or bound singly in fetters, and women, some on foot, carrying into captivity children on their shoulders. The dominant Assyrian theme was war, and the horrors of war.

In a nearby chamber, which turned into a great hall, Layard found a new collection of gigantic human-headed bulls and eagle-headed and lion-headed monsters. One creature had a human head and the legs and paws of a lion. In the half-light, underground, Layard was reminded of the gargoyles adorning Notre Dame. The strange creatures provided an eerie backdrop to the proceedings as Layard and his workers shoveled away debris, propped up wooden beams in the shafts, and went about their work like groundhogs.

Layard numbered the slabs and oversaw their removal. In a worn notebook, he jotted down a phrase next to each number, thusly: No. 39. Colorful winged figure. No. 45. Warriors on horseback pursuing enemy with spears. No. 62. Head.

An engrossing eyewitness account of Layard at work in this period turned up in 1851 in the journal of Lieutenant F. Walpole, Royal Navy, who used his home leave to travel in the region.

"We were frequently visited during my stay by furious gales from the north-north-west, hot as fire, of great violence, and heralded by clouds of burning dust, which penetrated everywhere," Walpole said. The winds were so hot that Layard's paper dried and curled, and ink stagnated, and he reported, "dinner was as much earth as anything."

Walpole inspected the subterranean passages firsthand. "Descending a few rudely cut steps, a narrow passage leads to one of the regular excavations; there were long galleries, some ten or more—perhaps fifteen feet high, and four or five broad, with the earth cut in an arch overhead, so as to render it less likely to fall in," he recorded. "Every fifteen or twenty feet a hole was cut in the top, open to the surface. . . . It was impossible to enter these [tunnels] without a feeling of awe." He described the bas-reliefs in situ as "beautifully cut" and added, "The inscriptions are as fresh as on the day they were executed." They recalled to him passages from the Books of Nahum and Ezekiel. "These [passages], as I sat," Walpole said, "I saw portrayed on the walls."

The very gloom and twilight of the setting was straight out of the Old Testament. Had not Nahum prophesied, "Not open, but half revealed, thou shalt be hid"?

On October 18, with Hormuzd Rassam at his side, Layard rode off for Nimrod, the mound closest to his heart. The people of the area slew a sheep to celebrate his return.

Like Kouyunjik, nothing there had changed either. Assyrian sentinels astride the mound greeted him. "A few colossal heads of winged figures rose calmly above the level of the soil," he wrote. They were the two pairs of winged bulls, which had not been reburied on account of their mutilated condition.

Layard and Rassam hastily recruited their old work gangs and reopened the excavation. The pay scale was still pitiful, but so was the local economy. First-class diggers, exposed to hard labor and danger, received the equivalent in piasters of 13½ cents per day; second-class diggers, 9 cents. Those who filled baskets with debris also received 9 cents; general workers, 7 cents; and young boys, who sifted rubbish for treasure, 4½ cents daily.

For the first several days, Layard stayed at the nearby village of Nimrod—until the vermin drove him to living in a tent atop the mound.

On the second morning of his return, as he ascended the mound at dawn, he spied a group of travelers on the summit, their horses picketed in the stubble. He approached warily but was relieved to recognize his *bairakdar*, who pointed excitedly to an excavated chamber in the mound. Layard peered in and saw a man wrapped in a great cloak, deep in slumber. It was Rawlinson, wearied by a long and harassing night-long ride, exhausted after a bout with chills and fever.

"For the first time," Layard said, "we met in the Assyrian ruins."

The East India Company's resident was en route from his post in Baghdad to London, via Constantinople. Layard and Rawlinson spent three days together, but for the first couple of days Rawlinson was too ill to walk among the ruins. On the third day, his health improved slightly, and he and Layard made a hasty survey of the excavations. Rawlinson then continued his journey, wishing him well and lamenting that Layard had not been assigned to replace him at Baghdad.

At Nimrod Layard was also visited by Walpole, whose journal again supplied some interesting details. "I ought to mention," he wrote, "that the Arabs on the mound are all well armed, all have good serviceable muskets; these are long barrelled, and the stock short and light. It is a cumburous weapon to use without a rest." The young naval officer found the barrels "excellent" but observed that the springs in the locks were often faulty. "The shots, however, they make with ball are wonderful, and our table was supplied with hare or gazelle daily." The game, he added, was washed down with strong coffee "cooked on splinters of cedar wood, dug from the [ancient] buildings."

The camp itself was lively. The Arab workers shouted as

they carried their loads. "They cursed the people who had made the place so strong, and the work so hard," Walpole wrote. Layard, if he was not directing the digging of a new tunnel or studying a new find, "was hard at work copying off inscriptions."

With the excavations at Kouyunjik and Nimrod reopened, Layard set in motion a whole new series of digs. He inspected the Assyrian ruins near Baasheikah, where a mound about the size of Nimrod stood, irregular in shape, furrowed by deep ravines worn by winter rains. He surveyed the Makloub Mountains, where he suspected the Assyrians quarried their stone. He scurried over the countryside, sextant in hand, taking bearings on the location of mounds (called *tels* in Arabic), among them Tel-Ermah, Tel-Shibbit, Tel-Duroge, Tel-Addiyuh, Tel-Abou-Kubbah, and Tel-Kharala. He also revisited Khorsabad, the scene of Botta's triumph, and picked his way through his old friend's debris. "The sculptures in the palace itself had rapidly fallen to decay," Layard wrote, "and of those which had been left exposed to the air after M. Botta's departure, scarcely any traces remain."

Fortunately, however, in some places, Botta's trenches had collapsed, re-covering and preserving the bas-reliefs. "Here and there a pair of colossal bulls, still guarding the portals of the ruined halls, raised their majestic but weather-beaten man-heads above the soil," Layard said.

Once again Layard waved his magic wand. He assigned several workmen to an unexplored part of the Khorsabad mound and—presto!—they no sooner touched their shovels to the ground than they found inscribed tripods and a collection of magnificently ornamented bricks with Assyrian figures and designs.

Layard spent Christmas Day, 1849, at Nimrod, with Stewart Erskin Rolland, late of the 69th Regiment, and his attractive wife Charlotte—a pair of English travelers who had attached themselves to the expedition—Rassam, Cooper, and Sandwith. The previous Christmas he had sat at the Cannings' table in Constantinople and the Christmas before that he had been in London with his mother and the Austens. He wondered half-aloud where he would celebrate Christmas, 1850.

By February, within six months of reopening the excava-

tions, Layard had collected enough new archaeological treasures to fill another wing of the British Museum.

At Kouyunjik, he discovered panels which showed in detail
how the Assyrians moved the winged bulls and lions into
their palaces—man-hauled on rollers with an assist from
levers, blocks, and tackle. "I used almost the same means!" he
exclaimed.

He also unearthed a façade of the Nineveh palace which
consisted of ten colossal bulls and six human figures, some of
them more than 20 feet high, grouped together and extending
a length of 180 feet. One figure in particular took his fancy,
that of a bearded giant holding a struggling lion in one arm
and a sickle-shaped saber in the other. Layard dubbed him
"the Assyrian Hercules." Actually, the giant was Gilgamesh,
the hero of the epic poem of the same name, of Sumerian and
Babylonian origin, which dealt with the Creation and the
Flood.

Among the important finds was a continuous cuneiform
inscription of 152 lines which neither he nor anyone else
could yet read but which soon would be deciphered and
would turn out to be the annals of the Assyrian king Sennacherib.

Many of the colossal figures in the chamber had been
knocked over, and Layard felt the havoc had been wrought by
a terrestrial catastrophe. "The same convulsion of nature—for
I can scarcely attribute to any human violence the overthrow
of these great masses—had shattered some of them into pieces,
and scattered the fragments amongst the ruins," he said.

Layard also discovered a complete series of thirteen bas-
reliefs, "sculpted with a spirit and truthfulness worthy of a
Greek artist," depicting the Assyrian assault on Lachish,
which, according to the Book of Joshua, was among "the
uttermost cities of the tribe of Judah." Other finds included
several glyptic or cylinder seals, which looked like a roll of
postage stamps. Four bore Egyptian hieroglyphics, and one
contained the seal of an Assyrian monarch and the cartouche
of an Egyptian pharaoh. The double seal had apparently been
affixed to a long-forgotten treaty.

At Nimrod, Layard unearthed another spectacular find—a
chamber which appeared to serve as a repository for royal

arms and sacrificial vessels. The room was a treasure chest of
Assyrian history and art. Among the numerous items in it
were a throne chair of wood overlaid with bronze; copper jars;
bronze plates, cups, goblets, tripods, and cauldrons. The
cauldrons looked as if they belonged in Homer's *Iliad*. Many
of the bowls were covered with figures; on one, Layard counted
six hundred. Some vessels were ornamented with bosses of
silver and gold.

The chamber also disgorged objects of ivory and glass. One
glass bowl, he would soon learn, bore the name of Sargon the
Great, the scourge of the East, who lived almost a millennium
before Christ.

As he studied these works of art, especially the repoussé
work, Layard marveled at the detail. How did the artists of
Assyria work in such microscopic detail? He found part of the
answer in that same chamber: a rock-crystal lens. The convex
side had been fashioned on a lapidary's wheel and was
tolerably well polished. It had been employed as a magnifier.

Another prize in the chamber was a stockpile of arms,
including swords, daggers, shields, and the heads of spears
and arrows, "which being chiefly of iron fell to pieces almost
as soon as exposed to the air," he recorded. The shields stood
upright, one against the other, just as they had been stacked
thousands of years earlier. They were bronze and circular, the
iron handles fastened by six nails, the heads of which formed
an ornament on the outer face of the shield. The diameter of
the largest and best-preserved shield was 2 feet 6 inches. But
the shields were in such an advanced state of decay that with
"great difficulty" Layard was able to procure only two of
them and ship them to England.

In his own mind, however, his most important discovery
was learning more about the secret of the strange "pyramid"
which rose in the northwest corner of the Nimrod mound.
Thirty men tunneled into it, and after penetrating 84 feet into
the base, ran into a wall of solid stone masonry. They burrowed
another 34 feet into the masonry and, in the process, discovered
a flooring of sun-dried bricks. Among the bricks was a yellow
earthen jar, rudely colored with simple black designs. "And
in it [I] found bones, apparently human," Layard wrote.

Then it dawned on him. The cone was "a square tower, and

not a pyramid." The ruin, because of its structure, had simply taken a pyramidal form. He pressed ahead. Finally, within the core of the tower, at the base, he uncovered a vaulted chamber, 100 feet long, 12 feet high, and 6 feet broad. "No remains whatever were found in it," he said, "neither fragments of sculpture or inscription, nor any smaller relic."

But he uncovered evidence that the chamber had once been broken into and he surmised that, like the pyramids of ancient Egypt, which housed the pharaohs, tomb robbers had rifled the chamber of its embalmed king and treasure.

Unknown to him, Layard had penetrated the mound's ziggurat. A feature of Sumerian, Akkadian, Babylonian, and Assyrian places of worship, the ziggurat symbolized the interdependence of heaven and earth, "a tower whose top may reach into heaven," according to Genesis. Layard estimated that the ziggurat at Nimrod rose above the mound for more than 200 feet, a superb feat of engineering.

Nimrod's ziggurat was unique. No arched chamber has ever been found again in the core of a temple tower, although modern archaeologists have torn apart countless mounds and ziggurats in search of a duplicate.

In the midst of these activities Layard still found time to arrange for the removal of the two great human-headed lions he had discovered earlier at Nimrod and for their transportation by raft to Basra.

To protect them from the weather, prior to his departure in 1848 he had covered them with earth. The British Museum had directed Layard "to remove them entire," and in December his laborers had started building a road through the ruins to the edge of the mound. By the end of February the road was completed and the lions man-hauled down it with enormous levers and tilted over the mound onto two carts, their fall restrained by blocks, tackle, and curses. The carts were then dragged to the bank of the Tigris. The Arabs insisted that Mrs. Rolland, an object of uninterrupted attention and curiosity, ride the lions for good luck. She did so, and in this manner the carts finally reached the bank. But it was not until April, when the torrents of spring flooded the Tigris, that the lions were sent on their way aboard two keleks. One raft went aground in the delta and was given up for lost. But Felix Jones, Layard's old friend who had been promoted from lieutenant to captain while Layard was in England, skillfully sailed his steamer abeam of the shoal and rescued the precious cargo.

While removing the lions from Nimrod Layard again confronted the question which has haunted archaeology from its inception: the morality, or immorality, of disturbing the dead, the past.

In *Nineveh and Babylon*, Layard expressed his feelings about the lions solemnly, eloquently, and romantically: "We rode one calm cloudless night to the mound, to look on them for the last time before they were taken from their old resting-places. The moon was at her full, and as we drew nigh to the edge of the deep wall of earth rising around them, her soft light was creeping over the stern features of the human heads, and driving before it the dark shadows which still clothed the lion forms. One by one the limbs of the gigantic sphinxes emerged from the gloom, until the monsters were unveiled before us.

"I shall never forget that night, or the emotions which those venerable figures caused within me. A few hours more and they were to stand no longer where they had stood unscathed amidst the wreck of man and his works for ages. It seemed almost a sacrilege to tear them from their old haunts to make them a mere wonder-stock to the busy crowd of a new world. They were better suited to the desolation around them; for they had guarded the palace in its glory, and it was for them to watch over it in its ruin."

Oh that my words were now written!
—JOB

XXXIII While clearing
out the repository for royal arms and sacrificial vessels at
Nimrod, Layard's workers accidentally discovered two door-
ways leading from the chamber into separate apartments. Each
entrance was formed by two collosal bas-reliefs of Dagon, the
Philistine fish-god.* The head of a fish formed a miter above
the head of the man, while the fish's scaly back and fanlike
caudal fin fell behind as a cloak, leaving the man's limbs and
feet exposed.

Layard, the first to cross the threshold of the first doorway,
found himself in a hall which led to two small chambers, each
opening into the other. The chambers were paneled with bas-
reliefs, but the greater part of them had been destroyed. Layard
beheld a strange sight: the two chambers were entirely filled
with cuneiform tablets. Layard had entered the royal library
of Assyrian kings!

The electrifying discovery recalled to his mind Darius' order
in the Book of Ezra to search "the house of rolls," and Layard
christened the twin rooms "the chambers of records."

"We cannot overrate their value," he said jubilantly. "They
will furnish us with materials for the complete decipherment
of the cuneiform character, for restoring the language and
history of Assyria, and for inquiring into the customs, science,
and we may perhaps even add, literature, of its people."

* See page 172.

(242)

The bricks, or tablets, were in different sizes. The largest measured 9 inches by 6½ inches; the smallest, not more than an inch in length and containing one or two lines of writing. The nail-shaped characters were in pristine condition, singularly sharp and well defined. In some instances, the cuneiform was so minute that it could be read only with a magnifying glass. All told, he collected more than 25,000 tablets from the library.

Walpole, who joined Layard and Rassam in the libraries, noted that the tablets reminded him of cakes of Windsor soap, the most popular of the day in London. "Except," he said, "instead of 'Old Brown Windsor,' they are covered with most delicately cut arrow-headed hieroglyphics [sic]."

News of the discovery spread to the Continent rapidly. When Rawlinson, who only a couple of years earlier was so discouraged by the difficulty of decipherment that he said he was sometimes disposed "to abandon the study altogether in utter despair," heard of the find he was overjoyed. "A perfect cyclopaedia of Assyrian science," he forecast.

And he was right. When the cuneiform code was shortly cracked by Rawlinson and a tiny band of scholars, including, notably, Hincks and Fox-Talbot, it turned out that Layard's library contained dictionaries and grammars, treatises on botany, astronomy, astrology, metallurgy, geology, geography, chronology, tracts on religion and history, and a collection of royal edicts, proclamations, laws, and decrees.

Layard's discovery confirmed the tradition of Seth, the third son of Adam and Eve, who wrote the history and wisdom of the ages before the Flood on burnt and unburnt bricks that the record should never perish. If water destroyed the unburnt bricks, the burnt would remain. If fire destroyed the baked tablets, the unburnt ones would only harden.

At Kouyunjik, the site of Nineveh, Biblical archaeology was born.

Love among the ruins.
—BROWNING

XXXIV With the excavations at Kouyunjik and Nimrod running smoothly, the impatient Layard undertook a series of short forays into the countryside in 1850 in search of more mounds, more ruins—and more adventure. He found them all.

He charted the position of mounds like a ship's captain charting shoals and reefs in strange waters. His list of discoveries boggles the imagination, and he wrote about them casually. "[At Gla] I discovered traces of Assyrian buildings and several inscribed bricks bearing the name of Sennacherib," he said. He also enriched his own background in history. He traveled to Gaugamela (Arbela), where Alexander defeated Darius, put an end to the Persian empire, and altered the destiny of the world; revisited Khalah Sharghat, the Ashur of Genesis; and inspected the rock sculptures at Bavian.

As for adventure, he had plenty of that. For example, as he rode through a patch of jungle along a stream, a wolf rose before him from its lair. "I wounded it with one barrel of my pistol, and was about to discharge the second, when my horse slipped on some wet straw left by a recent encampment and we fell together upon the wolf," Layard said. "It struggled and freed itself, leaving me besmeared with its blood." Fortunately, the cock of the double-barreled pistol broke as he fell, otherwise he would have been killed since the muzzle pointed at his head. As it was, he escaped with a badly bruised hand, "the complete use of which I did not recover for some months."

But these soujourns into the surrounding country were hit-and-miss forays. In the back of his mind, now that he had the resources, was a more ambitious project. He longed to mount a major expedition into untrod country, in particular the terrain along the uncharted Khabour River, which rose in northern Mesopotamia and ran west of the Tigris. But he needed an excuse to satisfy the trustees of the British Museum.

In March 1850, Layard received his excuse. A band of Bedouins from the friendly Shammar Arab clan descended on Mosul bearing a letter from their sheik. The sheik announced that "two colossal idols, similar to those of Nimroud," had suddenly appeared in a mound along the Khabour's banks, and he invited Layard to come to see for himself.

"I lost no time in making preparations for the journey," Layard said.

Such a journey meant traveling in open desert for two or more months. Since there were no permanent settlements along the way, the expedition had to be self-sustaining.

"We were obliged to take with us supplies of all kinds," Layard said. Camels were loaded principally with flour and rice. Over Layard's feigned protestations, Rassam loaded one camel with "luxuries," tea, sugar, coffee, and spices. He also packed bolts of silk and cotton and pairs of red and yellow boots as presents for chiefs they might meet in the desert. Baskets, spades, pickaxes, tents, cooking utensils, and other equipment formed the rest of the baggage.

Layard selected fifty of his best Arab excavators and a dozen Tiyari and Chaldean workers to accompany him. The party also included several Bedouin guides, as well as the indispensable Hormuzd Rassam, the Rollands, Cooper, and Dr. Sandwith. "Our party had swollen into a little army," Layard said with a laugh. In truth it had. The caravan boasted twenty-five camels, twenty-five horses, and one hundred well-armed men who followed on foot. It had "a strange and motley appearance," he noted. "Europeans, Turks, Bedouins, town-Arabs, Tiyaris and Yezidis, were mingled in singular confusion; each adding, by difference of costume and a profusion of bright colors, to the general picturesqueness and gaiety of the scene." Charlotte Rolland was the only woman of the expedition.

Several days out of Mosul, Layard ascended a peak to take bearings. "The vast level country, stretching to the Euphrates, lay like a map beneath me," he said enthusiastically, "dotted with mounds." One in particular stood out, the mound of Abou Khameera, which consisted of a lofty, conical heap surrounded by a square ridge of earth, which Layard recognized, based on his experiences at Kouyunjik and Nimrod, as the remains of ancient walls.

"I ordered the tents to be pitched near the reedy stream and galloped to the mounds, which were rather more than a mile distant," he said. When possible, camps were made alongside rivers and streams, the source of water for drinking, bathing, cooking, and washing, rather than at the site of a dig itself.

At Abou Khameera his workmen opened deep trenches and tunnels in several directions. In the debris he found potsherds and unsculptured slabs of alabaster. "[But] after the most careful search, I could find not even the smallest fragment of sculpture," he complained.

As the expedition rode deeper into the uncharted desert country along the Khabour, "on all sides of us rose Assyrian mounds." His chief guide, Suttum, explained to him that the Bedouins used the mounds to take bearings on their nomadic wanderings.

Layard cursed his lack of funds, that he was unable to undertake a systematic search of each and every mound. At one point, with his naked eye, he counted nearly a hundred mounds. "The great tide of civilization had long since ebbed, leaving these scattered wrecks on the solitary shore," he wrote in his journal. "Are those waters to flow again, bearing back the seeds of knowledge and of wealth that they have wafted to the West? We wanderers were seeking what they had left behind, as children gather up the colored shells on the deserted sands."

The desert air exhilarated Layard like nothing else. The feeling of independence which he had first experienced when he and Mitford embarked on their journey to Ceylon a decade earlier again coursed through him. Like the nomadic Arab, Layard was a son of the desert. The desertscape was uncluttered, unlittered. Only in the desert did he feel as free as the air he breathed. Suttum, his Bedouin guide, was also exhilarated.

"What delight has God given us equal to this?" Suttum exclaimed. "It is the only thing worth living for. Ya! what do the dwellers in the cities know of true happiness . . . ? May God have pity on them."

At the ruins of Sinjar, they encountered friendly Bedouins. Layard was enchanted by the girls. "Among them were several of considerable beauty," he reported, and he described them as possessing dark rich olive complexions, large almond-shaped and expressive eyes of "extraordinary brilliance and fire." Among them was a girl with light flaxen hair and blue eyes. Layard was surprised to see that she "wore necklaces of coins, coarse amber, agate, carnelian beads and cylinders, mostly Assyrian relics picked up amongst the ruins after rain."

On April 3, the caravan reached its ultimate destination, Arban, on the banks of the Khabour, the encampment of Sheik Mohammed Emin, Layard's host and a leader of the Shammar Arabs. Layard immediately went to the spot where the colossal stone monsters were said to have suddenly risen from the earth. He was not disappointed. The river had gradually worn away the mound astride its bank and, during a recent flood, left uncovered a pair of winged, human-headed bulls, some 6 feet above the water's edge and fully 50 feet beneath the level of the ruin. They were pygmy-sized bulls, sculpted from coarse limestone and about 5½ feet in height and 4½ feet in length. Their style of art also differed considerably from previous bulls he had found. The wings on the Arban specimen were small in proportion to the body and did not have the majestic spread of the Ninevite bulls. Also, the sockets of their eyes were deeply sunk.

Layard's first impulse was to start excavations. But, ever sensitive to the culture of the people around him, his first order of business was a reception for the sheik and his camp. Accordingly, he pitched a tent large enough to hold two hundred people. The party lasted two days. Charlotte Rolland, in her European costume, drew much attention from the Bedouins. So did the European men. It was the first time the sheik's camp had ever gazed on the notorious Franks. "They soon, however, became used to us," Layard said, "and things went on as usual."

Whether the Shammar Arabs envied the Franks is doubtful. But Layard certainly envied the sheik. "I must endeavor to convey to the reader some idea of the domestic establishment of a great Arab sheik," Layard noted in his account of the journey. "[His] weakness arising either from a desire to impress the Arabs with a notion of his greatness and power, or from a partiality to the first stage of married life, was to take a new partner nearly every month and at the end of that period to divorce her. The happy man thus lived in a continual honeymoon."

At Arban Layard hired fifty of the Bedouin warriors to supplement his work force and launched a massive attack on the mound with spades and picks. Tunnels were opened behind the bulls. Trenches were dug into the surface of the mound. Immediately, a number of objects were recovered, including fragments of bricks with arrow-headed characters, jars, vases, funeral urns, highly glazed pottery, fragments of glass, and a small green-white bottle with "Chinese characters."

For three days they searched for walls but without success. "I then directed a tunnel to be carried toward the center of the mound," Layard recorded. "I was not disappointed." On the fifth day a second pair of pygmy-sized winged bulls was discovered and a few days after that a magnificent lion in bold style with five legs. The lion was about 5 feet in height.

Among the most startling discoveries was a collection of Egyptian scarabs, some bearing the cartouche of the pharaoh Thotmes III, the Egyptian Napoleon, and another that of Amenophis III, who was succeeded to the throne by the heretic Akhenaten, the first monotheist in history, a precursor of Moses and father-in-law of Tutankhamen, whose gold-filled tomb was not discovered until a half-century ago.

Several tombs were also found in the ruins. "They contained

human remains turned to dust," Layard reported, "with the exception of the skull and a few of the larger bones."

As April drew to a close, hot weather approached uncomfortably near, and Layard and his party broke camp for the return journey to Mosul.

The expedition ended, however, on a troubled note.

Layard was disgusted with Cooper and Sandwith. During the trip neither of them contributed much to the proceedings. Sandwith spent almost all his time on shooting parties (the region abounded in ibex, gazelles, hares, and the bustard, an edible bird), and Cooper kept mooning over his bride. Worse, on the return journey, Cooper and Sandwith came down with fever. So did Rassam, who became "dangerously ill." The caravan halted for five days while Layard and Charlotte nursed Rassam back to health.

These troubles were compounded by deepening tension between Steward Rolland and Layard over Rolland's wife. During the two-month-plus journey, Rolland's admiration for Layard had developed into open hatred and jealousy as Layard's attentions to his wife became more and more obvious.

Coincidentally, on March 6, when the expedition set out for Arban, the London *Times* printed a glowing report from Rolland on what the *Times*'s editors characterized as "Capt. [sic] Layard's ... endeavors to bring to light the hidden antiquarian treasures of Nineveh."

In the report, Rolland described Layard flatteringly.

"You can have no idea of the difficulties Layard has to contend with, or the energy, talent and perseverance, and shrewdness with which he surmounts them, or the equal tact and good humour with which he manages the different people he has to deal with," Rolland wrote.

Rolland also recounted how "Mr. Layard, Charlotte and I and our servants embarked on a raft and floated down the Tigris in seven hours to Nimroud." And at another point, quite innocently, Rolland explained how Charlotte assisted Layard in preparing several Assyrian relics for shipment to England.

"My wife was employed the night packing them," he said.

On one occasion in mid-April, as Rassam and the others

recuperated from a bout of malaria, Layard, with Charlotte mounted behind him and clinging onto him for support, took off across the desert on a swift camel to visit a neighboring sheik's encampment.

Rolland apparently thought he had been made a cuckold, and several days later Layard reported a "painful scene" between the Rollands. Rolland beat her "most cruelly," Layard said in a private letter to a friend, adding, "I was alarmed by her screams and, seeing her struggle with him in an open tent, had him immediately seized."

When Rolland recovered from what Layard described as "his mad fit," he apologized, but Layard refused to accept the apology unless he packed his bags and left for England immediately. This is the chord on which the expedition arrived back in Mosul on May 11. The Rollands left the following day.

Several weeks later, in a letter to Henry Ross, who was then in Constantinople, Layard confessed, "I shall feel her loss much as she is the only [English] person who has given me the slightest assistance—copying inscriptions, notes, M.S., and taking bearings."

Layard enclosed a sealed letter for Ross to give to her and added, "She will probably write a few private lines to let me know how they have got on, which she will entrust to you." Layard underlined the word "private." If Charlotte wrote, there is no record of it. In any event, she dropped out of his life. Like two caravans passing each other's paths in the desert at night, they went their separate ways after their brief encounter.

> I marched by difficult roads
> over steep mountains.
> —ASHURNASIRPAL

XXXV The Rolland incident and the behavior of Cooper and Sandwith took some of the edge off the successes of Layard's second expedition into Assyria.

After the Rollands departed for England, things at the camp grew progressively worse. Cooper and Sandwith came down with new attacks of malaria. During the frightful heat of the summer of 1850 they retreated into the hills around Lake Van, where Layard mounted another excursion in search of far-flung Assyrian sites while they tried to recover their health. But the mountain air did them little good, and they informed Layard of their intention to "throw in the sponge" and return home. Layard was disgusted. He and Rassam were as ill as they were, but clearly Sandwith and Cooper—who now had taken to drawing sketches of his wife from memory—lacked the desire and drive to see the expedition through to the end.

Sandwith was not replaced. But in November the British Museum dispatched T. S. Bell, a former student at the government's School of Design, as Cooper's replacement. Bell turned out to be a young, brash, insensitive colonial type who lorded it over the misbegotten "natives." He reached Mosul at the end of February and barely lasted three months. Against the advice of the "natives," he took a swim in the Gomel River, a tributary of the Tigris, was swept under by the swift current, and drowned. His drawings were lost en route to London. There is nothing to show for his brief role in the formative period of Assyrian archaeology except a death notice in the London *Times*: "In carrying on his excavations amongst the ruins of Nineveh, [Bell] unfortunately drowned."

Except for the dedicated and devoted Hormuzd Rassam, Layard was now alone. "I have had but very little assistance [from England]," Layard complained in a letter to the trustees of the Museum, "and am now without any."

But if Layard expected help from the trustees, he was disappointed. They objected to meeting the expenses of Layard's Kharbour explorations. In a state of pique, Layard wrote the trustees a steaming letter in which he declared that he would bear *all* the expenses except for the pittance spent by the workers on the actual dig at Arban. He accused London of treating him "shabbily," and his log of the Khabar expedition bears him out. The expedition's supplies cost a mere 824 piasters (about $41), including 90 piasters for three sheep, 22 piasters for barley, and 6 piasters for salt.

But the letter from the trustees arrived as his funds ran low, and at Nimroud he had all but suspended excavations for lack of money. "At Kouyunjik they were still carried on actively as my means would permit," he said. His means were limited to royalties from *Nineveh and Its Remains.*

Without Rassam, the expedition would have collapsed then and there. In *Nineveh and Babylon,* to the embarrassment of the Museum, Layard flatly stated that to Rassam "the trustees of the British Museum owe not only much of the success of these researches, but the economy with which I was enabled to carry them through."

Sandwith, back in London, spoke as highly of Rassam, "a Chaldean by birth, English in tastes and education and regarded by Layard with considerable affection. His duties," Sandwith said, "are multifarious. He acts as interpreter and secretary. He marshals the servants, keeps the money-bags, speaks all unknown languages, and keeps [everyone] amused by his gaiety. . . ."

As before, Layard sought to overcome his sense of isolation and desperation by plunging into work. As long as he was in motion he felt all was not lost. He rose at daybreak and pushed himself until past midnight. He directed the dig, sketched architectural plans, copied inscriptions, arranged for the crating and shipment of relics, and kept the expedition's journal. Rassam, for his part, shared in the general supervision of the operations, paid the workers, maintained liaison with the Turkish authorities and local sheiks, and settled unending disputes among the workers.

Both men were ill with malaria. "Fortunately our ague attacks did not coincide," Layard said later. "We were prostrate on alternate days, and were therefore able to take charge alternately of the work."

Layard's only flight from work in this period was spending an occasional evening at the home of Hormuzd's brother Christian. Her Britannic Majesty's vice-consul had furnished his house with European comforts—a settee and a goodly store of the most recent books. The "latest" Punch, usually three months old, was always on the table, and an exhausted Layard would often sit and stare at it, drink in hand. England was so distant that it was a vague memory.

By the end of summer, however, half delirious from malarial attacks, the depressed Layard himself retreated from Mosul and took refuge in the mountains. "Few European travellers can brave the perpendicular rays of an Assyrian sun," he apologized.

And yet, in England and the Continent, as Rawlinson soon discovered on his return to London, Layard was a hero of the day. He was popularly referred to as either "the lion" or as "Mr. Bull," a nickname which stuck. His first winged bull and human-headed lion had just arrived at Chatham aboard H.M.S. Apprentice. They were quickly put on display to the delight and astonishment of the general public. Layard's "duplicates" also arrived, crates of Assyrian relics as gifts to Oxford University in repayment for their honorary degree and to the Guests at Canford. Indeed, Charlotte Guest added a new wing to Canford Manor and filled it with Assyrian antiquities— a lion, bull, bas-reliefs, and cuneiform tablets. She called it their "Nineveh Porch." Enid, Charlotte's third child, now seven years old, played hide and seek among her uncle's strange gifts.

That summer, too, a new edition of *Nineveh and Its Remains* rolled off Murray's presses and was soon followed by Layard's first foray into the scholarly world, *Inscriptions in the Cuneiform Character from Assyrian Monuments*, a handsome, coffee-table tome bearing the imprint of the British Museum and edited by Edward Hawkins, the Museum's new secretary. Each line of inscription contained a descriptive phrase by Layard identifying the place of its discovery; for example, "between hind-legs of Bull No. 2. Entrance e, Chamber B, Kouyunjik."

As a critic of the last century expressed it, "These books, published during his absence from England, created an extraordinary impression throughout Europe far beyond anything Layard could ever have dreamed of."

Rarely a month passed in this period that some eminent journal such as *Athenaeum*, *The London Monthly Review* or *The Journal of the Royal Asiatic Society* did not have a squib on his latest activities. Enthusiastic letters from home, primarily from his mother and the Austens, also assessed him of his growing celebrity. But these letters, instead of cheering him, served only to further depress and embarrass him. Layard took a dim view of "celebrities."

"I despise the mere flattering and lionising which follows the kind of success I have had," he wrote home, "and I do not think I shall be deceived by them." Nor was his attitude a case of false modesty. As Rassam later described this side of his character, "He hated humbug."

In his heart, Layard believed he was a failure, and nobody could convince him otherwise. The facts spoke clearly for themselves. Aside from the paltry job of embassy attaché—clerk, really—he had a token income and no future. Doubtlessly, his repeated bouts of malaria and the abominable heat strongly reinforced this state of mind. Physically and mentally, Assyria was draining him, exhausting him.

Whether it was his nasty letters to the trustees, the success of his books, the arrival of new shiploads of Assyrian treasures, the strengthening of Evangelicalism through Layard's discoveries, or a combination of these factors, the British Museum surprisingly appropriated another £500 to his fieldwork and implied that there was more to come.

There may have been another, more subtle, reason for

England's upsurge in interest in Layard. As an Oxford scholar later put it, "One cannot help thinking that these enormous bulls had something very much in common with the ponderous, conservative philosophy of the mid-Victorian period, with its unshakable faith in this best of all possible worlds, with its definite social castes duly prescribed by the Catechism, all doubtless to be maintained in *saecula saeculorum*."

Be that as it may, with the infusion of new funds, Layard turned his eyes southward. "The winter was now drawing near," he wrote in his journal, "and the season was favorable for examining the remains of ancient cities in Babylon." His decision made news in London.

"Mr. Layard," the press reported on October 11, 1850, "has now proceeded to Babylon."

To Babylon you shall go.
—JEREMIAH

XXXVI

Press reports aside, Layard did not leave Mosul for Babylon until six days later. He spent a week feverishly crating a new shipment of sculptures for the downstream journey by raft to Basra, where a British vessel waited to transport them to England. Then Layard, Rassam, and thirty of their best Arab workers, each heavily armed, clambered aboard keleks to ride them shotgun-style down the Tigris.

Mesopotamia was now in the grip of anarchy. Turkish authority had broken down; the Bedouins and other tribes plundered the countryside at will. The situation was so chaotic that, even with an armed party of his own, Layard for the first time deemed it expedient to pay the Bedouins "protection money" to ensure the safe passage of the rafts. "The navigation of the river as far as Khalah Sharghat was so insecure," he said, "that I deemed it prudent, in order to avoid a collision with the Arabs, to engage a Bedouin chief to accompany us."

The strategy worked. For three days they were borne swiftly downriver without incident, stopping briefly at Tekrit, the only permanent settlement between Mosul and Baghdad, a nondescript place remembered chiefly as the birthplace of Saladin, hero of the Crusades and chivalrous foe of Richard the Lion-Hearted. During the passage to Tekrit, armed Bedouins periodically appeared along the banks to reconnoiter the movement of the rafts, but, Layard reported, "under the protection of our sheikh we met with no hindrance."

Although this was Layard's third voyage down the Tigris, he busied himself taking fresh notes and bearings on the confused heaps of mounds the convoy passed. "On both sides of the river, as the raft is carried gently along by the now sluggish current, the traveller sees huge masses of brickwork jutting out from the falling banks or overhanging the precipices of earth which hems in the stream," Layard wrote. "Here and there are more perfect ruins of buildings . . . the remains of the palaces and castles of the last Persian kings and of the first Caliphs."

On October 25 the keleks drifted within sight of the colored domes, minarets, and date groves of Baghdad. The following day the flotilla anchored "beneath the folds of the British flag," opposite the stately mansion of the political agent of the East India Company where Layard first met Rawlinson.

In the absence of Rawlinson, who was still on home leave regaining his strength and being promoted to the rank of colonel, Layard was welcomed by a Captain Kemball, the acting Company resident.

To Layard, Baghdad was still the city of his youth, of the *Arabian Nights*, of the Hanging Gardens, a glittering oasis. Before setting off for Babylon, he spent some time unwinding in the vaunted, vaulted bazaars of the old quarter, with their polyglot mix of Turks, Arabs, Persians, Jews, and Hindus, their painted palaces and unsightly hovels and their renowned fleshpots.

Unexpectedly, but not unhappily, Layard found himself stuck in the city. "I found the country around Baghdad so overrun with Bedouins and other tribes in open revolt against the government," he said, "that it was some time before I could venture to leave the city for the ruins of Babylon."

On December 5 it was finally safe enough for him to form a caravan and travel to Hillah, 60 miles south of Baghdad, just north of the ruins of ancient Babylon.

As Layard pushed south, the Old Testament sprang to life. This was the land of Shinar, where the children and flocks of Noah first gathered after the Flood, where men had built a

lofty tower to heaven as a beacon so they would not lose their
way in the desert, where the children of Judea were carried
into captivity, and where King Nebuchadnezzar sat on a throne
of gold.

Hillah was a misbegotten place, not unlike Mosul, a disheveled town of about eight thousand people, several half-
ruined mosques, a bazaar filled with dates and coffee, Sheffield
cutlery, and a few bolts of Manchester cloth. The Euphrates
careened langorously through the town, "a noble stream with
gentle current admirably fitted for steam navigation," Layard
recorded, with the Englishman's eye on trade. Most of Hillah's
houses were built of bricks taken from the nearby ruins of
Babylon.

At Hillah, where Layard established "winter quarters" and
celebrated Christmas, 1850, the Turkish garrison commander
sent out a column of irregulars to escort his caravan to a
spacious town house which had been set aside for his party.
"It had once contained rich furniture and handsomely decorated rooms in the Persian style," Layard said, "but was now
fast falling into utter ruin." Cold wind whistled through the
rotted wooden panels of the windows (there was no glass),
the ceiling was crumbling, and the floor threatened to give
way under his weight.

Late in the day, he called on the Turkish commander and,
to his astonishment, was presented with a gift of two lions.
One was a cub, which died shortly thereafter; the other was
nearly full grown and became Layard's fast friend. But the
beast was too old to send to England, and Layard said
unhappily, "I was thus unable to procure specimens [for
England] of the Babylonian lion, which has not, I believe, been
seen in Europe." This species of lion, portrayed in glazed
Babylonian mosaics and in Assyrian bas-reliefs, was about the
size of the North American puma.

Layard also paid his respects to the mudir, or local governor,
an aged, infirm man who was incapable of conducting public
affairs and entrusted the task to his favorite son, a twelve-
year-old. "It was with this child that, in common with the
inhabitants of Hillah, I transacted business," Layard said.

The boy proved surprisingly capable and displayed warm

interest in Layard's expedition. Each morning the boy would cross the Euphrates with a retinue of attendants, servants, and slaves and visit Layard's dig. "We trust that it has pleased God to preserve your excellency's health," the boy would say with stilted solemnity. "Our heart begs your excellency's acceptance of sour milk and francolins [partridge]. May we show that we are your slaves by ordering the irregular troops to accompany you on your ride? Your person is more precious to us than our eyes, and there are evil men, enemies of our Lord the Sultan, abroad in the desert."

Suppressing a smile, Layard would nod gravely.

The boy was a daily joy, and Layard presented him with a kaleidoscope before leaving Hillah. "On the whole," Layard commented, "he made as good and active governor as I have often met with in an Eastern town, and was an instance of precocity which is frequently seen in Eastern children."

Hillah's setting—the ruins of Babylon—confused Layard. "The mounds seem to be scattered without order," he observed, "and to be gradually lost in the vast plains to the eastward." Everywhere were ruins, and Isaiah's judgment was in the air: "Babylon is fallen, is fallen; and all the graven images of her gods hath broken unto the ground."

Layard's initial focus of interest was a great ruin about 5 miles from Hillah which dominated the horizon and was the first great mound he had seen on approaching Babylon from the north. Layard immediately recognized it as the remains of a "square tower," similar to the one at Nimrod. The Arabs told him it was the Mujellbe, "the overturned," the site of the Tower of Babel.

Layard went to the spot and assaulted it with pick and spade. He employed Rich's memoirs as a guide and in particular searched for the underground chamber where Rich had found a wooden coffin and skeleton. Success was almost immediate. Within a few days Layard had not only located the lost chamber but had also amassed a splendid collection of burnt bricks inscribed with two lines of cuneiform. In another year or two, with the deciphering of cuneiform, the lines turned out to be the name and titles of Nebuchadnezzar.

Beneath the chamber Layard unearthed several coffins.

"They still held skeletons, more or less entire, which fell to pieces as soon as exposed to the air," he said. "No relic or ornament had been buried with the bodies. The wood of the coffins was in the last stage of decay, and could only be taken out piecemeal. A foul and unbearable stench issued from these loathsome remains."

Clearly, the coffins were of a comparatively recent period. But Layard's disappointment was assuaged by the discovery of small glass bottles, bronze and iron arrowheads, earthenware in different forms and shapes, and some vessels glazed with an especially rich blue color, like a Tintoretto painting.

Then he realized that if original ruins existed in the mound they must be at ground level. He abandoned his ghoulish work in the trench atop the mound, and opened tunnels at the base.

"A few days labor enabled me to ascertain that we had at last found [an] ancient building," he said. In great excitement, he and his workers tore at the mound and were rewarded by the discovery of a series of walls. Layard had reason to believe that he was hot on the trail of a major discovery. "But I failed to trace any plan," he said in disappointment, "or to discover any remains whatever of sculptured stone or painted plaster."

Nevertheless, compulsively, he pressed ahead with the underground tunnels. He found the limestone fragment of a slab or frieze with two odd figures wearing stovepipe-like hats trimmed with rosettes and feathers. "With the exception of a few rudely engraved gems and enamelled bricks," he said, "this was the only relic I obtained from the Mujelibe."

While his work gangs tackled the core of the Mujelibe, Layard and a few armed men rode out to inspect Birs Nimrod, "the palace of Nimroud," actually the site of ancient Borsippa, about 6 miles from Hillah. The mound rose 198 feet above the plain of Shinar, a bare yellow heap of bricks, slag, and broken pottery.

Until Layard inspected the mound Birs Nimrod was thought by most visitors to be simply another shapeless mound, perhaps a former palace. But based on his experience in northern Assyria, he immediately spied the terraces in the mound and recognized that it was a square tower. (In their general appearance, the terraced temple towers of Assyria and

Babylon were not unlike the terraced skyscrapers of New York millenniums later.)

Layard intended to return to the site after completing his work at the Mujelibe, but the region soon became a shooting gallery between Bedouins and Turkish irregulars, mostly Albanians, and the tumult precluded further excavations.

Layard now turned his attention to the site of Babylon itself. The area was a shambles of debris. "On all sides," he recorded, "fragments of glass, marble, pottery and inscribed brick are mingled with that peculiar nitrous and blanched soil which, bred from the remains of ancient habitations, checks or destroys vegetation, and renders the site of Babylon a naked and hideous waste."

In the few low shrubs among the ruins, Layard frequently saw flocks of large gray owls, recalling Jeremiah's prophecy that following Babylon's destruction "the owls shall dwell therein."

Once again, however, an area of promise turned into a quagmire of futility. His prize discoveries there were fragments of glass inscribed on the inner surface with letters "in form not unlike Hebrew." He shipped the fragments to England, where Thomas Ellis, a celebrated mid-Victorian Hebrew scholar in the British Museum's manuscript division, identified the writing as belonging "to the descendants of those Jews who were carried captive by Nebuchadnezzar to Babylon and the surrounding cities."

But beyond these bits and pieces, Babylon was a bust.

In search of an explanation, he cited the tradition that Xerxes, to punish and humiliate the Babylonians, ordered the utter destruction of their temples and other structures, and that Alexander later employed 10,000 men in a vain attempt to clear the rubbish alone from the temple of Belus, the Babylonian Zeus. "It is not surprising that with a small band of Arabs little progress should have been made uncovering any part of the ancient buildings," Layard, who had grown accustomed to easy triumphs in Assyria, said defensively.

But a more logical explanation for his failure to uncover significant remains was the nature of the materials the Babylonians employed in the construction of their cities. In southern Mesopotamia there were no quarries of alabaster or limestone as existed near Nineveh. The Tower of Babel, for example, according to Genesis, was built with brick for stone and slime for mortar. Moreover, for more than two millenniums the ruins of Babylon served as a mine from which builders, after the fall of Babylon, obtained their materials. "To this day," Layard wrote, "there are men who have no other trade than that of gathering bricks from this vast heap and taking them for sale to the neighboring towns and villages, and even to Baghdad. There is scarcely a house in Hillah which is not almost entirely built with them and as the traveller passes through the narrow streets, he sees in the walls of every hovel a record of the glory and power of Nebuchadnezzar."

Turning his back on Babylon, Layard attacked in other directions. The mounds lying east of Hillah appeared especially enticing, but because of the insecurity in the region, he was again compelled to travel under the protection of a sheik. He sent a special messenger to the chieftain of the Afaij Arabs, who inhabited the area around Niffer, the site of ancient Nippur, and asked for an armed escort. The sheik was extremely hostile to the Turks but "well-disposed towards Europeans" and consented. He probably considered the Franks potential allies against Turkish rule. Losing little momentum, on January 15, 1851, a bright and intensely cold Wednesday, Layard organized a caravan and set out east through the deserts of southern Mesopotamia.

For the first time in years, he was not accompanied by Rassam. Hormuzd had succumbed to another severe attack of malaria and was so desperately ill that Layard had sent him to Baghdad to be treated by Dr. M. Hyslop, the East India Company's physician.

Unlike most deserts of Western Asia, the area Layard now crossed was not a sandy plain with clumps of occasional stubble. Rather, it was composed of shifting sand hills extending far and wide on all sides, the most forboding desert he had ever experienced. The hills of sand were just high enough to block out the view of the surrounding country. It was impossible to take bearings, except on the sun during the day and the stars at night. The caravan moved like a ship through the troughs of a building sea. When the wind rose in the south it raised dense, suffocating clouds of sand, blinding the way of the traveler and leaving him to perish in the trackless labyrinth.

The first mound the party came across was called Haroun. "Human skulls and remains scarcely yet bleached by the sun," Layard recorded, "[are] scattered over the ruins mingled with bricks, pottery, broken glass and other relics of ancient population."

As they moved on, a war party of Bedouins rose on their flank and followed Layard's caravan for some distance before bearing off into the surrounding desert. "They deemed it prudent not to venture an attack," Layard said. "We were fully prepared for them."

Soon the caravan came upon another series of artificial mounds littered with fragments of bricks, pottery, glazed tiles, and richly colored glass. Layard recognized the clues. "The site of Babylonian ruins," he recorded. Now, for the first time, dried-up canals, no longer fed by the Euphrates, also crossed his path like the hatching on hot cross buns.

Although Layard was still 10 miles from his objective, the mounds of Niffer suddenly towered on the horizon "like a distant mountain." It was a mirage. "Magnified as they were by the mirage they appeared to exceed in size and height any artificial elevation that I had hitherto seen," Layard said.

With the caravan moving at the rate of about two knots, they reached the ruins five hours later. The Niffer mounds were unlike those of northern Assyria. They had more the appearance of ruined buildings than a platform surrounded by walls.

Layard went to work immediately.

"Commencing my search after antiquities as soon as we had reached the summit of the principal mound," he said, "it was not long before I discovered in one of these newly-formed ruts, a perfect vase, about five feet high, containing human remains."

The following day Layard told his protector, the local sheik, of his plan to camp with his workers beneath the very mounds themselves during the excavations. The sheik was stunned.

He warned Layard that he would be stripped of everything within twenty-four hours, and perhaps be killed in the bargain, by marauders. Even if, by a miracle, he escaped this fate, Layard would find it "utterly impossible to avoid a still greater danger in the Jinns and evil spirits who swarmed after dark among the ruins," the sheik counseled. To complete the litany of perils, the sheik continued soberly, "Wild beasts without number live amongst the mounds."

Judiciously, Layard decided to camp at Souk, the sheik's fortified camp. Each day the sheik and several of his armed followers accompanied Layard and his workers to the mound, ostensibly to guard them against raiders but more likely to be on hand in the event gold was discovered.

On this occasion, the local people had good cause for such a belief. From time to time, Arabs picking among the crumbling ruins turned up ornaments of gold and silver. According to tradition, a ship of gold filled with bullion and a great black stone were still hidden within the mound of Niffer.

In cold weather—during midwinter temperatures drop into the forties from the Indus River in the east to the Nile in the west—Layard started to dig. Dividing his workers into kar-khanehs, or gangs, he placed them in different parts of the ruins.

On the very first day they found a series of brick cells, 6 feet deep and 3 feet wide, containing human remains. During subsequent days they unearthed vases and jars, some glazed and others plain. One of the bowls was covered with ancient Hebrew characters, the same as Layard had found in Babylonia.

But the most common relics found were fragments of highly glazed pottery, rich blue in color, very coarse and fragile in texture. "I was at a loss to conjecture the nature of the objects of which they had originally formed part," Layard said.

On the fourth day the mystery was solved. A party of workers uncovered a sarcophagus of precisely the same material, and inside were human remains, which crumbled to dust almost as soon as exposed to the air.

Soon they were turning up scores of coffins, some ornamented with scrollwork.

"Sometimes, as the lid was carefully removed, I could almost distinguish the body, wrapped in its grave clothes, and still lying in its narrow resting place," he said "But no sooner did the outer air reach the empty crust of humanity than it fell away into dust, leaving only the skull and great bones of the arms and legs to show what these empty cases had once contained."

The sheik watched intently. Layard may also have had a touch of gold fever as he burrowed into Niffer. If he did, he was disappointed. "It is remarkable, however, that there were no ornaments whatever in metal in nearly a hundred coffins which I opened at Niffer," he said.

Impatient as usual, Layard decided to shift his attention from Niffer to Wurka, which, unknown to him at the time, was the site of Biblical Erech. But again his plans were thwarted. "Unfortunately," he explained, "the state of the country to the south of the marshes was such that I was unable even to make an attempt to reach the remarkable ruins of Wurka."

At the point, the mosquito-infested marshes around Souk and the dampness of the soil under his tent caught up with his state of near physical exhaustion. He came down with an almost fatal attack of malaria complicated by pleurisy. He lost weight rapidly and was soon so weak he was unable to lift himself from his bed. To worsen matters, unceasing torrential rains fell during this period and water soon coursed through his tent.

In a state of desperation and delirium, Layard took as medicine a "blistering fluid" given to him for an injured horse. "Fortunately," Layard said later, "[it worked] or I should probably not again have left the Afaij swamps."

Hormuzd, meanwhile, had recovered his health and had set out to rejoin his companion. When Rassam found him, Layard appeared to be crossing into the Assyrian *arallu*, the land of no return. Rassam was determined to remove him to Baghdad for medical attention.

A week later, with Layard barely well enough to mount a horse, he and Rassam and two armed guides from the sheik set off for Baghdad. If the ride did not kill Layard, perhaps nothing would. He rode for fourteen straight hours, and this after complete abstinence from food during his two-week battle against malaria and pleurisy. Layard could hardly summon enough strength to carry himself through Baghdad's gates.

His Arab workers fared worse. They had left Niffer for Baghdad by foot and en route, in search of water, approached the tents of some Arabs. They had fallen in with a Bedouin plundering party. Robbed of all their possessions, they were left naked in the desert to fend for themselves. Miraculously, they reached the small Arab hamlet of Bashayi and were clothed and fed.

In Baghdad Layard was attended by the same Dr. Hyslop who had saved Rassam's life. As it was, Layard did not regain sufficient strength until February 27 for the overland return journey to Mosul.

Layard's southern expedition had been a disaster.

The luck of Nineveh was either running out or did not extend as far south as Babylon, once a province of the Assyrian empire. In any event, Layard sensed that he had reached the end of his journey into bygone worlds. He was ill, tired, and depressed. He had found the outer limits of his determination and endurance.

Layard was now thirty-four years old, lean and bearded. He had been out of touch with his own world, except for the brief interlude in England, since 1839, a dozen years. He knew nothing of the rapidly developing pre-Raphaelite school of British painting. New books and plays were unknown to him. He had not lunched on shepherd's pie in ages. He had forgotten the taste of a pint of half-an'-half. He had not read a newspaper on the day of its issue in years. He missed the creature comforts of mid-Victorian England, of the cricket on the hearth, and, above all, Canford Manor. He recognized that for a true archaeologist and Assyriologist there was no journey's end. Yet he had reached the end. The terrible heat, the vermin, the repeated bouts of ague, the coarse way of Mesopotamian life, the parsimony of his financial backers, his uncertain future— all combined to bring him to a dead end in his search for a lost world.

The moment had come to return to England.

I departed from Nineveh.
—ASHURNASIRPAL

XXXVII

By the middle of March, Layard was back in Mosul. He stayed long enough to put his affairs in order, and a month later, he left for England via Constantinople, just before the heat of summer descended on the Assyrian plain.

Layard recognized, of course, that much was left to explore. He had blazed a path across the heartland of Assyria; it was now for others to follow him.

But it was doubtful if anyone could equal his capacity and match his productivity. In the mound opposite Mosul alone he had uncovered seventy-one halls, chambers, and passages whose walls, almost without exception, had been paneled with slabs of sculptured alabaster, recording the annals of a supposedly mythical empire. A year later, with the initial breakthrough in cuneiform, he learned that the walls of Kouyunjik were those of Sennacherib's palace.

"By a rough calculation, about 9,880 feet, or nearly two miles of bas-reliefs, with twenty-seven portals formed by colossal winged bull and lion-sphinxes, were uncovered in that part alone of the building explored during my researches," he wrote in his journal. "The greatest length of the excavations was about 720 feet, the greatest breadth about 600 feet."

Most of the chambers of the Ninevite palace ran 20 to 35 feet below the surface of the mound.

More important than statistics was that, on the eve of his departure, he had taken a step toward a new and refined method of excavation, although it would not be fully understood or appreciated for another generation. At Nineveh it slowly dawned on him that the temples and palaces of the Assyrians had been built at different levels in different time frames. "As buildings there appear to have been erected at various times on the mound," he wrote, "we accordingly find in the rubbish remains of various periods."

Thus, he sowed the seed of horizontal excavation. In time, this technique gradually replaced the bulldozer methods of the heroic age of archaeology—pell-mell trenches, tunnels, and shafts.

Although he was worn and sick, Layard regretted leaving an uncompleted job. He especially regretted never having dug at Nebbi Yunnus, the mound adjacent to Kouyunjik and the purported site of the tomb of the prophet Jonah. "The sanctity of the place prevented any attempt to excavate openly," he said.

A small village had risen around the mosque containing the tomb while the slopes of the mound itself had been converted into a Moslem burial ground. For years Layard had turned over the problem in his mind. How could he dig into the mound and under the tomb of Jonah without exciting the emotions of Islamic religious zealots?

As he completed arrangements for his departure for England, fate provided an opportunity. Layard learned that the owner of one of the larger houses on Nebbi Yunnus planned to dig an underground apartment as a retreat from the summer heat. Layard immediately offered to excavate the basement at his own expense "on condition that I should have all the relics and sculptures discovered during the excavations." The so-called stones meant nothing to the owner, and he agreed.

After a few days of digging, Layard's workers came to the walls of a chamber paneled with inscribed but unsculptured alabaster slabs. He recognized the inscriptions as similar to those of Nimrod. When the arrow-headed characters were decoded a little more than a year later, he learned that they bore the name of Esarhaddon.

That was the extent of his excavations at Nebbi Yunnus and, indeed, to this day, nobody has yet launched a massive assault against the mound—although Hormuzd Rassam tried—nor is anyone likely to do so as long as it is revered by Moslems as a religious shrine.

Ironically, when Layard left for England, he was still uncertain about the location of Nineveh. Although in *Nineveh and Babylon*, Layard blithefully identified Kouyunjik as the site of Nineveh, he still exhibited uncertainty about it. He even speculated that perhaps Nebbi Yunnus, the adjoining mound, might be the site of Nineveh.

Thus, when Layard left Mosul, he left not knowing what he had unearthed. It was a dilemma which was to plague Schliemann at Troy a generation later.

Schliemann found nine cities atop each other in the mound at Hissarlick, in northwestern Turkey, the Troad where Layard had vacationed with Lord Cowley. Schliemann knew one of the levels was the Troy of Homer and *The Iliad*, but he went to his death never knowing which was the city of his dreams.

As Layard prepared to leave Mosul, the countryside grew more insecure daily, and he was compelled to delay his departure until a heavily armed caravan set out for Constantinople. "It was doubly necessary for me to have proper protection," he explained, "as I took with me the valuable collection of bronzes and other small objects discovered in the ruins."

On April 27, 1851, he walked among his beloved mounds for the last time, and he pondered the meaning of meaning. Without success, he tried to understand the sudden resurrection of a great and glorious empire "in the midst of modern ignorance and decay."

The next day he bid a last farewell to his friends at Mosul "with a heavy heart," and turned from the ruins of ancient Assyria.

He knew he would never return. But Assyria was not done with him—nor he with her.

> I can forgive Layard for finding Nineveh;
> I cannot forgive Nineveh for finding Layard.
> —EMILY EDEN

XXXVIII The thirty-five-year-old Layard could not have timed his return home more dramatically. In 1851 a new mood of national pride and unity swept England. He arrived in London in July, two months after the opening of the Great Exhibition, the first modern world's fair. The fair's central attraction was the Crystal Palace, a towering mass of iron and glass which rose 282 feet above Hyde Park.

Much to Layard's astonishment, Nineveh was the topic of the moment. Public schools offered prizes for essays based on Ninevite themes—composed, of course, in Latin. Walter Savage Landor, the author-hero of an impressionable young Layard when he struggled with Uncle Ben's law books, published a poem in Layard's honor. "Layard!" he sang, "who raisest cities from the dust." Amid the commotion, Layard was made a Citizen of London and given the keys to the city.

Books on Nineveh were the rage, and bookstalls at the Great Exhibition displayed them prominently. Layard's friend and admirer James Fergusson, the author of several volumes on art and architecture, brought out *The Palaces of Nineveh and Persepolis* and dedicated it to Layard, "the indefatigable explorer and able illustrator of Assyrian antiquity." The year before Layard's return, a member of the British Museum's staff, W. S. W. Vaux, cribbing from the reports of Layard,

Rawlinson, and others, wrote "an account of recent researches" entitled *Nineveh and Persepolis.* By 1851 Vaux's book was in a third printing.

But Layard's first thought on reaching London was neither the Great Exhibition nor Nineveh. It was on Canford Manor and Lady Charlotte Guest.

Ignoring his mother, brothers, and the Austens, Layard beat a track straight to Dorsetshire. Charlotte, now thirty-seven, as lovely as ever, warmly greeted her "Ninevite," as she called him, and, despite his state of weariness, arranged a swirl of soirees for him. He was put on display like an Assyrian trophy. After a fortnight of this, Layard threw up his hands. "I am heartily sick of London," he wrote, "and its great people."

Thereafter, life at Canford Manor quieted down. Layard contented himself playing games with the children, eight-year-old Enid, her brothers and sisters, and their friends, including another nine-year-old girl, Janet Duff Gordon, who, in a memoir written fifty-four years later, vividly recalled her first meeting with Layard.

"Here is the man who dug up those big beasts you saw in the British Museum," she was informed, "and he is called Mr. Bull."

John Guest was bedridden at the time, and Layard spent Christmas week that year at Canford. Lord Bessborough, a relative of Charlotte's and the editor of her diaries, said, "He made himself responsible for entertaining the ten children, so leaving Lady Charlotte to look after her husband."

When Sir John died the following year at the age of sixty-seven, Charlotte went into mourning for six months, and on her first venture in public, she joined Layard at Covent Garden to hear *Fidelio.* "I felt some scruples on the matter of this first going out again," she wrote in her diary, "but I muffled up going and coming, and sat at the back of the box, and so escaped notice." The gossips were having a field day, however, and Layard's name became linked romantically with his cousin's.

In London, Layard made the rounds—his mother's place, the Austens, the British Museum, the Foreign Office, and John Murray, who urged Layard to cash in on the Nineveh craze by coming up with an edited, popular account of *Nineveh and Its Remains*. While recovering his health, Layard worked on the project and completed the editing in September. Murray rushed it into print. Fourteen thousand copies were sold within a year. The book was so popular it was reissued in 1867. In New York, Harper's brought out an American edition; at Leipzig, a German edition appeared.

"I have just published an abridgement of the first work in one volume," Layard wrote Ross on November 30, 1851, "which has sold exceedingly well and will bring me in something."

Simultaneously, in a tour de force, Layard also worked on two other books, his mammoth *Discoveries in the Ruins of Nineveh and Babylon* and a new coffee-table volume, *Second Series of the Monuments of Nineveh*.

"My [Babylon] book is still far behind," he wrote in a letter shortly before Christmas, "and there is no chance of its being ready before spring." It took longer than even the industrious Layard expected. He did not complete *Discoveries* until January 1853. "It has been fortunate for me," he told Ross later, "that I have not broken down."

Murray published the Babylon work and promptly sold the American rights to Putnam in New York. Layard had scored another literary success. But, for readers, there must have been confusion.

With one hand, Layard edited a volume which identified Nimrod as Nineveh; with the other, he wrote a book which pinpointed Kouyunjik as Nineveh. If there was a contradiction in his mind, or that of John Murray, neither of them referred to it in their voluminous correspondence.

Archaeology's growing popularity prompted the British Museum to put Layard in charge of a third expedition into Assyria. To the trustees' consternation, however, Layard balked. He had at last had his fill of the Arab world.

"I shall certainly not leave England again if I can help it," Layard confided to Ross. "I shall make a desperate effort not to return to the East, not even to Stamboul [Constantinople], which does not agree with me in any way—the climate always disagrees with me and I can find neither books nor society."

Layard also made known his views to Rawlinson, who was

about to return to Baghdad for another tour as British proconsul in Mesopotamia, and Hormuzd Rassam, who had recently returned to England, with Layard's connivance, and hoped to take up permanent residence there. "Mr. Layard had suffered so much from the common fever of the country [Mosul]," Rassam wrote later, "that he did not care to venture again to that inhospitable clime."

Matters quickly came to a head.

A subcommittee of the trustees met with Layard and Rawlinson at the British Museum Saturday, August 2, 1851, "to confer with Mr. Layard and Colonel Rawlinson as to the continuance of researches in Assyria." The Museum passed the ball to Rawlinson and agreed to finance a new, two-year expedition under his charge at a rate "not to exceed £1,500 per annum." However, since Rawlinson would be preoccupied with political affairs, the trustees left it up to him to appoint an assistant to carry on the work under his general supervision.

Layard's decision not to return to the East left him in an awkward and familiar predicament. Other than royalties from his books, he had no source of income. Pride—and gossip— would not permit him to continue living indefinitely at Canford. But what kind of employment should he seek? Frequently, he and Charlotte talked it over. Why not capitalize on Nineveh, as Canning and others had suggested, and enter politics? "I should like," he confessed to Ross, "to get into parliament in England and think that, if once there, I could push my way."

With the new year Layard's fortunes altered, abruptly and favorably. On January 2, 1852, the prime minister, a Liberal, invited him to No. 10 Downing Street for an interview. Lord Russell had heard much about the young man from Canning, and Canning's replacement, Lord Cowley, who was now taking up a new post as Her Britannic Majesty's envoy to France, the foreign office's most attractive and sensitive mission.

Cowley promptly offered Layard a plum, the position of embassy secretary at Paris at £500 pounds a year. Before Layard could leap at the opportunity, however, Russell's foreign minister, Lord Granville, astonished Layard—and London—by naming Layard undersecretary of the foreign office.

The reason for surprise was Layard's lineage. His family did not belong to that small cluster of names that ruled the empire, a coterie of power brokers who played musical chairs as Liberal and Tory governments rose and fell during Victoria's reign. Indeed, nepotism was one of the critical weaknesses of Victorian England, not only at the top but right down the line. The spoils system, based on family connections, was encouraged; advancement on merit, discouraged. On occasion new blood was pumped into the system. Layard was one example; Disraeli another.

Layard's appointment was enthusiastically received by public and press. Canning wrote a note of congratulations; so did Disraeli, who was pushing his way in parliament in a manner that Layard envied. The Austens were delighted. Sara told everyone that the Austen influence during his adolescence probably had much to do with sweeping him into the corridors of power. Uncle Ben termed the appointment "an accomplishment of all my hopes."

The euphoria lasted nine days. On February 20 Russell's ministry fell. But when the House of Commons was dissolved, Layard saw the opportunity to enter politics, and grabbed it.

"I am now making arrangements for entering parliament," he wrote Ross April 10, 1852. "Once in the House I have a career open to me . . . of course it will depend upon myself how far I shall be able to take advantage of it."

Layard contested in Aylesbury township, where his parents had lived and his father had died eighteen years earlier. Although Aylesbury was considered a safe Tory seat, Layard was confident of victory. "My election is almost a certainty," he wrote a friend. And it was. He swept the polls. "It was a complete triumph," Layard said July 9, "and most gratifying."

Lady Charlotte threw a wild victory celebration for him at Canford. "By the first train from London (about 12:30 P.M.) Henry Layard arrived," she wrote in her diary July 8. "Nothing can have been more triumphant and satisfactory than Henry Layard's election," she wrote. "The bells rang. . . . Some of the village people had guns and fired off cannons."

Upon his election, Lord Granville proffered him words of counsel: "I believe the best advice which can be given was given to me by an excellent judge, when I first went into the

House of Commons. Never, till your reputation is established, speak on any subject but those that you both know and are supposed by others to know, and never, however tempting the occasion may be, condescend to personalities."

Layard, as impatient, impetuous, and independent-minded as ever, promptly ignored the advice. For five stormy years he represented Aylesbury. "Public life in England is a tempestuous sea," he complained, "in which it is difficult to steer clear of the rocks and sand-banks."

In Parliament, he lived up to his nickname Mr. Bull. He was a bull in a china shop—and was thus depicted in a cartoon in *Punch*. He was a maverick, a liberal conservative and a conservative liberal. No label, no slot, no pigeonhole, no political party fitted him. Ardent liberals and conservatives misunderstood him. "My position is . . . a delicate one," he told Ross. "Taking an independent line, I cannot, of course, expect much from the government that is now in power, and, on the other hand, I have completely broken off with the other party."

He was denounced on both sides of the House as either "Mr. Lie-hard" or as "the Bedouin of Parliament." In a classic remark, one of his critics, the author Emily Eden, declared that she could forgive Layard for discovering Nineveh but she could not forgive Nineveh for discovering Layard.

In parliamentary debates, Layard bristled. He descended into personalities, and on one occasion his remarks in the house had to be bowdlerized for the permanent record.

Lord Aberdeen, who had blocked his appointment to the diplomatic service more than a decade earlier, was his bête noire. He assailed Aberdeen's appeasement of Russia. "Where are you to stop Russia?" Layard asked. "How many centuries did they not throw back the civilization of mankind!" During the Crimean War he visited the front and was appalled. He accused the government of sacrificing thousands of British lives "on the shrine of inconsistency and neglect." He toured India, the jewel of empire, shortly after the Indian mutiny of 1857, and was shocked. "The people we govern are treated like a distinct race, inferior to us—more, indeed, as if they were a lower order of creatures," he declared.

Layard defended Cavour and the emergence of liberal in-
stitutions in Italy, and he rallied to the cause of the Turk while
a horrified, evangelical Gladstone denounced the Sublime
Porte as a "barbarian." Layard raised almost everyone's hack-
les, including Victoria's, on about every issue that came before
Parliament.

Yet, in private, he had admirers. Disraeli, who soon emerged
as the most colorful and powerful prime minister of the
century, described Layard as "a genius" and often joshed him
for not joining the Tories.

In 1857, when Layard opposed reprisals against India for
the "mutiny," he was defeated for reelection. Three years later
he was returned to Parliament.

In her memoirs, Janet Ross, who had played with Charlotte's
children at Canford and first met Layard there, brilliantly
summed up Layard's predicament.

"The impulsiveness which made him so lovable in private
stood in his way in public life," she wrote. "Generous and
high-couraged to a fault, he would rush into the fray, and
occasionally make assertions he could not prove without
giving the name of his informant and getting him into trouble—
a thing he would rather have died than do. A sentence in one
of his letters to me as a young girl: 'I *am* always getting into
hot water,' was only too true."

These endless parliamentary rows convinced Layard that
he was unsuited for Parliament, a conclusion that terrified
him. If he could not hack it in politics, how was he to earn a
living? "The split between myself and the ministries is now
complete, and I suppose all chance of employment out of the
question," he wrote a lady friend after a particularly bad day
in the house. "I do not mind. I have done what I believe to be
my duty and I trust I shall always be able to refer back to what
has occurred some conscientious satisfaction."

But, inwardly, he did mind.

And yet, outspoken as he was, he attracted, developed, and
maintained strong friendships, particularly in the worlds of
arts and letters. Among his staunchest allies, for example, was
Charles Dickens, whom Layard first met in 1853 as Dickens
completed *Bleak House*. Like the fire-eating Huguenot, Dick-

ens empathized with mistreated minorities, railed against social injustice, and assailed the spread of soulless, sordid urban blight in Britain as the Industrial Revolution gathered uncontrollable momentum.

Among the Layard Papers in the British Museum is a neatly tied bundle of letters from Dickens, 1854–69, really notes, on light blue stationery, signed in a scrawl, "CD." Among them is one which reads: "Now that I am at home again, will you come to us this Christmas?" Imagine! Christmas with the creator of Ebenezer Scrooge and Tiny Tim.

Nor was Assyria still too far removed from his mind. When the Great Exhibition of 1851 closed down, there was a public outcry against destroying the fabulous Crystal Palace, that "giant greenhouse," as Robert Furneaux Jordan, the architectural correspondent of the London *Observer*, called it. In truth, the Crystal Palace was the first miracle of prefabrication, and Joseph Paxton's concept was not duplicated for nearly another century.

The Crystal Palace, moved to Sydenham Hill, included a new section called the Assyrian Court. Layard and James Fergusson, his architect friend, were commissioned to design the Court, and in Paris they received the most cordial cooperation of the government, the Louvre, and the Ecole des Beaux Arts. The French also gave them permission to make casts of objects retrieved from Mesopotamia by Botta. The Court at the newly situated Crystal Palace was 120 feet long, 50 feet wide, and 40 feet high.

Entering the Court, which was guarded by colossal bulls, the visitor found himself in a large hall, in the center of which stood four great columns copied literally from columns found by Botta and Layard. The walls were covered with sculpture cast from the originals Layard found at Nimrod. To many visitors, the exhibit, which was popularly called the Nineveh Court, outshone the Crystal Palace itself.

Layard was commissioned to write a brochure on the exhibit, and the result was a book-in-miniature, consisting of eighty pages, *The Nineveh Court in the Crystal Palace*. The booklet was published in 1854 and immediately became a collector's item. In the introduction, Layard stressed that the French went out of their way to collaborate in the construction of the Court and gave full credit to Botta as the first to discover Assyrian ruins.*

Assyria was not his only diversion during these turbulent political years. As a bachelor he was in steady demand, and obviously a splendid catch. There were affairs with a "Miss A" and a "Miss C." Gradually, the lust for life affected his physical appearance. He put on considerable weight and, with his short frame, developed a portly silhouette. His face filled out, his already heavy brows thickened, and by the end of the 1850s he took to regrowing a beard.

Aunt Sara tried her hand at matchmaking; she thought domestic tranquillity would absorb his nervous energy. Charlotte Guest apparently thought similarly. But Layard artfully dodged their intrigues. One reason was that, despite his wayward affairs, he genuinely believed marriage should be "deep . . . enduring."

Clearly, finding Nineveh was easier than finding a wife.

* The Court was destroyed in the fire of 1866.

XXXIX

Rawlinson, on his return to Mesopotamia, sought to pick up where Layard left off. In the fall of 1851 and through the spring of the following year, he labored among the ruins of Kouyunjik and nearby mounds. Rawlinson's blind spot, however, worked against his success as an excavator. He ignored art, architecture, and artifacts. He made no effort to remove, for example, the great sculpture at Kouyunjik depicting Sennacherib before Lachish, which Layard had left intact when he ran out of money and energy.

Instead, Rawlinson hunted for an Assyrian "Rosetta Stone." To the exclusion of everything else, he was possessed by a desire to decipher Assyrian writing.

During this period, as anarchy in Turkish Arabia spread, Rawlinson came close to losing his life. As he was descending the Tigris on a raft after a reexamination of Khalah Sharghat, roving Bedouins fired on his kelek. At the moment of the attack, Rawlinson was writing and held an ink bottle in his left hand. A bullet struck it from between his fingers, and one of his raftmen was killed.

By the summer of 1852, Rawlinson became embroiled at Baghdad with political affairs and sent a signal to London for an assistant. There was a sense of urgency to his request: the French had recently reentered the competition for Assyrian antiquities. Paris had established the Ninevite Commission under the capable Victor Place and provided him with excavators, artists, and funds to resume the work abandoned by Botta more than a decade earlier.

When the French arrived in Mesopotamia, Place and Rawlinson reached an understanding not to infringe on each other's previous excavatory sites. This meant Khorsabad was French; Nimrod and Khalah Sharghat, British; as for Kouyunjik, where both nations had dug, Layard's tunnels, pits , and shafts at the southern end of the mound were considered a British preserve while the French occupied the northern end.

Back in London, Layard strongly recommended Rassam as Rawlinson's assistant, a suggestion which both Rawlinson and the British Museum heartily approved. Rawlinson was delighted to have a man who "graduated under Layard, and was thoroughly competent to the task." On August 14, 1852, Rassam completed arrangements and booked passage for the Near East aboard the "screw steamer" S.S. *Pirate*.

Three days before Rassam's departure, Layard sent a memorandum to the trustees and urged that Rassam's first order of business should be "the removal to England of several series of bas-reliefs remaining in different chambers at Kouyunjik, and amongst them the sculptures representing the siege of Lachish."

Layard also took the occasion to press the trustees for payment of a medical bill for a former superintendant in his service, whose foot was broken in a fall in one of the tunnels. Obviously, Layard was not one to forget his men.

Rassam, accompanied by the English artist Charles Hodder, arrived in Mosul in October and for the next two years regularly plied Layard with reports on his excavations. In effect, Layard directed the third Assyrian expedition by remote control. The trustees were aware of this arrangement and were grateful for his guidance.

For example, a typical entry in the minutes of the British Museum contained an extract of a February 8, 1854, report from Rassam to Layard "respecting some sculptures discovered in the northern part of Kouyunjik mound, which had not been thoroughly examined" (italics added). Thus, the official record shows that only excerpts of the Rassam letter were received by the Museum. In point of fact, the excerpts avoided a report on one of the more explosive episodes in Assyrian archaeology.

When Rassam first returned to Mosul, it seemed that there was a Frenchman hiding behind every mound. He set up his base of operations at Nimrod and sent excavation parties scurrying around the countryside—in effect, implanting the British flag. The French flew the tricolor at Khorsabad and embarked on a similar strategy.

At Khalah Sharghat Rassam discovered a French camp atop the mound and was outraged. "The place is crown property," he stormed. "As a matter of etiquette no agent of any national museum [may] attempt to interfere with the operation of the other." But Rassam was diplomatic. His mission at Khalah Shargat—probably at Layard's suggestion—was to reexcavate in the area where Layard had unearthed the headless black statue of Shalmaneser and the Tiglath-Pileser terra-cotta cylinder containing eight hundred lines of cuneiform inscription. Accordingly, he told the French they could dig wherever they liked in the mound except at that spot. Rawlinson supported Rassam's position.

While digging in Layard's tracks, Rassam made a remarkable find, a duplicate terra-cotta cylinder in almost a perfect state of preservation. The cylinder was destined to play a major role in the decipherment of cuneiform.

But Rassam's "great aim," he confessed in a memoir he wrote some forty years later, was to excavate the northern end of Kouyunjik, "which, in my opinion, had never been thoroughly explored." The northern part of the mound, of course, was French. "My difficulty was how to do this without getting into hot water with M. Place," Rassam said.

Stealthily, on the night of December 20, 1853, Rassam and a work party armed with spades, picks, and kerosene lamps ascended the northern slope of Kouyunjik and began to dig. "I told them they were to stop work at dawn. and return to the same diggings again the next night," Rassam said. "The very first night we worked there one of the gang came upon indications of an ancient building."

For three nights, undetected, the furtive work continued. In those three nights, Rassam uncovered a fantastic Ninevite palace, complete with halls, chambers, and walls covered with bas-reliefs. He then proceeded to lay claim to it for England by relying on "the established rule that whenever one discovered a new palace, no one else could meddle with it."

News of the palace's discovery spread like brush fire through Mosul, and Victor Place, superintending excavations at Khorsabad, hurried to the scene. He was furious and accused Rassam of violating the Anglo-French accord agreed to by Rawlinson. The scene was ugly. The following February, as Layard reported "excerpts" of Rassam's letter to the trustees, Rawlinson sought to placate Place. After selecting from the newly discovered palace a number of bas-reliefs for the British Museum, Rawlinson invited Place to choose between seventy and eighty sculptures from the remainder for the Louvre.

Rassam continued to dig on the site, however, which later proved to be a palace built by Ashurbanipal at the time of Nineveh's fall. In the course of his excavations, Rassam recovered another Assyrian library, equal if not superior to the library unearthed by Layard. It consisted of inscribed terracotta tablets of all shapes and sizes; the largest of these, which were in superb condition, were stamped with seals, some in hieroglyphics and others in Phoenecian characters. Obviously, the library included the state archives, and among the items were the texts of treaties the Assyrians signed with foreign powers.

At the end of his two-year stint in Mesopotamia, Rassam was able to ship to England 360 cases of bas-reliefs, sculptures, and cuneiform inscriptions. It was an impressive accomplishment. Rassam, however, lacked Layard's intellectual curiosity and did not possess a semblance of Layard's discipline. He rarely took notes on what he found or where he found it. His collections of relics were thrown together like scenes in a kaleidoscope. But it would be wrong to fault him. It took more than another generation before archaeology developed into even a rudimentary science. In the middle of the last century, archaeologists were largely "collectors."

Rassam was uncertain about his reception on his return to London in 1854. Layard was both elated and embarrassed by his protégé's work. Rawlinson, however, felt Rassam had carried out his duties "with zeal and prudence"—obviously, more zeal than prudence. Neither Layard nor Rawlinson condoned Rassam's furtive actions, but they felt he was justified in his behavior because the French had broken an earlier understanding on Khalah Sharghat.

If there was uncertainty in Rassam's mind, it vanished at his first meeting with the trustees of the British Museum. "They asked me to go out again for them to Assyria," Rassam said proudly. "I accepted their offer with great pleasure."

Rawlinson and the foreign office, however, had also been closely watching Rassam's work. They were impressed with his command of languages, knowledge of local customs, daring, and initiative—and his loyalty to the crown. He was more English than the English. As Rassam began organizing a fourth Assyrian expedition, the foreign office offered him a political appointment at Aden, a sensitive post on the Red Sea.

"I was at a loss what to do," the twenty-eight-year-old Rassam said. He turned to his mentor for advice, and Layard did not hesitate. Take the diplomatic posting, he counseled Rassam, and for once, look forward to a regular job and regular pay. Working for the Museum was a dead end. The job was temporary at best, the pay a joke, and who ever heard of making a career out of digging up the past?

The Museum's trustees released Rassam from his commitment. "They were glad I was going to have a permanent employment," Rassam said ruefully.

The question now was: Who would take Rassam's place? Layard was in Parliament and expressed no interest whatever in returning to Mosul.

Fortunately for the Museum, the previous year Layard had helped set up an Assyrian lobby in London as a form of public pressure on the Museum, and he promptly offered his organization's assistance.

The Assyrian Exploration Fund, as it was called, enjoyed the active financial support of Prince Albert, Lord Russell (the former prime minister), and other luminaries. Its purpose was twofold: to build a fire under the Museum, which continued to operate in Assyria on the cheap, and to backstop continued exploration there if the Museum suddenly backed out.

Rawlinson had taken a dim view of the Fund's creation. He

considered it a rival. "The institution of an Assyrian Society with independent funds, independent powers, and perhaps independent views, must be expected, more or less, to embarrass the operations which I am now conducting on behalf of the Museum," Rawlinson wrote the trustees September 26, 1853, two months after the Fund was set up.

The friction between the Fund and Museum in the field started almost immediately. Before the end of 1853 the Fund sent out its own expedition, comprising William Loftus, a geologist with experience in the region, and William Boutcher, an artist whom Layard hand-picked and who subsequently put rings around the Museum's earlier choices, Cooper, Bell, and Hodder. In the Layard tradition, Loftus was to write about his activities in *Researches in Assyria, Babylonia and Chaldea.*

"Really," Rawlinson wrote the trustees, "to appear as a competitor, whilst our works are still in full activity, seems to me not only indelicate, but prejudicial to the interests both of our own party and of the other."

Rawlinson's disapproval is surprising, because he apparently did not complain about the formation of a Crystal Palace Company that same year as a commercial venture aimed at exploiting Nineveh and its remains for profit. The unsavory details are not clear, but the British Museum apparently granted the company permission to dig up duplicate relics Layard had left *in situ* in Assyria and offer them for sale to European and American interests. It was through this sort of wheeling and dealing that the Berlin Museum acquired its impressive Assyrian collection. Significantly, Layard had no connection with the company, and in retrospect it appears he helped promote the Fund to head off the Crystal Palace Company at the pass.

Loftus arrived at Mosul shortly before Rassam wound up the third expedition and immediately began excavating at Kouyunjik. A three-way tug-of-war over Nineveh now erupted, involving the British Museum, the Louvre, and the Assyrian Fund.

The conflict of interests sharpened when Loftus struck pay dirt, a magnificent series of sculptures at a level lower than those disinterred by Rassam. "In following up his discovery,"

Rawlinson warned the Museum, "he [Loftus] is continually encroaching on the *terrain* reserved for the Museum operations, and risking *collisions between rival workmen*." The emphasis was Rawlinson's.

As it turned out, the squabbles over the future of Assyrian excavation coincided with the outbreak of the Crimean War, involving Russia on one side and Turkey, backed by Britain and France, on the other. Continued exploration in Mesopotamia became academic. The public lost interest in Nineveh just as it had during the French Revolution of 1848.

On February 20, 1855, with the war in full swing, the Assyrian Fund's promoters summoned a general meeting to "wind up the affairs of the association, consequent upon the exhaustion of finances, and the present disturbed state of the East."

Ironically, the collapse of public interest in Nineveh and the termination of excavations coincided with one of the great moments in the history of Assyriology—the decipherment of cuneiform.

Favorable signs in heaven and earth . . .
favorable oracles.

—ESARHADDON

XL Ever since the days of
Claudius and Mary Rich, scholars had labored in vain to
decipher cuneiform. Progress was made but, as one Assyriologist later put it, "there was too much chaff mixed with the
few grains of wheat which remained after sifting."

As the Crimean War spread in 1855 and the Assyrian digs
closed down, the last breakthrough occurred. The achievement
was largely the work of an Irish clergyman, Dr. Edward Hincks,
whom history has treated shabbily. Through the late forties
and into the fifties, piece by piece he solved the mystery. But
his accomplishments were consistently downplayed. Part of
the explanation lies in his lack of scholarly credentials, part,
that he was not a member of the Victorian Establishment. For
example, when Hincks reported some major advance in translation, he was accorded a short paragraph in *Athenaeum*.
When Rawlinson, who was later knighted, made some observation, the commentary filled three columns.

Yet the decipherment of cuneiform is worthy of being
included among the great achievements of the nineteenth
century. "Only a hundred years ago it was still possible to
maintain that there was no such thing as cuneiform," A. J.
Booth wrote at the turn of the century, "and that the mysterious
figures that went by that name were merely a grotesque form
of ornamentation."

Almost simultaneously with Hincks's discoveries, parallel breakthroughs occurred in England and France. Many scholars, however, remained skeptical. In 1857, shortly after the Crimean War ended, the claims of these Assyriologists were put publicly to the test. Rubbings of the almost perfect clay cylinder Rassam retrieved from Khalah Sharghat four years earlier served as the litmus. Copies were distributed among four claimants. The quartet included a Protestant soldier (Rawlinson), an Irish clergyman (Hincks), a Jewish refugee (Jules Opert, who had moved to France, since Jews were not permitted to pursue academic careers in Germany), and the gadfly mathematician, astronomer, and inventor of photography whose hobby was cryptography (William Henry Fox-Talbot). The Royal Asiatic Society established a committee to check their independent translations against one another.

It was a tense moment, and not only for Assyriology and Assyrian archaeology. Evangelicalists and agnostics nervously awaited the outcome.

While the four translations were not precisely the same, there was no doubt that each of the participants could read the nail-headed inscriptions. Now, for all time, the shroud of mystery which had hung over cuneiform for thousands of years was lifted. The Rassam cylinder, it turned out, contained the annals of Tiglath-Pileser, who reigned in 1400 B.C., more than three millenniums earlier. The cylinder was by far the oldest historical inscription which had—up to that time—been discovered among Layard's mounds.

"All the Assyrian kings mentioned in the Bible have now been identified," Rawlinson proclaimed shortly afterward, "and many others mentioned in the works of profane writers." As for the debate between Biblical students and doubters, while the Reverend Ussher's chronology of the world was consigned to the hellbox of history, the agnostics were forced into a retreat. "An erroneous impression was at one time in circulation that the information obtained from the inscriptions was adverse to Scripture," Rawlinson lectured the British Association at Glasgow. "But so much was it the reverse of this that if they were to draw up a scheme of chronology from the inscriptions, without having seen the statements of the

Scriptures, they would find it coincided on every important point."

And J. W. Bosanquet, in *The Fall of Nineveh*, based on the first translations of Layard's discoveries, wrote, "There can be little doubt that, within a few years from this time, we shall know as much of the date and history of Sennacherib, king of Assyria, as we now know of the reign of William the Conqueror of England."

"The chamber of records in his palace has been laid open by Mr. Layard," he said.

Layard himself was equally delighted by the breakthrough. "We cannot overrate [cuneiform's] value," he exclaimed. "The tablets furnish us with materials for the complete decipherment of the cuneiform characters, for restoring the language and history of Assyria. . . . The documents which have been discovered at Nineveh probably exceed all that have yet been afforded by the monuments of Egypt."

In new editions of *Nineveh and Babylon*, and other works, Layard updated his material to include the translations of the inscriptions he had unearthed more than a decade ago. He also rushed to draw attention to the unsung hero of Assyriology, Hincks: "In any other country but England a man of such attainments and so eminently calculated to confer honor upon the nation to which he belonged, would have received some reward, or would have been placed in a position of independence to enable him to pursue his studies. But in spite of numerous representations to government and of the European reputation he had established, Hincks was allowed to remain without any public recognition of his literary and scientific acquirements."

Actually, Hinks received some recognition of his work, the Conyngham Medal of the Royal Irish Academy. But among the scholarly snobs of the big English universities, this was viewed as a "provincial" honor.

Incredible as it may seem today, some scholars refused to believe the evidence of 1857. A French savant as late as 1864 flatly argued that cuneiform was not decipherable. In England, some years later, Sir George Cornewall Lewis, who consumed almost nine columns in *The Dictionary of National Biography* (Hincks received one column), went a step further. "Neither

Egyptian nor Assyrian can ever be restored," he declared. He did not even believe in Champollion's stunning decipherment of the hieroglyphics on the triscript Rosetta Stone.

Layard followed these academic pyrotechnics with wry amusement. But while he was stimulated by the work of Hincks, Rawlinson, Opert, and Fox-Talbot, and immersed himself in new editions of his popular books on Nineveh, he was never stimulated enough to return to Mosul. The second time around was a lasting cure.

Yet, his interest in art deepened, and his involvement was strongly influenced by his experiences among the Assyrian mounds. For example, he was among the first to understand the urgent necessity for a civilization to protect from decay and destruction the indelible, undoctored history of its age—its art.

Thus, in 1858, a century ahead of his time, Layard launched a spirited drive to save the relics of Venice from the encroachment of the Industrial Revolution. "Talk of London smoke," he exclaimed, "why, Italian neglect, indifference and ignorance have done more to deprive the world of some of its noblest and most precious monuments of art than could be accomplished by the atmosphere of ten Londons!"

He also went, single-handedly, to the rescue of the dying Arundel Society, which had been founded a decade earlier for "the preservation of the record ... of the most important monuments of paintings and sculpture by engravings and other mechanical means of reproduction."

"The success of the Society seemed for some time very doubtful," Sir William Gregory, the president of the organization, confessed later. "But Layard, having returned from the exploration of Nineveh, turned his energies to Italian art ... [and] was elected to the Council [sic]." As a result of his election, Layard at once proposed that the Society should reproduce the frescoes of the Italian masters which were falling into decay. When the Society protested it lacked funds, Gregory recalled, Layard "volunteered, at his own expense," to underwrite much of its work. He saved the Society. His actions reflected a return to his old love, Italian art.

Thus, during his volatile years in Parliament, each summer Layard took refuge in Italy from the broil, embarking on a comprehensive restudy of Italian painting. Starting in 1858, he regularly filled the columns of the *Quarterly Review* with lengthy articles on Italian painting, with occasional forays into the world of Dutch, Flemish, and German art. Many of his readers must have been astonished by his versatility and virtuosity. For every column on art there was a column on foreign affairs—the Crimea, Cavour, Russian expansionism, the Eastern Question, Abyssinian affairs, and so on. "What a wonderful man you are to find time for everything," a friend wrote, "and how I envy you that great and rare faculty."

In Italy, Layard also made tracings in outline with his own hand from the decaying frescoes of the fourteenth- and fifteenth-century masters for the Arundel Society's annual. He also wrote a series of monographs on the paintings of Ottaviano Nelli, Domenico, Ghirlandajo, Giovanni Sanzio, and Pinturicchio, among others. But the arrest of decay was his prime interest. "I have been very busy making fresh plans for the Arundel Society, and endeavouring to find some means of preserving records of the great works of art with which the sanctuary of St. Francis at Assisi abounds, but which are fast perishing," he wrote Aunt Sara from Rome on November 11, 1858. "Every time I return to Italy I find fresh progress in the work of decay. ... The most important frescoes [must] be copied before it is too late." How many times had he written the same lines to the British Museum about Assyrian art! Nobody seemed to appreciate the need for urgency.

Layard's interest in Italian art was a continuing affair. Ten years later he was writing Aunt Sara from Venice about his founding of the Murano Glass and Mosaic Work Company, for the purpose of reviving these art forms. The company was almost in perpetual need of subsidies. Pulling strings, Layard won it a fifteen-year contract to repair the mosaics of St. Mark's Church. "This enables us to form a regular school of young mosaicists, which will be very useful to the art," he wrote her January 6, 1868. "Moreover, I have now a department for painting on glass, which promises exceedingly well, and employs young artists. ... The glass blowers have made wonderful progress, and are improving every day."

His friends had grown accustomed to his losing himself in art on these trips to Italy, a form of escapism from the pressures of British parliamentary life. But he was also a well-known political figure in Italy and a staunch supporter of Italian unification. He could not escape politics completely. "I have been so much occupied with politics and art that I have really had scarcely any time to write anyone," Layard wrote on one occasion from Rome to Janet Duff Gordon, a friend of Enid Guest, who was now, like Enid, a young woman of twenty-four. "When I take my run abroad for a couple of months I usually eschew all manner of letter writing, leaving my afflicted friends in darkness as to my movements and whereabouts."

Layard did not finance his cultural pursuits out of his earnings as a member of Parliament. The explanation for his affluence and largess lies in the financial jackpot he hit in 1856, barely five years after his return to England.

In the aftermath of the Crimean War, trade in the Near East burgeoned, the Sublime Porte was in need of developmental loans, and Turkish reformers—Layard's allies in his youth—had surfaced at Constantinople. French and English banks scrambled for the business. Two prominent London bankers conceived the idea of setting up the Imperial Ottoman Bank to handle large transactions. They cast around for a front man, and Canning recommended his protégé. The bankers invited Layard to join them as the Ottoman Bank's chairman. At last, his long years and extraordinary contacts the length and breadth of the Ottoman empire produced dividends.

Layard found international banking akin to politics, and he was fascinated by its diplomatic intricacies. Within a short time he was playing an active and pivotal role in the bank's success. The bank soon reaped profits, and among his intimate friends Layard jestingly referred to it as the bank "which supplies me with that which is dearest to me—pounds, shillings and pence."*

* The bank has since dropped the word "imperial" from its masthead. But it continues to flourish. At its 110th general meeting of shareholders, held in London, Liverpool Street, May 4, 1977, the chairman, M. J. Babington Smith, a Layard successor, reported that "our business has once again shown an increase in all fields, particularly in Turkey." He added, ". . . our branches have been able to increase their activities in a satisfactory manner and in this way continue to make their contribution to the economic development of the country." The Ottoman Bank's assets totaled £333,003,745 and on June 3, 1977, paid a dividend of £2.50 per share in Istanbul (Constantinople), London, and Paris.

Thus, quite suddenly and unexpectedly, Layard found himself financially independent. For the first time, he no longer worried about money. For Layard, life was truly beginning at the age of forty.

In 1860, after an absence of three years, as noted earlier, he was returned to Parliament. The advancing years had softened him, although he was always at the ready to mount a barricade if he felt the issue before the house warranted it. Primarily he spoke out on the need for administrative reform (the domestic issue of the day) and foreign affairs. His expertise in the latter field attracted the notice of both sides of the house. "The ability, and what is more, the personal knowledge and experience, which he brought to bear on [various] subjects, drew general attention to him," Lord Aberdare, a close associate, later wrote in a memoir. Disraeli, relentlessly moving to the pinnacle of imperial power, watched him carefully.

Layard's vision of foreign affairs was a mix of imperialism and reform. Observers of the post-mid-Victorian period took to calling him "the first Liberal Imperialist."

In 1861 Palmerston formed a new Liberal government and Layard's old admirer Lord Russell was named foreign secretary. The new government offered back Layard his old post as undersecretary of state for foreign affairs. Layard jumped at it. Public, Parliament, and press applauded the appointment. But behind the scenes Palmerston had engaged in a push-and-shove match with the Queen. Victoria thought of Layard as a brash, incandescent critic of her regime. She did not understand that his endless calls for reform were designed to preserve the empire. In an exchange with Palmerston, she tartly reminded the prime minister that the post should be held by "a thorough gentleman," and in her view, Layard was no gentleman.

But Palmerston had his way. The age of the divine right of queens was long past. Layard's polished performance in the foreign office, however, soon won over Victoria, and the Queen became one of his ardent admirers, although she never forgave him for his past indiscretions, especially his attacks on the bloated aristocracy and its blundering of the Crimean War.

Aunt Sara, now seventy, beamed over her godson's appointment and predicted that Layard was on the high road to No.

10 Downing Street. A month later, however, the joy was taken out of her life. After a long illness, Benjamin Austen passed away. In his last will and testament he left Layard, his apprentice law clerk and godson who bore his cognomen, a token bequest of £500. Sara died seventeen years later.

Layard plunged into foreign affairs, his forte, with zest. He profited from his early travels and adventures. With aplomb, he dealt with the election of the Greek king in 1863, the Serbian Question (which ultimately led to World War I), the American Civil War, Bismarck and Schleswig-Holstein, Theodore in Abyssinia, and so forth. But Layard still had some rough edges.

"Endowed with an independence of character, which was often rather rough in its manifestations . . . ," Lord Aberdare wrote later, "he was also hampered in his political career by the fact that he represented a combination of views and opinions which was in his time quite strange and exceptional."

In 1868, when Gladstone assumed the prime ministership for the first time, the new head of government promptly removed Layard from politics and shunted him into the post of chief commissioner of works and buildings, a position which admitted Layard to the Privy Council and empowered him to rule over urban renewal and the construction of new buildings in the seat of empire.

Layard took the new appointment in stride. He had always considered the British Museum "a monstrous building" and London an architectural mess. He immediately drew up imaginative—and costly—plans to beautify the Museum and the capital. Based on his excavations in Assyria, he entertained definite ideas on the subject. But the cost of the projects horrified the treasury. When the exchequer informed Gladstone, the prime minister blanched.

Layard lasted on the job ten months.

He was accused of throwing away public funds on architects, sculptors, painters, and "market-gardeners," i.e., landscapers. When he ordered mosaics to be imported from Italy and installed on the Houses of Parliament, there was an uproar over waste. "The only condition is to be," Mr. Bull bellowed, "not how well but how cheaply can a thing be done and that will not do for the arts!" His political enemies unjustly accused him of profiting from the mosaic project because of his financial interest in Murano, the Italian company which received the contract.

Layard was outraged. He was fed up with domestic politics.

He was also an embarassment to Gladstone, and in 1869, a year after taking office, the prime minister eased him out by offering him an appointment abroad, as minister in Spain. In an unexpected way, his return to the diplomatic fold drew him inexorably back to archaeology.

I caused my lady to dwell . . .
in joy and happiness.
—TUKULTIURTA

XLI

For Layard, the year
1869 was a watershed. Not only did he give up his desire to
"push his way" through politics, but he also abandoned his
bachelorhood.

For years, there had been gossip about Layard's incessant
visits to Canford Manor. Lady Charlotte, of course, was the
focus of the petty talk. But within two years of Sir John Guest's
death, she silenced that gossip and provided rumormongers
with another field day—by marrying her son's tutor!

At the time of her husband's death, Charlotte had engaged
one Charles Schreiber, at a salary of £400 a year, to coach her
sixteen-year-old son Merthyr. Schreiber was eleven years Merthyr's senior and fourteen years Charlotte's junior. On April
10, 1855, she married him. Schreiber's mother was ambivalent
about the wedding. "This is nothing to be ashamed of, though
there may be much to be said for and against, on both sides
. . . ," she had written the couple when they revealed their
plans to her the previous November.

Layard had no such ambivalence. He strongly disapproved
of her action, and relations between Layard and Charlotte
cooled appreciably. Charlotte felt hurt. There were stories,
unsubstantiated, that he had hoped to marry her.

Apparently Charlotte's ten children also took a dim view of
their mother's remarriage, and life at Canford Manor lost much

of its festive air and attractiveness for the Guest children, just as it had for Layard.

In 1857, in an August 1 diary entry, Charlotte again expressed dismay over Layard's behavior. "He cannot forgive my marriage," she wrote.

But not longer after, Layard appeared to have undergone a change of heart. Within two years he was visiting Canford Manor frequently as in the past. Victorian tongues wagged the more—but inconclusively. Now what was the object of Layard's incessant trips to Canford?

During this period the ranks of Layard's bachelor friends from his adventurous days in Constantinople, Baghdad, and the other fleshpots of the East thinned noticeably. Henry Ross, at the age of forty, had wed eighteen-year-old Janet Duff Gordon; Rassam, at forty-three, married a girl half his age, Anne Elizabeth Price, the daughter of a captain formerly in the 77th Highlanders; Rawlinson, at the age of fifty-two, wed a twenty-three-year-old beauty, Louisa Seymour.

Then, in early January 1869, Layard titillated London society. He proposed—to Enid, Lady Charlotte's daughter, the tyke he had bounced upon his knee when he first returned from Assyria. Tiny Enid had ripened into a tall, slender, and lovely young woman of twenty-five. She possessed classic features, aquiline nose, blue eyes, and honey-colored tresses that fell to her shoulders. Mr. Bull had always been the love in her life, first paternally (her father died when she was eight), and, after adolescence, in a surprisingly and completely different way. Whether or not she was waiting for him and whether or not he was waiting for her is not known and will never be known. Layard and Enid were private about their most intimate relationship.

Whatever the case, Enid did not hesitate a moment. She readily accepted Layard's proposal. As an engagement present, he snapped around her thin left wrist—it was slender enough for him to encircle it with his thumb and index finger—an exquisite bracelet fashioned from Esarhaddon's seal.

The reaction of the prospective in-laws was mixed. Now it was Lady Charlotte's turn to be discomfited. Her daughter's decision took her by surprise, and it took a couple of months to turn her around. Layard's mother, who had never remarried and was now sixty-six (she died in 1879 at the age of eighty-nine), also harbored reservations. "I hope that she [Enid] will never regret the change," Marianne Layard wrote Charlotte.

Many of the couple's friends entertained similar misgivings. Not only was Enid twenty-seven years younger than Layard, but she had led a relatively sheltered, almost cloistered existence at Canford. By contrast, Layard was worldly, roisterous, restless, and explosively aggressive.

Marriage bonds were posted March 3 and the wedding took place swiftly, six days later. As a wedding gift, Layard presented his "darling Enid," as he fondly called her, a unique piece of jewelry, a necklace fashioned from several cuneiform cylinders.

The couple honeymooned at Dorking, in Surrey, then the lush valley of the Mole River, between the escarpment of North Downs and the sandy heights of Leith Hill. Layard found time to drop Lady Charlotte a note; he apparently always had time to write letters. "I am," he wrote unabashedly, "more in love with her than ever."

Enid kept a copious diary, but her entries more closely resembled a ship's log or an appointment book than diaries in the Samuel Pepys or Charlotte Guest-Schreiber tradition. The day after their wedding, she wrote: "We breakfasted rather late."

It rained heavily that March, and the inclement weather provided the newlyweds with the opportunity to avoid people. "Wet day," she wrote March 20 from their new home in central London, "and we gave up our plan of going over to [illegible] to lunch." It rained the next day, too, and she wrote: "Wot again and we did not attempt to go to church."

The marriage was a brilliant success and outlived many of the gossipers of the day. It was an idyllic union. Layard never left her side and never looked at another woman. Early in their marriage, Enid confessed "with astonishment" that her happiness with Layard was complete, although they were destined to be childless.

In physical appearance they were in striking contrast. She stood a head taller than he, and she retained a slim figure while Layard's silhouette grew increasingly rotund. She frequently dressed in sparkling white, a color that matched Layard's egret-white hair and beard. In company, Layard was his usual witty and explosive self; she, low-keyed, demure, and radiant.

When Gladstone offered Layard the Spanish embassy with the rank of minister extraordinary, Layard talked it over with Enid at breakfast, their most intimate meal. This was their first big decision together. He deferred to her. She approved and he promptly notified the prime minister that he accepted the appointment.

Layard's career in domestic politics was at an end. So was his life in England. Thereafter, like Canning before him, he lived largely abroad. Inevitably, power politics led him back to Constantinople and, from there, by remote control, back to Assyrian archaeology.

Is this the son of my successor?

—ESARHADDON

XLII

During Layard's early years in Spain, Assyrian archaeology continued to languish in the doldrums which enveloped it during the Crimean War—despite the breakthrough in the decipherment of cuneiform. Logically, that wonderful discovery should have dictated burgeoning interest in Assyriology. But logic is not mankind's strong suit.

In his final report to the Assyrian Exploration Fund, Layard recognized this human condition. Interest in Assyria, he forecast, will revive only when there is "some discovery so important as to excite attention and curiosity."

In 1873, almost twenty years later—and three years after Layard and his bride settled at Madrid—the "exciting curiosity" exploded on the front pages. The trigger was pulled by George Smith, who flashed across the archaeological firmament like a meteor.

Smith was born into an impoverished Chelsea family in 1840 and was apprenticed to Bradbury & Evans to learn banknote engraving. This was the firm that in 1854 published Layard's guide to the Nineveh Court at the Crystal Palace. The booklet fascinated Smith. Just as Layard's imagination had been fired from an early age by the *Arabian Nights*, Smith's was set aflame by Layard's discovery of Nineveh and his adventures in Assyria.

Smith spent the greater part of his lunch hour each day at the British Museum, studying Layard's finds. He spent the greater part of his modest earnings on books by Layard, Rawlinson, Fergusson, Vaux, Loftus, and others. Over a period of time, Rawlinson, who maintained a workroom at the Museum, took notice of the youth's almost daily visits to the Assyrian section. His curiosity was aroused, and he introduced himself to the boy. Impressed by Smith's enthusiasm and astonishing knowledge of cuneiform, Rawlinson gave him permission to study paper casts of cuneiform tablets in his workroom. There Smith displayed a rare gift for deciphering cuneiform, and after a short while Rawlinson landed him a position as an assistant in the Museum's department of antiquities.

"Everyone has some bent or inclination which, if fostered by favorable circumstances, will color the rest of life," Smith wrote later. "My own taste has always been for Oriental studies, and from my youth I have taken a great interest in Eastern explorations and discoveries, particularly in the great work in which Layard and Rawlinson were engaged."

In 1872, while rummaging through the thousands of cuneiform tablets Layard and Rassam had recovered from the royal libraries of Nineveh, Smith made an earth-shattering find. Among the items collected by Rassam was "a curious tablet" which recounted a story with a familiar theme: a great flood, a ship aground, a dove sent out when the waters subsided . . .

Smith had found the Assyrian version of Noah's Ark!

For twenty years the tablet had been lying on Rawlinson's workbench awaiting a deliverer. That December, at a meeting of the Society of Biblical Archaeology, Smith announced his discovery.

It created a sensation. Smith casually remarked, however, that about fifteen lines of the story of the Flood were missing.

This was an era of robust circulation wars. Newspaper publishers underwrote expeditions to the North Pole and engaged in other stunts. In New York, for example, James Gordon Bennett's *Herald* assigned Henry M. Stanley, a reporter, to join the British 1868 expedition against King Theodore of

Abyssinia, who had taken several British subjects hostage, among them none other than Hormuzd Rassam.* This was the Stanley that the *Herald* later sent in search of Dr. Livingstone.

In this atmosphere, the London *Daily Telegraph* profferred Smith £1,000 if he would take charge of an expedition to Assyria in search of the missing fragment. "I resolved to start at once," Smith said.

On May 7, 1853, Smith, who had never before been outside of England except on a short visit to Wales, arrived at Mosul and two days later descended into one of the old Layard-Rassam trenches at Kouyunjik. In a denouement that Hollywood producers would reject out of hand as belonging to the theater of the absurd, five days later, while poking around in the trench, Presto! Smith recovered the missing piece.

"I sat down to examine the store of fragments of cuneiform inscriptions from the day's digging, taking out and brushing off the earth from the fragments to read their contents," he said. "On clearing one of them I found to my surprise . . . that it contained the great portion of seventeen [sic] lines of inscription belonging to the first column of the Chaldean account of the Deluge, and fitting into the only place where there was a serious blank in the story."**

Naïvely, Smith expected his newspaper to continue to lavish money on further exploration in Assyria. But Edwin Arnold, the *Telegraph*'s editor, had his circulation-builder, and was already in search of a new sensation. Arnold ordered Smith home.

On his return to London Smith, in the tradition of Layard, rushed into print with a two-volume *Chaldean Account of Genesis.* John Murray, of course, was the publisher, and the book was an immediate success.

---

* Upon his rescue, Rassam published a two-volume account of the adventure, *Narrative of the British Mission to Theodore, King of Abyssinia.* The Reverend Percy Badger, his brother's father-in-law, the same Badger who first approached Stratford Canning with the scheme to dig up the mounds of Mesopotamia, edited the manuscript.

* *Assyrian scholars have since determined that the fragment Smith found did not belong to the original tablet. As Rassam noted in 1897, "The *Daily Telegraph* fragment is in the third person, whereas mine is in the first person." But in quest of newspaper circulation, why kill a good story?

Victorian England was then riding the crest of the Evangelical wave. The public clamored for the government to return Smith to the field. The British Museum bowed to public pressure and underwrote two more Smith expeditions to Mosul. On the second of these, in 1876, Smith fell ill and died at the age of thirty-six.

Smith's death did not stifle interest in Assyria; on the contrary, the perils of archaeology excited the public. The Museum was in a quandary over whom to select as Smith's replacement.

After his wild adventures in Abyssinia and his subsequent marriage, Rassam had retired from government service to spend his time "quietly in England." He had, of course, ravenously followed the *Telegraph*'s accounts of Smith's adventures. The trustees turned to him as Smith's replacement, and the fifty-one-year-old Rassam leaped at the opportunity.

Pride was also a factor in Rassam's decision. In a speech some three years later, November 4, 1879, before a meeting of the Society of Biblical Archaeology, Rassam confessed, "It was expecially gratifying to me to feel that my former services in connection with Assyrian researches had not been forgotten at the British Museum."

Money was still the Museum's principal bugaboo, however. As usual, the trustees explained, they were a bit short of funds. Like Layard before him, Rassam put them down gently, but firmly. "I offered to go out without a stipend," he said, "provided I should be allowed to carry on my excavations the way I deemed best."

But Rassam never got beyond Constantinople. The Sultan refused to issue a firman permitting him to excavate the mounds.

The notoriety attendant on Smith's discovery of the missing fragment and Heinrich Schliemann's discovery that same year, 1873, of mythical Troy and a hoard of gold at Hissarlik, Turkey, had shocked the Turks. They had been right: so-called archaeology was a cover for treasure hunters, gold seekers. As a result, the Turkish government summarily shut down all digs in the Ottoman empire.

For months, Rassam stagnated in Constantinople. Even the

grand vizier was unable to help him. "The Sultan alone can give the permission and privileges asked for," Rassam was informed. Empty-handed, in disgust, Rassam returned to London.

At this critical stage, Layard rushed to the rescue of Rassam, the British Museum—and Assyrian archaeology.

Like Layard, Prime Minister Disraeli believed strongly that the collapse of the tottering Ottoman empire would be detrimental to Britain's imperial interests. Stratford Canning had long since retired—he died in 1880 at the age of ninety-four—and Layard argued that Britain needed a strong representative in Constantinople to put spine into a flabby Sultan.

"We want another Lord Stratford, if we can find him," Layard wrote a friend from Madrid. "To break up the Turkish Empire in its present state would be to run the risks of forming two great European powers—Russia and Germany."

Disraeli was precisely of the same opinion. "What we want is a man of the necessary experience and commanding mind at this moment in Constantinople—and one not too scrupulous," he said. "But such men are rare everywhere."

In the back of his mind, however, Disraeli had his man: Layard.

As 1876 drew to a close, the prime minister offered Layard the job. Layard snapped it up. As part of the arrangement, with Victoria's connivance—she had changed her mind about Layard and now viewed him favorably as a defender of the empire—Disraeli arranged for the Queen to bestow a knighthood upon him. For good measure, Layard also received the Grand Cross of the Bath. Shrewdly, Disraeli surmised that in Constantinople a Sir Austen Henry Layard would carry more weight than a Mr. Layard.

The Ninevite plot at this point is as incredible as Smith's discovery of the needle in the haystack. Who needs fiction with the following cast of characters?

Disraeli, who insisted more than thirty-five years earlier at Aunt Sara's brunches that he would one day occupy No. 10 Downing Street, and did.

Layard, who had cooled his heels in the cold reception room of the British embassy at Constantinople a generation earlier and, like a Cinderella pumpkin, was now miraculously transformed into the Great Elchi.

And *Ahmed Vefyk*, Layard's companion during his early escapades in the Turkish capital, who, at the age of seventeen, proclaimed that one day he would be grand vizier of the Ottoman empire, and shortly after Layard's appointment as ambassador emerged in that role!

Rassam was delighted by Layard's posting. "His appointment was naturally a harbinger of joy to me," he said. Rassam knew Layard perhaps better than any other man, and he said, "I knew that he still took a lively interest in all Assyrian discoveries." The British Museum was equally delighted. The secretary wrote Layard, "Do get a *firman* by hook or crook as ere long Mesopotamia will be lost to Turkey. . . . [and] if Aremenia and Assyria are lost, Russia will allow no excavations."

Neither Rassam nor the Museum was disappointed. With Enid on his arm, her eyes sparkling as she viewed the Golden Horn for the first time, Layard arrived in Constantinople on April 20, 1877. He no sooner unpacked than he brought his influence to bear directly on the Sultan and effortlessly extracted a firman for Rassam. This is all the more astonishing because Czar Alexander was about to declare war on Turkey, and a firman to dig up mounds should have been the farthest subject from the minds of the Sublime Porte and Her Britannic Majesty's new envoy at their first meeting.

Indeed, Layard was so confident of his success that he ordered Rassam forthwith from London to Mosul to organize the dig while the firman was being processed through the grand vizier.

On his arrival at Mosul, Rassam promptly called on the local pasha to find out if he had heard about the coveted firman.

"I was not a little relieved when he told me that he had received telegraphic orders from Constantinople to allow me to commence my explorations because, though the *firman* had been granted, it would take some time before it reached Mosul," Rassam said. "The British Ambassador, Sir Henry Layard, for the purpose of saving time, had begged this boon from the Porte, and it had been accorded him, though it was contrary to rule to allow any one to carry on excavations without possession of the royal mandate."

Coincidentally, Schliemann, who had smuggled Trojan gold out of Turkey, was in bad odor with Constantinople. He had no luck in acquiring a new firman to reopen his dig at Hissarlik, and turned to the British ambassador for help. Once again, Layard's diplomatic magic produced results. Thus, single-handedly, in a tour de force, Layard went to the rescue of not only Assyrian but also Greek archaeology. Indeed, Layard played so critical a role in Schliemann's work at Troy that Schliemann publicly attributed his later success there to "the aid of my honored friend . . . Layard . . . who smoothed away all my difficulties with the Turkish government."

In his third book on the rediscovery of Homer's Troy, *Ilios*, published in 1880, Schliemann's dedication read: "The Right Honorable Sir Austen Henry Layard, G.C.B., D.C.L., the Pioneer in Recovering the Lost History of the Ancient Cities of Western Asia by Means of the Pickaxe and Spade, in Acknowledgement of his Kind and Effective Aid to the Excavations on the Site of Troy, as Ambassador to the Sublime Porte, This Work is Respectfully and Gratefully Dedicated By the Author."

Thus, as a direct result of Layard's influence at Nineveh and Troy, Rassam and Schliemann, respectively, resumed their historic missions. More than a generation after he had gazed in awe at the mysterious mounds of Mesopotamia and had brought to light the lost cities of Assyria, Layard's life was still inextricably interwoven with the worlds of the past.

Let the prince who comes after me,
when that temple shall fall to ruins,
restore it.

—ASHURBALLIT

XLIII

The British Museum's instructions to Rassam were "... to try to find as many fragments as possible from the libraries of Ashurbanipal and Sennacherib." But Rassam was in search of greater things— new palaces, lost cities, new art treasures. Like Layard and the Assyrian kings, he sought a place for himself in the sun.

Nearly twenty-four years had passed since Rassam had closed the excavations at Kouyunjik, and he attacked his new assignment with relish. "It was impossible for me to lose my interest in the old explorations," he said.

At Mosul, where he recruited an army of five hundred Arab, Kurdish, and Chaldean diggers, many of Layard's old workers and their children flocked around him. "I felt sorry that I could only recognize a few of them, because a large number had died, and some who were still living had grown so old that I could not recollect their faces."

Among them, however, he recognized several Arabs who had worked for Layard in 1845 and for himself a decade later. One was Mahmood Alfaraj, whom Rassam immediately appointed the expedition's overseer, a man of "fidelity and honesty." Two others who had served Layard had grown too feeble to be of any use in manual labor, and, out of pity, Rassam employed them as suboverseers "on small pay."

Indeed, so many people lined up to work for him that a

majority returned home disappointed. "Most of these came to serve me for the sake of gratifying their wives or parents, who had either served Sir Henry Layard or myself, or who remembered us when they were children," Rassam noted. "They did not covet much gain, but they wished to be in my employ for the sake of old associations."

By the spring of 1878, with Mosul as his base of operations, Rassam had scattered his work force across the face of Assyria, spreading them out over a 200-mile area. His effort was on an heroic scale—as envisioned by Layard a generation earlier.

The conditions under which Rassam labored were as difficult as ever. An infestation of flies that spring attacked his transport animals, and left many of them "literally covered with blood." He walked with a green twig during this epidemic "and beat them off right and left."

He also suffered repeated attacks of malaria. "I did not give way to the debilitating attacks, which came on, with few exceptions, regularly every other day, and almost at the same hour," Rassam said. But he conceded that he suffered a loss of energy and that his enthusiasm for the dig slackened.

And there were other perils. "One night while encamping on the mound of Kouyunjik," he reported, "and I was fast asleep in my tent, there was a tremendous storm of hail and rain, and all of a sudden I felt myself going down a pit, with bed, tent and everything else I possessed." He was engulfed by a deluge, as if the Flood of Genesis was again covering the earth. A group of Arab workers came to his rescue and raised him, half-drowned, from the pit which was rapidly filling with a torrent of water.

At dawn, he discovered what had happened: "It appeared that my tent had been pitched over one of the large tunnels dug at the time of Sir Henry Layard's excavations, which had been lost to the sight, and the quantity of rain which had fallen had undermined it."

These hardships and mishaps notwithstanding, under Layard's protective diplomatic umbrella, Rassam embarked upon a series of dazzling campaigns between 1872 and 1882.

The first firman Layard secured for Rassam was good only for one year. It gave Rassam the right to explore any Assyrian ruin not occupied by a Moslem cemetery. The firman, however, reflected, for the first time, rising Turkish interest in archaeology. It allotted one-third of Rassam's discoveries to the British Museum, one-third to the newly established Archaeological Museum at Constantinople, and one-third to the owner of a given mound or piece of land on which excavations were conducted (if there was no owner, the one-third reverted to the Turkish government). Furthermore, the imperial decree provided that a representative of the Sultan must accompany Rassam at all times to ensure that the finds were properly reported to the authorities. The Turks had been burned by Schliemann when he smuggled the gold of Troy from Hissarlik to Athens, and they were determined not to be robbed again in the name of science by foreigners. Rassam considered this stipulation an impertinence and a nuisance, and Layard succeeded in having the odious condition withdrawn. (Schliemann had no such luck.)

Rassam's methods of excavation left much to be desired, however. It was physically impossible for him to supervise each dig simultaneously, and he delegated authority to a number of his Mosul cronies, including a nephew, Nimrud Rassam. The digs were conducted on a catch-as-catch-can basis. Rassam led a flying squad which galloped from mound to mound to sift evidence and collect material. No records were kept. Notes were haphazardly written up. Rassam's letters to Layard constitute the only regular flow of reports on his work.

Rassam lacked patience and discipline. The pressure on him, in his own mind, was very great. He suffered from an inferiority complex. He was a Chaldean, a Nestorian Christian, a native of Mosul, and inwardly, he felt he had to prove himself better than the natives of his adopted country, England.

In complete disregard of the trustees' order that he concentrate on the Ninevite libraries, Rassam's first dig was at Balawat, the ancient Assyrian fortress city of Imgur-enlil, 15 miles east of Mosul and 9 miles north of Nimrod. Through contacts, Rassam had learned of the discovery in the area of two pieces of bronze adorned with inscriptions and figures. The place, to his chagrin, turned out to have been converted into a Moslem graveyard, but Rassam was determined to dig there "even for one day" in defiance of the firman.

"I thought that the prize was well worth the risk of a row," he said, "or even a riot."

Rassam no sooner put his spade to the soil than he uncovered seven magnificent strips of bronze, each 8 feet long, richly ornamented and inscribed. They bore the annals of Shalmaneser III, who reigned some 2,500 years earlier. It was a spectacular discovery—the famed Balawat Gates, among the greatest treasures of the British Museum.

But the discovery caused such an uproar at Balawat that Rassam was compelled to abandon further excavations.* Orthodox religious leaders were enflamed over the desecration of an Islamic burial ground.

In March 1878, Rassam's firman expired and he was detained at Mosul with his treasures as a dispute erupted between him and the Turkish authorities over the disposition of one-third of the relics. "If it had not been for Sir Henry Layard's influence at Constantinople ... ," Rassam conceded, "it would have been quite impossible for me to [remove the relics]."

Layard arranged for the collection to be shipped to Constantinople and told Rassam to "leave it to me to settle with the Porte about the division."

Rassam arrived in the Turkish capital with the treasures June 21, 1878. He spent the next twelve days as the personal house guest of Layard and Enid. Because he was one of her husband's closest friends, Enid was especially fond of him.

At Layard's suggestion, Rassam also brought with him some old bas-reliefs from Nimrod "as a present to the Sultan from the trustees of the British Museum." Such a gracious gesture had never entered the minds of the trustees—nor anyone else's, except Layard's. Although the Sultan considered the Assyrian trophies "old stones," Layard's thoughtfulness was warmly appreciated, and thereafter Rassam encountered no difficulty, not even with sticky Turkish customs officials, while loading his share of the treasures onto a Messageries

---

* In 1956 British archaeologist M. E. L. Mallowan discovered a second set of decorated bronzes at the very same spot.

Maritimes Company vessel for the journey to England via Marseilles (a rather roundabout way of getting to London).

By then, the first firman had expired and Layard again interceded directly with the Sultan on behalf of Rassam and the British Museum. This time Layard extracted an imperial decree for two years, 1878–80, with the option of extending it another two years, until 1882. The new firman was extraordinary. It invested in the holder the unprecedented power of conducting excavations anywhere in the Ottoman empire. But following the cemetery incident at Balawat and the dispute at Mosul over the finds, Rassam was suspect in Turkish eyes. Accordingly, instead of being issued in Rassam's name, the firman was made out in Layard's name, a tribute to the Great Elchi's unique relationship with the Turkish ruler, Abdul Hamid.

Rassam lost little time taking advantage of the new firman. In late 1878 he extended his excavations from Mosul south to ancient Babylon. His discoveries were truly spectacular, rivaled only by those of his mentor, Layard.

In addition to the Bronze Gates of Balawat, Rassam's major finds included 100,000 clay tablets and fragments of tablets, some containing new and important versions of the Creation and the Flood; the cylinder of Nabonidus, with its checklist of early Babylonian kings; Nebuchadnezzar's palace at Birs Nimrod; a new series of Ninevite lion-hunting scenes (surpassing those of Layard in beauty and execution); the discovery of ancient Kuthu at Tel Ibrahim; and the identification of the Hanging Gardens of Babylon at the mound known as Babil.

Like many of Layard's discoveries, Rassam's finds were the gift of Luck. At Kouyunjik, for example, the capricious goddess stood at his side as he discovered a hidden recess in a brick wall in Ashurbanipal's palace and within it the almost perfect, ten-sided terra-cotta cylinder inscribed with 1,300 lines of cuneiform, detailing the conquests of that Assyrian king. In a talk later before an archaeological group in London, Rassam recounted his discovery:

"Generally speaking, we do not waste our time and money in digging out thick solid brick walls to no purpose; but as I had given orders that when the workmen came to a broken wall they were to search it ... I was asked by the overseer superintending the work in the palace of Ashurbanipal if he was to demolish a small remnant of a brick wall which was left in digging out two chambers or leave it to be covered over with the debris that came out of the excavations. On seeing that its removal would entail very little expense, I ordered it to be pulled down, and it appears that I had not gone two hours on my way to Nimroud [to inspect another mound], before they came upon this rare object, buried in the center of the solid wall."

Both Layard and Rassam were troubled, however, by the emergence in these years of a new species in archaeology—the antique dealer or broker. The excitement in Europe over the discoveries of Smith and Schliemann demonstrated that there was a market for "antiquities." Indeed, in this period, "on or about the 15th of June, 1877" Scotland Yard reported the first theft of Assyrian relics. A thief or band of thieves made off from the British Museum with a collection of Assyrian pieces, including a rectangular ivory panel from Nimrod (a drawing of which appeared on page 60 of Layard's *Monuments*), a lapis lazuli cylinder, several intaglios with cuneiform inscriptions, and several Assyrian seals decorated with figures. They were never recovered.

But the major marketplace for brokers was in Mesopotamia. Armenian and Jewish merchants there cornered the field. They bribed Arab diggers to sell them relics, especially those bearing Inscriptions This in turn stimulated independent treasure hunts among the Arabs.

The damage done by these sub-rosa operations was incalculable, far exceeding even Rassam's blunderbuss approach to archaeology. "In nine cases out of ten they [the brokers] break or lose a large part of their collection," Rassam wrote Layard, "and worse than all, they try to make a good bargain by breaking the inscribed objects, and dividing them among their customers."

But like latter-day archaeologists, however dissatisfied with this state of affairs, Rassam admitted he was not adverse to dealing with the brokers. "I myself bought, when I was at Baghdad, a most valuable Babylonian terra-cotta cylinder for the British Museum, which had met with the same fate," he said. "The discoverer had tried to saw it in two, and in doing so the upper part broke into fragments, some of which were lost altogether." The saw gnawed off nearly half an inch of inscriptions.

The pilfering of archaeological monuments by "antica dealers," as they are known in the Arab world, persists to this day wherever there are grounds for digging up the past.

Although Rassam was tight-fisted in money matters, he often rewarded his workers for important discoveries. The dealers, however, offered his workers double rewards. In truth, both Rassam and the Armenian and Jewish brokers cheated the ignorant Arabs. A wretched digger, living in a hovel, would be rewarded with twenty or forty cents for an object which later brought upwards of $50 in Baghdad. In one instance, a marble tablet from Khalah Sharghat was sold by a digger for $1.25 and resold by a broker to the late George Smith for $350. It is now in the British Museum's priceless collection.

In 1880 the Disraeli cabinet fell and Gladstone, the Turkophobe, returned to power. "One of the first things I expect is the return of Henry and Enid from Constantinople," Lady Charlotte Schreiber wrote in her diary. "He is sure to be superseded." Enid's mother astutely judged the political situation. Indeed, one of Gladstone's first acts was to order Layard back to England on home leave. "This is a great blow," Enid confided in her diary, "as I believe we shall never return."

They never did.

Rassam was stunned by the news of Layard's removal. So were the Turks. Rassam raced to Constantinople to renew the two-year-option on Layard's firman. He just made it. The firman was renewed, and Rassam excavated unmolested for the next two years. In his last dig, on April 21, 1882, before the firman expired, he completed the recovery of the lost Biblical city of Sippara or Sepharavim in the Abu Habba mound, another of archaeology's greatest finds.

But when Rassam applied, on his own, for yet another firman, he was turned down. The new British ambassador was equally powerless. Without Layard, a firman was out of the question. On November 11, 1882, the fifty-six-year-old Rassam sailed for England and arrived in time for Christmas dinner with his family.

Ten years later, at the Ninth International Conference of Orientalists, Rassam publicly confirmed Layard's influence in promoting Assyrian archaeology as Great Elchi. "There are still very valuable records and monuments to be found in Assyria and Babylonia . . . ," Rassam told the Congress. "Had Sir Henry Layard remained a little longer at Constantinople, I should have been enabled to add more important acquisitions to my late discoveries."

Neither he nor Layard ever again dug in Mesopotamia. The heroic age of Assyrian archaeology had ended.

Thus, they took me and made me reside far away.

—GILGAMESH

XLIV

Layard's recall to London terminated his public career. Although he longed for the embassy in Rome, Gladstone offered him no other diplomatic assignment. For all practical purposes, the fiery and outspoken Layard was forced into early retirement. The word "retirement" is a misnomer, however. Layard was sixty-three, and still robust; Enid, a sparkling thirty-six. As she quickly learned, for Layard "retirement" was a full-time job, with overtime.

They tarried in England and soon withdrew to Venice where Layard acquired a fourteenth-century, three-story *palazzo*, Casa Capello or Ca Capello, as Italians referred to it. The ornate, stately building was perched astride the Grand Canal, boasted a lovely roof garden, and commanded a sweeping view of the canal and one of its tributaries, Rio di San Palao. A gondola, with serpentine prow, was always tied up at Layard's private dock. Robert Browning, who, influenced by Layard's discovery of Nineveh, wrote *Love Among the Ruins*, was a neighbor.

At Ca Capello, Layard devoted himself to the three great passions of his waning years—Enid, art, and writing.

The first four years he worked steadily on his two-volume *Early Adventures*, which John Murray brought out in 1887. Like *Nineveh and its Remains*, it was highly autobiographical and led him to resume work on his *Autobiography,* which he had ended abruptly in 1869, on the eve of his marriage and departure to Spain as ambassador. This uncompleted work was published posthumously in 1910.

During this period Layard also wrote extensively on art, and as a disciple of the revolutionary Giovanni Morelli, whom Layard considered the greatest living authority on Italian painting, the bull found himself in the familiar role of wrecking a china shop. Layard assailed the established art critics of the day and promoted a radical approach to the study of painting. Layard's views were contained in his revision of *Kugler's Handbook of Painting.* The latter was based on Morelli's theories and advanced the concept of analyzing paintings by a study of the original drawings and sketches of the artist in question—a commonly accepted method today but startling in Layard's time. Morelli also argued that in order to account for certain features and peculiarities which some schools of art and painters may have had in common, writers on art had attached too much importance to the influence which one school is supposed to have had over another.

In his introduction to the revised edition, entitled *The Italian Schools of Painting,* Layard observed, based on his experience among Assyria's mounds, that "hard and fast lines fixing periods of development are not to be drawn in the history of art." At best, he said, such lines are arbitrary and unscientific. If divisions are to be made, he argued, those of Morelli were preferable.

Morelli divided a school of art into periods. The first or "heroic" period abounded in religious sentiment, myths, and legends; the second gave itself up to the study of anatomy and perspective, and endeavored to imitate nature; the third sought to raise the forms closely imitated from nature to the highest order of ideal beauty; then followed the periods of mannerism, eclecticism, and, finally, decline.

Layard also wrote regularly for *Quarterly Review* and, as a gourmet, contributed as late as 1891 a lengthy article on Renaissance cookery for *Murray's Magazine.* "A banquet of the time," the now portly, white-haired, and white-bearded seventy-four-year-old Layard concluded, "would probably be

to us moderns more gratifying to the sight than to the taste."
Obviously, despite his chronological age, inwardly he considered himself quite youthful and "modern."

During these years when he was author and free-lance writer, Enid worked as Layard's editorial assistant, preparing indexes, typing notes, and proofing galleys. The typewriter, one of the wonders of the last century, had come onto the popular market in 1877, and she quickly mastered it (Layard never did). Judging from the volumes of typed copy among the Layard Papers at the British Museum today, Enid must have been employed steadily at the keyboard.

Life was pleasant in these last years, as Layard happily acknowledged: "I am leading the life which, from my earliest days, I aspired to lead—what more can I want?"

He was also pleasantly surprised by the honors bestowed upon him as the winter of his life lengthened. "I thought I was well forgotten by the world," he remarked.

He was appointed a trustee of the prestigious National Gallery and played a major role in the Gallery's acquisition of Italian masters; he was named a corresponding member of the French Academy; elected president of the Hugenot Society; selected to fill the seat of Robert Browning in the Royal Academy upon the latter's death in Venice in 1889; and made "honorary member of I don't know how many learned societies," he joked in private.

He took the honors in stride, albeit a bit cynically. "I am too old to care for any honor that may be conferred upon me," he wrote in 1891. "Honors are only of use to those who still have the world before them, not to those who should be making their preparations for leaving it."

But he was disappointed that the British Museum never appointed him a trustee and that during Victoria's silver jubilee—despite rumors—the Queen did not elevate him to peerage. He was not so much interested in the title as in the right to sit in the House of Lords and lend a voice to the making of foreign policy. He had made too many enemies at court, both Liberal and Tory. Victoria, however much she admired him, also considered him too outspoken, too caustic, and, worse, too independent-minded.

Although the Museum's trustees dodged the question of appointing Layard a trustee, a group of his friends commissioned Sir Edgar Boehm, the premier sculptor of the era, to do a bust of him (and later Enid), and the trustees announced that they would put it on display at the Museum. The group—including the royal family of Germany, which felt it owed Layard something for the help he had given Schliemann (the Germans still considered Schliemann one of their own, although he was a naturalized American and lived in Greece)—commissioned Boehm to do the bust in bronze. But Boehm, who described himself as an "admirer" of Layard, felt, fittingly, that only stone would do justice to the discoverer of the stones of Assyria. He did the bust in marble.

The sculpture was unveiled June 11, 1891, in the board room of the trustees. Layard was flattered, and Enid jokingly told him he would now be placed "amongst the embalmed corpses of ancient Egyptians." Layard replied that "when the typical New Zealander is sent over and commissioned to promote the excavation of the ruins of the British Museum, he will perhaps find the likeness of one who had something to do with the ruins of Nineveh."

But amid these honors, Layard was deeply disturbed over the British Museum's slighting of Rassam. In the natural course of things, new faces had moved into power at the Museum, among them E. A. T. Wallis Budge, the assistant keeper of Egyptian and Assyrian Antiquities, who could read Egyptian hieroglyphics, ancient Hebrew, and Assyrian cuneiform as easily as he read the London *Times* at breakfast each morning. Budge's scholarship notwithstanding, he was a caricature of the late Victorian period, a period afflicted by a deepening colonial mentality.

While Layard was color-blind in dealing with people, Budge was blinded by color. One word, almost conspicuous by its absence in Layard's vocabulary and employed excessively by Budge, delineates their world outlook. The word is "native."

Layard considered Turks, Baktiyari, Arabs, Kurds, and others (including Chaldeans like Rassam) simply as "people." Budge considered them "natives," in the pejorative stereotype of nonwhite, unwashed, and inferior peoples. In his *By Nile and*

Tigris, Budge could barely write a sentence without referring to "natives"—"native guides," "native watchmen," "native officials" ad infinitum.

Almost from the beginning, Budge rubbed Layard the wrong way. As early as 1888 Layard remarked in a letter to a friend, "From things that have come to my knowledge, I have not a very high opinion of the man." And in another letter, Layard complained that Rassam "is one of the honestest [sic] and most straightforward fellows I ever knew, whose services have never been acknowledged—because he is a 'nigger.' "

Manifestly, they were on a collision course, and the collision was not long in developing.

During the 1887–89 seasons in Mesopotamia, Budge made several trips to Mosul and Baghdad to inspect the dormant British digs at Nineveh, Calah, Ashur, and Babylon. In confidential reports to the Museum, he said he found in Baghdad lively trading of Babylonian and Assyrian relics "being carried on by the natives." The objects, he averred, were stolen from the British excavation sites. Furthermore, Budge claimed, he traced the thefts to "native watchmen" employed by the "native Mr. Rassam" before Rassam left Mesopotamia in 1882 at the expiration of Layard's firman. Finally, Budge observed that Rassam had engaged the "native watchmen" to guard the British sites and that the watchmen were his relatives.

As a result of Budge's reports, the "native watchmen" were fired—surely the use of the term "native" in this instance had to be gratuitous, since no individuals other than local persons were available for the job.

After returning from Mesopotamia, Budge was named the Museum's acting keeper of the Department of Egyptian and Assyrian Antiquities, a promotion which Layard considered a "shameful calumny."

One of Budge's first acts was to reorganize the Museum's Assyrian collection and to publish a new *Guide to the Exhibition Galleries of the British Museum.* Page XI of the introduction ascribed the Museum's "unrivalled collection" of Assyrian art and artifacts to "Layard, Rawlinson and others." There was no mention of Rassam, whose role in Assyrian archaeology was reduced to that of a spear-carrier.

Layard was furious. "I desire to protest," he wrote in a letter which appeared in the London *Times* July 27, 1892. He charged that Rassam was being done a "great injustice." Rawlinson, he protested, was indeed a great scholar but "he was not an excavator in Assyria. I fear that a deliberate attempt is being made to deprive him [Rassam] of the credit which is his due."

Two days later the Museum replied that there had been no intention to slur Rassam and pointed out that there were references to Rassam on pages 80 and 90 in the guide.

Layard, however, was not appeased. Although he made no reference to it in his letter to the *Times*, Layard seethed over Budge's dismissal of Rassam's watchmen and his character assassination of Rassam. Budge was now telling all who would listen within and without the Museum that Rassam was "a party to the theft of antiquities."

For his part, the dismayed Rassam appealed to the British Museum to convene a board of inquiry to look into Budge's allegations. But the trustees ignored him.

In the summer of 1892 Rassam sued the acting keeper for libel and slander and for £1,000 in damages. From his Venetian retreat at Ca Capello, Layard wrote Rassam that "I shall speak pretty openly when in the witness box, if I have an opportunity of doing so."

The following summer the case came to trial at the High Court of Justice, London, and Layard made good on his promise. The hearing lasted five days.

Budge's predecessor, the former keeper of the department, P. Le Page Renouf, joined Layard in a spirited defense of Rassam. It turned out during the testimony that the only relative Rassam had hired was his nephew, Nimrud Rassam, whom Budge had praised lavishly. Budge's allegations were untrue. Rassam won. The jury found in his favor and awarded him £50 in damages. The figure would have been higher, but the plaintiff was unable to prove "malice" on Budge's part.

Press accounts of the trial in London's *Times*, *Daily News*, and other papers were slanted in Budge's favor. Indeed the coverage was so unbalanced that the foreman of the jury felt constrained to write Rassam a letter in which he said he was "very indignant at the misrepresentations which have appeared in the press." The jury's vote, he told Rassam privately, was 10 to 2 in his favor. Now Budge's honor was on the line. To salvage the day, the Museum launched a subscription drive to raise money to pay his fine and legal expenses.

Layard almost went into cardiac arrest when he learned of this maneuver. "This, if true, is a most scandalous ending to a most scandalous business," Layard exploded. "The court found Budge a mendacious scoundrel but he got public sympathy and gets court expenses paid by British Museum employees. Poor Rassam will have to pay heavily his share of the costs."

Layard felt the urgent need for fresh air—to get out of London and to get away from its tawdry politics. He and Enid left for some salmon fishing in Scotland; like him, Enid was an enthusiastic angler. To his chagrin, she landed the pool fish, a 12-pounder. He landed nothing. "Too much wind for casting a fly," he grumbled in a letter to a friend. But he added cheerfully, "We eat voraciously and sleep soundly."

The British Musem's bail-out of Budge, however, was not the end of the "scandalous business."

The week the Layards returned from their fishing jaunt, the August 10, 1893, issue of the respectable scientific journal *Nature* raised new charges against Rassam. The journal claimed that "soon after Mr. Rassam began to dig in Babylonia, collections of tablets found their way into the London market." Budge, *Nature* said, allegedly found an agent appointed by Rassam who was actively engaged in the sale of antiquities and that "on visiting the sites of the excavations Dr. Budge found that clandestine diggings were going on."

An outraged Rassam tried to set the matter straight. "Excavations by the Arabs have been carried on in Babylonia from time immemorial, and as the land belongs to subjects of the Sultan and not to the British government, I do not know by what right you think that the British Museum can prevent others from digging and from selling what they can find to whomsoever they choose."

But in a rejoinder, *Nature* broadened its charges to envelop Layard. The magazine now charged that Canford Manor contained a gallery of Assyrian sculptures brought from Nineveh and "obtained at low price."

The relics at Canford were never purchased; they were gifts and duplicates found by Layard. "... I might have sold the whole of my discovery and could have made a considerable fortune thereby," the wounded bull charged, "I present[ed] them voluntarily to the nation ... I spent the whole of the little money I had, ... and I never received any renumeration in money from the trustees either for the marbles or my labors but only the base payment of expenses."

The Budge affair was Layard's last brush with Assyrian archaeology, and it was sordid. In disgust, he and Enid fled to Venice—and to the domestic tranquillity of Ca Capello.

The wild bull lives no more/
he is stretched out on the ground/
he lives no more.
—ASSYRIAN POEM, ANON.

XLV

In 1894, at the age of seventy-seven, Layard participated in his last dig. He and Enid spent the early part of the year in southern Italy "in search of warmth." At Pompeii, in his honor, the Italian archaeological authorities put on a *scavo*, or excavation. "We discovered a dining room, with its table and triclinia, the bronze brazier on which meats were kept hot, various utensils and many small objects," he wrote a friend in England on February 23. "The owner of the house had been probably entertaining his friends when he was disturbed by the ashes from Vesuvius."

In the letter, Layard expressed the hope that he and Enid would return to Ca Capello in time to celebrate the twenty-fifth year of their life together. "How time flies!" he said. "Well, I have been very fortunate."

They did get back in time, and their Italian friends "overwhelmed us with flowers," and gave them a champagne dinner, although both of them would have preferred to have a quiet dinner together. In another letter, dated three days later, March 12, Layard reflected on his silver wedding anniversary.

"I can say what few married men can—that during twenty-five years I have not had a single holiday, or a single quarrel

(322)

to relieve the monotony of wedded life!" he exlaimed. "It is perhaps too late to begin anew—so we may thus remain until the end—which in the nature of things cannot be far distant."

A fortnight later, April 3, he complained of terrible pains in the area of the groin. "On the advice of my doctor here," he recorded at Ca Capello, "I am leaving Venice for England tomorrow ... to consult Sir Henry Thompson on a matter which caused me some trouble four or five years ago, which cannot be neglected."

On April 9, six days later, he reported that "the case does not appear to be so serious as my Venice doctor feared." He had a tumor on the groin, but apparently the cancerous growth was not malignant, or so he was told.

He was immediately confined to bed, however, and thereafter deteriorated rapidly. Layard was shrewd enough to suspect something. "I am rather bad," he wrote May 3, less than a month later. "I cannot sit up without pain."

With Enid at his side, Layard lingered uncomfortably into July. Her diary is a poignant record of his journey into the Assyrian *arallu*, the vast land, the land of no return.

"This is the first day since his illness he has not asked for the newspaper," she wrote, alarmingly, July 4. "I was terribly anxious."

That night the physician informed her that "there is no hope."

"After the first shock, I was more or less prepared by my own observation," she said. "I managed to pull myself together but it was a terrible night, so restless and his breathing terrible."

On Thursday, July 5, 1894, the wild bull was stretched out on the ground. "This day, at 8:15 p.m., my husband died, and after twenty-five years that we had never been apart, he left me forever," Enid wrote in her diary.

Reserved and reticent to the end, a genuine Victorian, Enid rarely put her emotions on display—or paper. On the page of that last entry, in the lower left-hand corner of the diary, the lines of black ink ran together and turned into a gray blotch. The ink had been diluted by a teardrop.

Layard was buried at Canford, where he first met tiny Enid and bounced her on his knee.

Three years later Rassam wrote Layard's epitaph. He dedicated *Asshur and the Land of Nimrod* "to the loving memory of . . . Austen Henry Layard . . . the pioneer of Assyrian explorers. . . ."

Author's Note

There is a striking similarity between Austen Henry Layard, discoverer of Nineveh, and Heinrich Schliemann, discoverer of Troy. Both were men of action. Both were also men of letters. They left behind published works and mounds of correspondence, private and public journals.

Schliemann is widely recognized as "the father of modern archaeology." Yet his work, from digging techniques to literary accounts of discoveries, a generation *after* Layard, displayed the highest form of flattery. They were a Xerox of Layard's style.

Schliemann freely acknowledged his debt. In a letter to Bismarck, January 29, 1882, Schliemann wrote, "Many people, but especially Dr. Dorpfeld [Schliemann's Rassam] have been insisting that I combine interesting excerpts from my various works and publish them with numerous illustrations, just as Sir Henry Layard did with his great work *Nineveh* with which, as he and Mr. Murray [also Schliemann's publisher] told me, he had spectacular results."

Why, then, is Schliemann acclaimed as the father of modern archaeology when he was truly Layard's successor? Isn't the cart being placed before the horse?

The answer is found partly in the homage paid to Layard at his death. One eulogy (*Huguenot Society's Proceedings*, London, 1894, Vol. 5) observed: "Layard's career in middle life in the field of politics and diplomacy is of minor interest compared with the brilliant achievements of his earlier years" (italics added). A similar assessment appeared in the obituary published in *The Athenaeum*, July 14, 1894 (No. 3481). "Henry Austen [sic] Layard died on Thursday evening, the 5th instant, at the age of seventy-seven, one of the last of a famous generation of explorers," Stanley Lane-Poole, Canning's minibiographer wrote. "It is nearly half a century since he made his mark, and nothing he did afterwards can be said to have increased his fame." And in 1976, in Paris, while I researched this book, Pierre Amiet, *conservateur en chef des antiquities Orientales* at the Louvre, put it tersely: "Layard sacrificed his archaeological career for a political career."

Obliquely, this assessment is borne out elsewhere. Despite Layard's incredible accomplishments in raising the lost cities of Assyria, there has been only one attempt at a definitive Layard biography, the work of a former Reuters correspondent, Gordon Waterfield, *Layard of Nineveh* (London: John Murray [who else?], 1963). Waterfield, a great-nephew of Janet Ross, the wife of Layard's friend Henry Ross, did a splendid job. The biography is definitive. And therein lies its weakness, reflecting the sentiments of the Huguenot Society, The Athenaeum and Amiet. The biography is divided into six parts; Part II covers archaeology. The remainder of the book focuses largely on Layard's political and diplomatic career. That is the problem. C. J. Gadd, formerly of the British Museum, in The Stones of Assyria (London: Chatto and Windus, 1936), who dedicated his work to Layard, attempted a capsule biography of Layard in tracing the early history of Assyriology and concluded that Layard is "a man so all-pervading that it is difficult to observe the bounds of relevancy in writing of him." Botta would probably describe Layard as hors categorie—a man without a pigeonhole.

Yet as Layard's life recedes deeper into yesterday, his discovery of Nineveh looms ever larger while the rest of his life dissolves into nothingness. But this still does not answer why Layard is not known as "the father of modern archaeology." A closer inspection of his and Schliemann's careers, however, resolves the question. Layard discovered Nineveh in the springtime of life and then went on to other things. Schliemann discovered Troy in late autumn. Once Schliemann, a brilliantly successful financier, at the age of fifty, accompanied by his sixteen-year-old bride, quit the counting house and plunged into archaeology, he never abandoned it. That is how the public remembered him at his death—as an archaeologist. When Layard entered archaeology, it was a fluke; he had only a vague notion of discovering anything when he set out for Ceylon. It was the luck of Nineveh that catapulted him into politics and public life. At his death, he was remembered as a political figure of imposing stature in foreign affairs, not as a pioneering archaeologist. This state of affairs, I believe, explains why the sobriquet "father of archaeology" has eluded Layard.

Hopefully, this biographic account, with its emphasis almost exclusively on archaeology, may restore Layard to his true place in history.

Indeed, as I look back on my last two books on archaeology, The Dream of Troy (New York: Mason & Lipscomb, 1973) and The Search for the Gold of Tutankhamen (New York: Mason & Charter, 1976), I recognize the error of my ways. I have written about the heroic age of archaeology backhanded. I should have written about Layard first; everything afterwards would have fallen neatly into place. Now I, too, know better. It has taken me three books to learn.

Layard is an engaging figure to write about. Unlike the pompous Schliemann and the ascetic Howard Carter, who discovered the gold and mummy of Tutankhamen in the Roaring Twenties, Layard never took himself seriously. He possessed too much common sense for such foolishness. Thus, in a letter to a friend May 5, 1849, following the success of Nineveh and Its Remains, Layard wrote, "Now, if you wished to make your fortune you have only to give the world a biography of the author of Nineveh—of how he liked various kinds of jams and fruit pies—discovered a unique cone [mound]—and various other little anecdotes."

I don't know if I shall make my fortune with this biography, but Layard was certainly a marvelously satisfying character to work with, especially since he was such a positive individual. We live in a negative age. It was a pleasure to write about the positive accomplishments of a positive individual in a positive age.

Among the disciplines, archaeology is surely one in which nobody should take himself seriously. "I have seen yesterday," the papyric Coffin Text reads, "I know tomorrow." Yet some contemporary archaeologists are almost humorless. As Andre Parrot, the great French Assyriologist and Amiet's predecessor at the Louvre, put it, "Like the men of Nineveh and Assyria, they have lost the art of smiling."

One example is enough. I asked the present keeper of Assyrian antiquities at the British Museum, a dour Swiss, Edmund Sollberger (pronounced Soul-berjay), what he considered the missing link in Assyriology, thinking he would discuss Nebbi Yunnus or the continuing failure of archaeologists to find Resen and Rehoboth-Ir, two of the five Assyrian cities of Genesis (Calah, Ashur, and Nineveh are the others).

"What a stupid question," Sollberger said, unsmilingly. "The Assyrian Tapes are missing."

Holding a layman up to ridicule is hardly a scholarly accomplishment—in any discipline. Perhaps he was trying to make the point that nobody knows how to speak Assyrian and never will; and that many Assyrian secrets lie beyond the grave, unless tapes are discovered among the mounds. M. Sollberger's sarcasm, however, was hardly original. A. H. Sayce, the great Oxford scholar, at the Ninth International Congress of Orientalists in London in 1892 observed similarly among his peers. "The discussions about the pronunciation of certain Assyrian sounds, which are unfortunately too prominent in many a Assyriological publication, are a simple waste of time . . . ," Sayce said. "Unless we can raise an ancient Assyrian to life," he added with a laugh, "we shall never know."

As a starting point in researching Layard's story, I borrowed a line from The Quarterly Review, December 1848, in which the reviewer of Nineveh and Its Remains remarked, "Mr. Layard must excuse us if we acknowledge that he has irresistibly awakened our curiosity as to his own early history."

The principal mass of Layard material is in the British Museum. While my stringer-wife Aggie scurried around London's first- and secondhand bookshops, collecting the published works of Layard and his contemporaries, I buried myself in early 1076 in the Students' Room of the Museum. To my horror, the Layard Papers, "bequested by Dame Mary Evelyn Layard" (Enid), filled 234 volumes, ranging from special and general correspondence to manuscripts to field notebooks to confidential Foreign Office reports.

In the Catalogue of Additions to the Manuscripts in The British Museum, which I used in tracking through the Layard labyrinth as a mariner uses a chart, the descriptive material on the Papers alone consumed 27 pages, from Vol. I, his uncompleted, handwritten autobiography, through Vol. CCXXXIV, containing correspondence between Layard and Lord Lytton, viceroy of India. The latter dealt with Russia's "forward policy in Asia."

Layard's published works constituted the second major source of material. These covered the period 1849–91 and included Nineveh and Its Remains, 2 vols. (London: Murray, 1849); The Monuments of Nineveh (London: Murray, 1849); Inscriptions in the Cuneiform Character from Assyrian Monuments (London: The British Museum, 1850); A Popular Account of Discoveries at Nineveh (London: Murray, 1851); Discoveries in the Ruins of Nineveh and Babylon (London: Murray, 1853), A Second Series of the Monuments of Nineveh (London: Murray, 1853); The Nineveh Court in the Crystal Palace (London: Bradbury & Evans, 1854); Nineveh and Its Remains, abridged and updated with cuneiform translations (London: Murray, 1867); Nineveh and Babylon, an abridged version of Discoveries, 2 vols. (London: Murray, 1887); The Italian Schools of Painting, revised and in part rewritten by Layard (London: Murray, 1891); and Sir A. Henry Layard, his uncompleted autobiography, 2 vols., published posthumously and edited by William N. Bruce, a close friend (London: Murray, 1903).

In 1970, Routledge & Paul, London, brought out a new edition of Nineveh and Its Remains, cut to one volume by H. W. F. Saggs, department of Semitic languages and religious studies, University College, Cardiff. His introduction is nothing short of brilliant.

Relying on the subject's private and published papers, of course, provides a lopsided portrait. Accordingly, I turned to two other lodes, the memoirs of his contemporaries and such documents as transcripts of the meetings of the trustees of the British Museum.

Among the memoirs upon which I have drawn are *A Land March from England to Ceylon*, by Edward Ledwich Mitford, Layard's companion as far as Persia during his first trip into the interior of Asia Minor (London: Allen, 1884); *Assyrian Discoveries*, by George Smith (New York: Scribner, 1876); *The Ansayrii*, by Lieut. F. W. Walpole, whose travels included "a visit to Nineveh," 2 vols. (London: Bentley, 1851); *The Life of Lord Stratford de Redcliffe* by Stanley Lane-Poole, a monographic biography of Canning (London: Longmans, Green, 1890); *Discoveries at Nineveh*, a translation of Botta's letters to Mohl (London: Longman, Brown, Green and Longmans, 1850); *Lady Charlotte Guest*, edited by a friend, the Earl of Bessborough (London: Murray, 1850), and his companion piece, *Lady Charlotte Schreiber* (London: Murray, 1852); *The Fourth Generation*, by Janet Ross, Enid's childhood companion and later wife of Layard's friend (New York: Scribner's, 1912); *Letters from the East*, by Henry James Ross, edited by Janet Ross (London, Dent, 1902); *A Memoir of Major-General Sir Henry Creswicke Rawlinson*, by George Rawlinson, who taught ancient history at Oxford (London: Longmans, Green, 1898); *Humphrey Sandwith: A Memoir*, by Thomas H. Humphrey Ward, his nephew (London: Cassell, 1884); *Breifwechsel: Heinrich Schliemann*, 2 vols. (Berlin: Mann, 1953, 1958), which contains correspondence between Schliemann and Layard; *At John Murray's*, by George Paston, with many references to the production of Layard's works (London: Murray, 1932); *The Letters of Queen Victoria*, 3 vols., edited by Arthur Christopher Benson and Viscount Esher, containing her acerbic views of Layard (London: Murray, 1907); *Monuments de Ninive Découvert dé Decrit*, 5 vols., by Paul Emile Botta, containing Flandin's unsurpassed Ninevite drawings (Paris: Imprimere, 1849–50); *Travels and Researches in Chaldea and Susiana* by William Loftus, who worked for Layard's Assyrian Excavation Fund (New York, Carter, 1857); *Ninive et l'Assyrie*, by Victor Place, Rassam's nemesis (Paris: Imprimere Iperiale, 1870); *Asshur and the Land of Nimrod*, by Hormuzd Rassam (Cincinnati: Curtis & Jennings, 1897); *Reminiscences*, by A. H. Sayce, who visited Layard when the latter was ambassador at Constantinople (London: Macmillan, 1923); *The Palaces of Nineveh and Persepolis*, by James Fergusson, who designed the Nineveh Court at the Crystal Palace (London: Murray, 1851); *Guide to the Crystal Palace*, by Samuel Phillips, which contains a description and floor plan of the Ninevite exhibit (London: Crystal Palace, 1859); *Nineveh and Its Palaces*, by Joseph Bonomi, an example of the Evangelical upsurge accompanying the Layard discoveries (London: Bohn, 1857): *The Bible and The British Museum*, by Ada R. Habershon, another example of Evangelicalism (London: Morgan & Scott, 1909); *Nineveh and Persepolis*, by W. S. W. Vaux (London: Hall, Virtue, 1851); *The Nestorians and Their Rituals*, 2 vols., by the Rev. George Percy Badger, Christian Rassam's father-in-law, containing letters to Canning on excavating the mounds (London: Masters, 1852).

As for documentary material, my trail led from *Proceedings of the Huguenot Society of London* (London: Spottiswoode, 1911) to *Journal of Transactions of the Victoria Institute* to *Transactions of the Society of Biblical Archaeology* to the unpublished trustees' minutes of the British Museum, 1850–61.

Yet Layard's papers, various memoirs, etc., still provided an incomplete picture. Accordingly, I went back to Layard's youth and read what he read, starting with his favorite volume, *The Arabian Nights*. What child has not read those wondrous tales? And if not, why not even in this age of the idiot box? I reread my own copy. *The Arabian Nights' Entertainment*, by Richard F. Burton (New York, Modern Library, 1932), which I acquired in the late thirties as a little boy. The tales are as wondrous as ever. Equally fascinating were other Layard favorites, including *Narrative of a Resident in Koordistan*, 2 vols., by Claudius James Rich (London: Duncan, 1836), edited by his wife Mary, and *The Itinerary of Rabbi Benjamin of Tudela*, translated and edited by A. Asher (London: Asher, 1840), which was extraordinary, although, while the good Rabbi matched Marco Polo as a man of action, he offered no competition as a man of letters.

Subconsciously, Sir Robert Ker Porter's *Travels in Georgia, Persia, Armenia, Ancient Babylonia* (London: Longman, Hurst, Reese, Orme and Brown, 1821) must have put the idea of digging up the mounds into Layard's mind. Gazing upon the Mesopotamian mounds for the first time, Ker Porter wrote: "It is impossible to pass over such scenes without stopping to pause under the most awful impression; here lay the remains of a great city; with memorials of her past existence standing in such stupendous heights and breadths, and yet all that had concerned it was now buried in such deep oblivion, that not even a conjecture could be formed of what had been its name."

Other Layard favorites included *A Journal Written During an Excursion in Asia Minor*, by Charles Fellows (London: Murray, 1838), the explorer who thrilled him as a youth at Aunt Sara's brunches with tales of adventure and discovery; *The Spirit of the East*, by D. Urquhart (London: Colburn, 1838); and *Later Researches in Assyria*, by William Ainsworth (London: Parker, 1838), a member of the Euphrates expedition.

Much has occurred in Assyriology since Layard's era—new finds, for example, some of them spectacular. Sumer was unknown in Layard's day; today the invention of cuneiform writing is traced to the non-Semitic Sumerians who inhabited Mesopotamia 5,200 years ago. In 1977 Dr. Denise Schmandt-Besserat, assistant director, Center for Middle Eastern Studies, University of Texas, Austin, reported in *Discovery*, vol. 1, no. 4, June, a scholarly journal, evidence that amid the ruins of Layard's Uruk, the Erech of the Bible, pictographic writing may have developed the basis for cuneiform as long ago as 8500 B.C. In a communication, Professor Schmandt-Besserat confessed "my total ignorance of Layard and Botta" but recalled that they were "part of the fascinating figures which were mentioned in lectures in my training at the Louvre."

For background on Assyrian archaeology, I used the following sources: *The Discovery and Decipherment of the Trilingual Cuneiform Inscriptions*, by Arthur John Booth (London: Longmans, Green, 1902), which contains groping conclusions such as those of Rawlinson, who suspected that cuneiform was not a Semitic language but may have come from the uplands of Africa(!), the speech of Highlanders or Akkads; *A Century of Exploration at Nineveh*, by R. Campbell Thompson and R. W. Hutchinson (London: Luza, 1929), which is strong on Layard's impact on Victorianism; *The Call to Seriousness*, by Ian Bradley (New York: Macmillan, 1975), which evaluates the impact of Evangelicalism on the Victorian period, *The Stones of Assyria*, by Gadd, already cited, which contains the text of Layard's last report to the Assyrian Excavation Fund; *The Five Great Monarchies*, 2 vols., by George Rawlinson (London: John Murray, 1871), the brother of Henry Rawlinson, which contains a stimulating summary of what was known or suspected about Chaldea, Assyria, Babylon, Media, and Persia in that era; *A History of Babylonia and Assyria*, 2 vols., 6th ed., by Robert William Rogers (Cincinnati: Abingdon, 1915), who later wrote the introduction to Rassam's *In the Land of Asshur*, already cited; *By Nile and Tigris*, 2 vols., by E. A. Wallis Budge (London: John Murray, 1920), in which, in poor taste, Budge again tried to defend himself against the jury's verdict in the Rassam libel suit; and *Foundations in the Dust*, by Seton Lloyd (London: Oxford, 1949), who served as a post–World War II adviser to the Iraqi government's department of archaeology.

For the flavor of the Assyrian empire, the translations of cuneiform tablets are indispensable, among them, *Ancient Records of Assyria and Babylonia*, 2 vols., by

Daniel David Luckenbill (Chicago: University of Chicago, 1926–27); *Poems of Heaven and Hell from Ancient Mesopotamia*, translated by N. K. Sanders (London: Penguin Classic, 1971), which, although in paperback, is already out of print; *The Epic of Gilgamesh*, also by Sanders (London: Penguin Classics, 1960), still in print; and *The Ancient Near East*, edited by James B. Pritchard and a flock of Assyriologists (Princeton, Princeton University, 1958 [Vol. 1], 1975 [Vol. II]).

Several Assyriologists have been apologetic about their work. Many translations deal with war and its goriness. The Assyrian reveled in bloodshed and did not understand why he should not relate what he did. In *History of Assyria*, by A. T. Olmstead (Chicago: University of Chicago, 1951), the author goes after revisionist Assyriologists who have refused "to tell their readers about the horrors of war they read in their sources." Olmstead made the telling and obvious point that "the history of Assyria has one consolation, the blood of millions is not on [the historian's] skirts."

Indeed, since Layard and Rassam put down their spades, Assyrian archaeology has focused primarily on Assyriology, that is, on translations of cuneiform à la Rawlinson. One result was that the sculptures of Layard and Rassam were neither fully cataloged nor illustrated. In 1962, however, the British Museum, under Barnett, moved to rectify this oversight and put out the first in a series of illustrated works in a belated attempt to catch up to the Louvre and its reproduction of Botta's finds. The latest Barnett volume, *Sculptures from the North Palace of Ashurbanipal*, was published by the Museum in 1977. The volume weighs 35 pounds and costs £160 ($103), a price which draws as much criticism today as the Botta-Flandin volumes of more than a century ago. R. D. Barnett was former Keeper, Western Asiatic Antiqutis, British Museum.

Jacquetta Hawkes, who has written extensively on archaeology and is the wife of author J. B. Priestley, reviewed the tome for the *Times* of London, April 17, 1977, and treated it as a work of expiation, adding that Layard "will, of course, be eagerly awaiting the next volume."

Layard has received belated contemporary recognition in other ways; for example, in Mallowan's *Nimrod and Its Remains*, 2 vols. (New York: Dodd, Meade, 1962), which he dedicated "to my wife, Agatha Christie Mallowan, who shared with me in the joys and trials of excavating Nimrod. . . ." Mallowan, like Schliemann before him, acknowledged that the structure and style of his work was an imitation of Layard's. Incidentally, this is the Agatha Christie who is probably the most widely read British author in the world, with translations in 103 languages, fourteen more than Shakespeare.

Mallowan and Agatha Christie were married in 1930, and she accompanied him on numerous "digs." So many people asked her how she lived during an expedition that she broke down and wrote a witty, charming account, *Come Tell Me How You Live* (New York: Dodd, Mead, 1946). Much of it is downright hilarious.

During these Mesopotamian journeys she plotted several of her masterpieces of detection, such as *The Orient Express* and *Murder in Mesopotamia*. Often she served as an expedition's official photographer, and she also played a direct role in the expedition's work. For example, in 1951, a century after Layard's discovery of Nineveh, a British expedition led by Mallowan returned to the scene of Layard's triumphs and made fresh finds, including a new collection of ivories at Nimrod. Like Layard before him, Mallowan wrestled with the problem of preservation, the nightmare of archaeologists. The finds disintegrated on exposure to air. Agatha contributed to the solution by wrapping the ivories in wet cloth and standing vigil over them day and night until they successfully negotiated their passage through the millenniums into a new time frame.

Clearly, the Mallowans worked well together. As Sir Max once observed "Archaeology is really quite like whodunits—we use similar methods."

In London I heard a story in point. In the field, Dame Agatha watched in fascination as her husband pieced together a tale of murder and plunder at Nimrod in 614 B.C. After a month's labor, supervising 200 Iraqi diggers, he pointed out to her signs of looting at Nimrod—spent enemy arrowheads along the city's wall, by illustration. Then he traced the unmistakable signs of a drunken mob through the city's streets.

"But how did you know they were drunk?" Agatha Christie, the creator of Hercule Poirot, inquired.

"Elementary, my dear Agatha," Sir Max replied dryly. "They did not burn the wine cellars."

And in Paris, I was provided with another insight into this renowned couple. A French archaeologist who lunched with the Mallowans in Morocco laughingly recalled a remark she made to him. "When you marry an archaeologist," Dame Agatha said, "the older you become, the more he loves you!"

At this point, I wish to acknowledge the assistance of several individuals in the course of my work, notably Ann Hopley, Director's Office, Secretariat, The British Museum, who dredged up the trustees' minutes from the Layard period and arranged for my use of the Layard Papers; Nancy Kelly, my editor; Mary Kohn, reference librarian, Western Connecticut State College, Danbury, Connecticut, where I am a member of the faculty and who, in brilliant fashion, made rare finds such as Layard's booklet The Nineveh Court in the Crystal Palace, working through Ronald J. Mahoney, head, department of special collections, California State University, Fresno; my typist, a hopeless archaeological buff, Isabelle Bates; and Assyrian archaeologists who took the time to answer my questions, either in person or by mail, among the former, such eminent scholars as Professor D. J. Wiseman, University of London, over a cup of tea, and, over glasses of wine, Dr. Pierre Amiet, director of the department of Oriental antiquities at the Louvre, and his able Belgian assistant, Agnes Spycket; among the latter, the aforementioned Mallowan, whose wife passed away the week we arrived in London, and Professors Barnett and Saggs. It should be added that all the facts and opinions in this book are solely the responsibility of the author and that all dialogue and quotations are authentic; only spellings and verb tenses, on occasion, have been altered.

In some respects, I learned quickly, researching Layard and Assyriology is akin to piloting through a minefield. Occasionally a mine goes off. Rassam is a sample.

The most controversial individual in Assyrian archaeology, Rassam is usually idolized or hated. Until fifteen years ago he was treated shabbily by the country of his adoption, England. Despite the valiant effort of Layard and others on his behalf in the aftermath of the Budge libel case, Rassam was cast into oblivion. The British Museum ignored him. British publishers, including Murray, refused to print his memoirs. Aside from a few lectures, Layard's references to him in his own works, and a solitary article in the Illustrated London News, May 1856, "no record has appeared anywhere of the share I have had in Assyrian and Babylonian discoveries," Rassam complained in 1897 at the age of sixty-one. Indeed, many of his acquisitions were attributed to others. The great library he found at Nineveh was credited to either George Smith or Smith and Layard. The incomparable hunting scenes in bas-relief were said to be Rawlinson's discovery, although, to his credit, Rawlinson publicly denied they were his.

"It may be considered extraordinary that I allowed such a long time to elapse before I placed before the public the results of my discoveries," he wrote in the preface to Asshur and the Land of Nimrod, "but when the different unavoidable circumstances which intervened are explained, it will be seen that it was beyond my power to have my book brought out sooner."

On completing his memoir, Rassam disclosed, "I submitted it to different publishers in London, all of whom declined the responsibility of its publication, and, as I could not afford to have it brought out at my risk, there was nothing for it but to wait for a good opportunity."

The opportunity appeared in Robert W. Rogers, an American Assyriologist who taught at Drew Theological Seminary, Madison, New Jersey. "Among all the earlier explorers and excavators," Rogers said, "Mr. Hormuzd Rassam stands forth as a man of distinguished service. He struck the spade into many a mound almost unknown."

Rogers arranged with Curtis & Jennings of Cincinnati to bring out *Asshur* in 1897, fifteen years after Rassam completed it. The volume is subtitled *An Account of the Discoveries made in the Ancient Ruins of Nineveh, Asshur, Sepharvam, Calah, Babylon, Borsippa, Cuthah and Van.* It is excellent reading, modeled, of course, on Layard's format.

Controversy, however, continues to swirl around Layard's protégé. Some contemporary writers still treat Rassam with disdain. "There is something in Rassam's conduct as an explorer which induces peculiar distaste," Seton Lloyd, *op. cit.*, wrote. Grudgingly, Lloyd admitted, "Actually Rassam's accomplishments were considerable."

Justifiably, the French remember Rassam with distaste, as the rascal who outfoxed Victor Place by clandestine digging at night and other *opéra comique* stratagems. A senior Louvre official said scathingly, "Rassam was a pirate." Another French official held that Botta, Layard, Rawlinson, and Place were gentlemen who got along well together but whose relationships were disrupted by Rassam's chicanery.

As Rassam aged, however, he apparently mellowed. In 1892 the Ninth International Congress of Orientalists unanimously adopted a Rassam proposal that "all learned scholars, especially those interested in Biblical and scientific studies, should set aside national jealousies. . . ." Mellowed, indeed. But Rassam was still in disfavor, and did not attend the Congress; he sent his proposal to Sayce, who introduced and strongly supported it.

A thorough assessment of Rassam is contained in a private letter I received from Saggs.

"I have no intention of going into the rights and wrongs of the [Rassam] matter but undoubtedly Rassam was unduly touchy and Budge unduly tactless and unforgiving," Saggs wrote. "The legacy of this was that some Assyriologists have rather tended, long afterwards, to take sides as between H. Rassam and his patron Layard, and Budge and his patron Rawlinson.

"In my view," Saggs continued, "virtually everything found by H. Rassam can almost be regarded as a find by Layard at second hand. I think H. Rassam was a man of integrity and an excellent and loyal lieutenant to Layard, but he lacked the qualities of originality which I consider as essential if a man is to be considered a pioneer. Undoubtedly, Rassam has sometimes been robbed of the credit due to him and I think it is only belated justice that his name should now be better known to the public at large."

Saggs probably had in mind the July 1, 1963, Twelfth International Meeting of Assyriologists in London. On that occasion, the British Museum under Barnett atoned for the sins of the past. A special exhibit opened—"Layard and His Successors"— which restored Rassam to stage center. The pendulum swung widely. Not only did Barnett resurrect Rassam but he gave Rassam the most prominent position in the foyer of the famed Assyrian Basement. A large portrait of Rassam, hanging between the marble busts of Henry and Enid Layard, now dominates the entranceway.

Budge must have writhed in his grave, while Layard laughed.

When I pointed out the amazing reversal of Rassam's fortunes at the Museum to Sollberger, Barnett's successor grew defensive and protested that "there is no conspiracy, nothing sinister about it." When I contacted Barnett about the resurrection, he replied, "What you say about my resurrection of Rassam is correct."

Barnett, now working in retirement on reproducing the Museum's entire collection of Assyrian sculpture (see above), described Rassam's role in Assyriology as "a rather complex story which has never been dispassionately studied.

"He was a great discoverer, though an unscientific and rather unscrupulous one, attempting to do too much at one time," the former keeper said. "His clash, however, with Budge was a tragedy, and his treatment by Budge and the trustees was little less than a scandal."

There were other exploding mines.

Since Layard's day half a million cuneiform tablets have been recovered in Mesopotamia, half of them almost four thousand years old. The contents of many tablets bear a striking parallel to the Biblical stories of the Creation, the Flood, etc. What is the relationship, if any, between the Old Testament and these tablets? Scholars have struggled inconclusively with the question.

Even before Layard's discovery of Nineveh, as early as 1826, the cosmogony of Berosus* stirred controversy because part of it formed a remarkable parallel to the Mosaic theory of creation. Indeed, some people asserted that the Mosaic cosmogony was derived from it (see R. G. Niebuhr's *Lectures on Ancient History* [Philadelphia: Blanchard & Lea, 1852]).

According to Berosus, the world began in darkness, a chaos which was conceived as fluid and in which strange swimming animals abounded. The governor of the world separated darkness from light, and the monsters ("terrible lizards," i.e., dinosaurs in Greek) perished in the light. Other traditions, startlingly, said the governor of the world labored six days and rested on the seventh.

Then came Smith's discovery of the Flood tablet and an unending series of revelations since then. A recent translation of a Sumerian tablet, for example, described the creation of woman "from a rib" and described her as "the one who makes life." Other recent finds include tablets which discourse on Paradise and the Fall of Man, right down to a cylinder bearing two figures, a sacred tree and a serpent. Adam and Eve? No tablet has yet been recovered which expressly details the Biblical story of Adam and Eve, but Assyriology is, like archaeology, a relatively young discipline. Such a tablet may still lie buried at Sippara, the City of the Sun, which Rassam found as his firman expired and Layard was recalled to London. According to tradition, the history of the world before the Flood was written by Xisuthus, who was warned in a dream to do so. Did his history include the story of Adam and Eve?

These and other jarring revelations in cuneiform shook Christian and Jews alike in the last century. Sayce, who did for Biblical Assyriology (*The "Higher Criticism" and the Verdict of the Monuments* [New York: Young, 1894]) what James Henry Breasted later did for Biblical Egyptology (*The Dawn of Conscience* [New York: Scribner's, 1934]), cited Layard's discoveries as evidence of the Old Testament's historical accuracy. By 1903 some Assyriologists argued that the fundamental basis of Hebrew

---

* Berosus, a priest of Babylon, wrote circa 280–261 B.C. in Greek a history of Chaldea; only fragments of its contents are known at this writing.

traditions, laws, and temple rituals was of Babylonian origin. But as Budge pointed out in his *By Nile and Tigris*, there is a singular distinction between the Old Testament and the similar ideas and expressions found in the cuneiform tablets, i.e., "the spiritual character, the sublimity and the lofty and exalted conception of God ... is wholly lacking in the cuneiform tablets." Fifty years later, Wiseman made a similar distinction between the story of Creation unfolded in the Epic of Gilgamesh and the Old Testament. The Bible's lofty conception of God "bears a dignity unparalleled in any other known account," he said (*Illustrations from Biblical Archaeology* [London: Tyndale Press, 1970]).

The suggestion that there is a relationship between the Mosaic cosmogony and that of the Assyrians has a familiar ring in Egyptology, where controversy continues over whether Moses' monotheism may have been inspired by Akhenaten, the heretic pharaoh who destroyed the idols of the Egyptian pantheon and preached the existence of one God *before* Exodus (see *The Search for the Gold of Tutankhamen*, pp. 183–7).

Putting two and two together should equal four, but archaeology is not a pure science and two times two may add up to anything in the imagination of the multiplier; as Mallowan observed, archaeology is a bit like a whodunit (Howard Carter, incidentally, made a similar observation after discovering Tutankhamen's mummy; he said if he had not become an Egyptologist he might have wound up at Scotland Yard).

Since the archaeology of Egypt and Assyria finds echoes in the Old Testament, it suggests to this writer that the Israelites, bouncing back and forth like a shuttlecock between bondage in Egypt and captivity in Babylon, may have absorbed and, above all, refined Egyptian and Mesopotamian mythology and theology into the lofty conception of God which dominates the Old Testament and, in turn, was absorbed first by the New Testament and, still later, the Koran.

Clearly, in the search for the meaning of meaning there is unity in diversity.

Even more remarkable explosions were set off in Layard's minefield. J. W. Bosanquet, in *The Fall of Nineveh* (London: Longman, Brown, Green & Longmans, 1853), considered Layard's discoveries preordained, and a portent of things to come. Bosanquet drew a startling conclusion. Layard's discovery of the lost Assyrian empire of Genesis was a sign that "the time for Israel's redemption is surely at hand," he wrote. This rebirth, he felt, would draw Christian and Jew together to await the "deliverer," whether the interpretation was the Second or First Coming. "Are we not both waiting and looking for the same Deliverer?" he asked.

Bosanquet's book aroused skepticism. In 1853, the thought that the state of Israel would be reborn after two millenniums was viewed as ridiculous. But Bosanquet was convinced that the resurrection of Nineveh was a harbinger of Israel's resurrection and that Israel's restoration was in turn a forerunner of global spiritual rebirth. It may take another century to disprove or prove Bosanquet's thesis.

Yet other minefields exploded during my research. Layard, for example, the astute observer, concluded amid the ruins of Assyria that many of the colossal statues such as the man-headed, winged bulls had been toppled by a "convulsion of nature" (see page 238).

In *Worlds in Collision* (New York: Doubleday, 1950), the intellectual acrobat Immanuel Velikovsky relied on translations of astronomical observations found by Layard in Ashurbanipal's library—Mesopotamia is frequently called "the cradle of astronomy"—to prove that Venus was once a comet and that its tail lashed earth before it was transformed into a planet of our solar system. This event, Velikovsky argued, caused havoc on earth and gave rise to much of the mythology of mankind. "This star shattered mountains, shook the globe with such violence that it looked as if the heavens were shaking, was a storm, a cloud, a fire, a heavenly dragon, a torch and a blazing star, and it rained naphtha on the earth," he said. This lively overview dovetails with Ashurbanipal's account of the goddess Ishtar (Venus), "who is clothed with fire and bears aloft a crown of awful splendor, raining fire over Arabia."

Such a cataclysmic event may have been accompanied by a shift in the earth's orbit, accounting for the Ice Age and subsequent Flood. As early as the twenties, this theory was promoted by Multin Milakovich, a Yugoslav geologist, but it was not until 1975 that the American journal *Science* confirmed evidence that a rapidly melting ice sheet circa 10,725 B.C. may have resulted in the Flood described in the Assyrian cuneiform tablets and Genesis. Indeed, lately, the interaction between astronomy and archaeology has given rise to a new discipline, astroarchaeology.

An example of the latter is found in the research of Commander George Michanowsky ("Cuneiform Clues to an Ancient Starburst," *Explorer's Journal*, December 1975). His research was based on a recent confirmation that a supernova in the southern constellation of Vela exploded circa 9000 B.C., perhaps releasing cosmic gamma rays which penetrated the earth's atmosphere and reached the ground level of our planet, resulting in genetic consequences such as spontaneous mutations. Such a development could have either destroyed or created the monsters depicted in Assyrian bas-reliefs. Michanowsky cited an obscure passage in Job (who is believed to be of Mesopotamian origin), 9:8,9, in which reference is made to a monotheistic God "who alone stretched out the heavens, and trampled the waves of the sea—who made the Bear and Orion, the Pleiades and the chambers of the South." The word "chambers," Michanowsky observed, is the correct literal translation of the Old Testament, but the word also has a figurative meaning—"secret." In the cuneiform tablets discovered by Layard and his successors, Michanowsky discovered references, he said, "to the appearance of a mighty star in the Sumerian equivalent of what we today call the constellation Vela, where the supernova occurred." Vela is located in the southern sky. To enliven matters, he noted, philologists have recently confirmed that we currently have in English a cuneiform word related to this cosmic event. It is "abyss," which was long thought to be of Greek origin but is now known to be derived from the Sumerian word *ab-zu*. It was used by Mesopotamians as a synonym for "the great southern sea and heavenly vault above it." This ancient usage, Michanowsky feels, may be better appreciated when thought of as the conceptual equivalent of the present-day astronomical term "deep space."

"At the dawn of human history," he therefore concluded, "a powerful cosmic stimulus reached out toward mankind from a mysterious event in the far southern sky and may have influenced the fate of all of us for ages to come." Manifestly, the cuneiform tablets still have much to yield.

Other minefields also dot Assyrian archaeology and Assyriology. What, for example, lies under the mound of Nebbi Yunnus, adjacent to the mound of Nineveh and revered by Moslems as the tomb of the prophet Jonah? Calah, Ashur, and Nineveh have been unearthed. But where are Resen and Rehoboth-Ir, the other two cities of Genesis? They must be in the neighborhood.

In 1976 the archaeological ferris wheel was given a rude spin by Italian archaeologists working under Paolo Mathiae, professor of Near East Archaeology, University of Rome, and a colleague, Giovanni Pettinato, an Assyriologist.

Mathiae announced the stunning discovery, near Aleppo, Syria, the area Layard traversed with Mitford, of the seat of the ancient empire of Elba. In cuneiform tablets there are hazy references to Elba. In its day, the tablets recorded, Elba rivaled Egypt and Assyria. Among the ruins of Elba, the Italian archaeologists discovered the archives of the royal palace in much the same manner that Layard did before them at Nineveh. The archives contained 15,000 cuneiform tablets, including new versions of Genesis, the Flood, etc. They are still being translated.

Obviously, the words of H. V. Hilprecht (The Excavations of Assyria and Babylonia [Philadelphia: Holman, 1904]) hold as strongly today as when he wrote them. "Much more remains to be done before the resurrection of ancient empires will be completed," Hilprecht, the Assyriologist, wrote. "Hundreds of ruins scarcely yet known by their names await the explorer."

But there is a sense of urgency today lacking in Hilprecht's time. Turkey's economic development demands increasing amounts of power for industry and water for irrigation projects. Developmental plans include the erection along the Euphrates of dams, submerging many archaeological sites in a new, man-made Flood. The most stupid point of view is expressed by those who argue that Turkey—like Egypt, Greece, and Iraq—has so many archaeological sites that "a few hundred less will not matter[!]" The problem also has a Layardian strain. Some Turkish officials, according to a New York Times story, April 3, 1977, "have little interest in cultures that preceded the Islamic invasion of Asia Minor," and this view is often linked to a general suspicion of foreign archaeologists who find it increasingly difficult to obtain permits of any kind in Turkey. Yet the same newspaper, shortly thereafter, published a Sunday propaganda supplement for the Turkish government in which Dr. Sevin Buluc, curator, Museum of Middle East Technical University, alleged that "the most drastic harm was caused by the transportation of classical monuments from their original sights [sic] to great museums in the West." The same theme is heard in Baghdad. This is part of a campaign for the return of archaeological objects to their original sites. Although one may empathize with Turkish and Iraqi officials, their position is absurd. The record speaks for itself, and speaks eloquently.

In 1852 an Armenian Catholic priest reported that a colossal statue had been discovered by men plowing a field at Kouyunjik and that the farmers, devout Moslems, "ordered it to be broken, as they do with everything else that is brought to light." In 1891, when Budge was in Mosul, he found only one winged bull left intact. A year later, an aide reported that its head had been hacked off by local people. In 1914 W. A. Wigram, in Cradle of Mankind (London: Black, 1914), reported the fate of the remainder of the Assyrian monument: "The whole monument was sold for the sum of three shillings six pence (66 cents) to be burnt into lime by its purchaser."

In London I met one Iraqi official who ranted about the "theft" of archaeological treasures from Mesopotamia by the British Museum. He had been in London almost a year. When I asked him what he thought of Barnett's rearrangement of the Assyrian collection, he looked at me blankly. "Oh," he said, "I haven't yet had time to visit the Museum."

In Paris, the situation has a parallel. French archaeologists digging in Susia, now incorporated in present-day Iran, recovered in the last century the famous Hammurabi stele, which the Elamites had stolen in 1200 B.C. from Babylon, now present-day Iraq. "Who should we 'return' it to?" an official asked. "The whole business is nonsense."

Mallowan, in a letter to the author, zeroed in on Layard's true archaeological accomplishment: "Before all else comes the fact that he saved for posterity the Nimrod bas-reliefs which were locally being burnt for lime in the kilns" (italics added).

So much for the claims of militant nationalists, who demand the "return" of archaeological finds. Their energies would be better spent if diverted from propagandizing to continuing the work of Layard and his successors in the interests of everyone and in the Periclean sense that "the whole earth is the tomb of famous men."

But while nationalists clamor for the "return" of these "stolen" objects, the issue has an obverse side. The great museums in the West, like museums everywhere, have a moral responsibility to present—and past—to maintain these discoveries on permanent view, with access to all. The winged bulls and lions, and other treasures of Nineveh and Assyria, are magnificently displayed at the British Museum and the Louvre. The same may not be said of the most important museum in the United States, New York's Metropolitan.

As a young boy I saw my first winged bull and lion at the Metropolitan. They were 10 feet high, and I still remember, as probably does every child (or adult) who saw them, how impressively they guarded the museum's Mesopotamian transept. These monsters had guarded Ashurnasirpal's palace, 883–859 B.C., at Layard's Nimrod, and were acquired by the museum in 1932.

In the course of working on this book, after viewing the extraordinary Assyrian collections in London and Paris, I thought I would refresh my memory of the Metropolitan's pieces. To my shock, I could not find my bull and lion. Indeed, they have not been seen in public for a decade.

In 1968 the exhibit of the Ancient Near East Department was closed "temporarily." Ninevite treasures were stored in the Museum's North Garage, covered with plastic. At this writing, they are still there. Officials of the department, such as Vaughn E. Crawford, curator, who spent two seasons at Nimrod with the British Expedition led by David Oates, and others are quite unhappy about this shocking state of affairs. "If the public, including people like you," one Met official told me, "would express your sentiments to the Museum's administration, it might help."

During the period these treasures have been hidden from the public view, the Museum—in an era devoted largely to high-powered public relations under its former director, Thomas Hoving—put on politically motivated exhibitions such as "Harlem on My Mind" and "The American Indian." [The latter seemed particularly odd, because New York boasts a superb Museum of the American Indian, in a matter of speaking, just up the street.] As the London *Economist* suggested, "scholarship was sacrificed for showmanship." Let the record state that the Metropolitan was incorporated in 1870 for the "purpose of establishing and maintaining . . . encouraging and developing the study of the fine arts. . . ."

For a city like New York—which, like Nineveh in the past, dwells carelessly and says in her heart, "I am, and there is none beside me!"—one may fairly pose a question to the Metropolitan's administration:

Has Modern Nineveh no place for Ancient Nineveh?

Index

Karun river, 94 passim, 112
Kater's compass, 92
Kelek, 73–75, 126, 149, 180–181, 194–196, 256–258
Kellogg, Miner, 147, 210
keritlioglu, defined, 126
Kermansha, 81 passim
Khalah Sharghat, 70 passim, 279, 280
Khanumi, 87
Khorsabad, 115 passim, 123, 136, 219
Khoshor, river, 67
King Peacock, 155
Kings, Book of, 174, 199
Kirkup, Seymour, 21
Kouyunjik, 68, 114–116, 121, 146, 155, 173 passim, 197 passim, 219, 232–235, 244, 307, 310; origin of name, 67; first excavations, 97
Kugler's Handbook of Painting, 315
Kurdeston, 65, 159
Kurds, 62, 93, 140, 164, 193, 230, 317
Kuthu, 310
kymak, defined, 49

La Guiseppina, 110–111
Lachish, 238
Landor, Walter Savage, 270
Larissa, II, 128
Laveran, Alphouse, 152
Layard, Arthur, 95
Layard, Austen Henry: birth, vii, 18; Schliemann relationship, vii–viii, 325–326; first journey, 15; family background, 15–17; linguistic ability, 20, 24; fond of art, 20; impact of Thousand and One Nights, 19–21; interest in ancient history, 22; "adoption" by Austens, 25; alters name, 25; law clerk, 26 passim; youth in London, 27 passim; father's death, 28; interest in German, 30; visits France, 30; romantic encounters, 30, 109, 111, 278; visits Russia, 31; first lesson in archaeology, 31; to Ceylon, 35–36; overland route, 38 passim; passes bar, 42; first impressions Orient, 47 passim; love of freedom, 52; first brush with Assyria, 52; parts company with Mitford, 54; almost killed, 55; befriended by Jew, 59; malarial attacks, 68, 128, 213; first encounter with Nineveh, 60; at Kouyunjik, 68; fascinated by mounds, 72, 74; on Ottoman Empire, 77; narrowly drowns, 79–80; rejoins Mitford, 81; expenses on journey, 82; parts with Mitford, 83–84; prisoner of Persians, 89–91; abandons Ceylon, 93; inspects Nineveh first time, 100; encourages Botta, 99–101; first Canning meeting, 103; missions to Bal-

kans, 105 passim; horsemanship, 105; as journalist, 106–107; Turkish escapades, 109–111; reads Botta's dispatches, 120–121; Layard-Canning compact, 124; at Nimroud, 127–129 passim; meets Rawlinson, 132–133; Islamic, 137–138; receives firmon, 141; Cadi incident, 143–145; at Nimroud, 146–147, 171–176; transports bulls, 190 passim, 191–195; return to Constantinople, 203; in Paris, 204–207; return to England, 209 passim; need for Ottoman reforms, 210; appointment to foreign service, 211; turns author, 217–220; unpaid attacks, 222; literary acclaim, 224–226; style compared to Arabian Nights, 226; disgust with British Museum, 228; worker's payments, 236; moves enraged lions, 240–241; desert forays, 243 passim; Babylon expedition, 255–266; malarial bout anew, 266; second return to England, 266; honors, 270; under secretary of foreign affairs, 273–275; member parliament, 274–277; on Western art, 290; enters banking, 291 passim; returns to parliament, 292; clash with Gladstone, 293; joins Privy Council, 293; appointed minister to Spain, 294; knighted, 303; impact on Assyrian and Greek Archaeology, 305 (See also Author's Note) Rassam Affair, 318–321; last years with Enid, 314–323; death, 323–324; Rassam's epitaph, 324
Layard, Charles Edward, 16–17, 35–36, 38
Layard, Frederick, 95
Layard, Henry Austen (see Layard, Austen Henry)
Layard, Henry Peter John, 16; wedding, 18; death, 28
Layard, Lady (see also Guest, Mary Enid Evelyn), 297–305 passim; and Rassam, 309; in Venice, 322–324
Layard, Marianne, 93, 95, 120, 126
Le Commorant, 204
Le Havre, 204
Lebanon, 52
Lebanon, Cedars of, 7
Leghorn, 205
Leith Hill, 297
Lenormond, M., 207
Levinge bed, 41
Lewis, Sir George Cornewall, 288
Limehouse Reach, 209
Lind, Jenny, 209
Little St. Bernard Pass, 29
Livingstone, David, 35
Lloyd, Seton, 194